THE GEYSERS OF YELLOWSTONE

The Geysers
of Yellowstone
SECOND REVISED EDITION

T. Scott Bryan

University Press of Colorado

The University Press of Colorado is a cooperative publishing enter-
prise supported, in part, by Adams State College, Colorado State University, Fort Lewis College, Mesa State College, Metropolitan State
College of Denver, University of Colorado, University of Northern
Colorado, University of Southern Colorado, and Western State College.

The paper used in this publication meets the minimum requirements of
the American National Standard for Information Sciences — Perma-
nence of Paper for Printed Library Materials. ANSI Z39.48–1984

Cover Photo — Steamboat Geyser erupting over 300 feet high in 1963
(NPS photo by Robert Lang and William Dick).

Contents

Tables, Figures, and Maps

Figure

Maps

Preface

This is the second edition of *The Geysers of Yellowstone.* For it, every word has been rewritten, every description revised. The maps have been redrawn. Significant new features have been added. Every effort has been made to make this a thoroughly up-to-date and comprehensive reference to the geysers of Yellowstone National Park. I hope it will serve those who have been geyser gazers for years as well as those who have never before seen a geyser. Enjoy!

At first glance the maps will look the same as before. In fact, they are considerably more accurate. The locations of the roads, trails, streams, and thermal features are precise and to scale since these maps are strictly based on the detailed thermal maps of the U.S. Geological Survey. The only exceptions to this are the maps of the Gibbon and Lone Star Geyser Basins, for which no detailed maps exist, and the index maps to the Upper and Lower Geyser Basins; these are all based on enlargements of USGS topographic maps.

Some special words of note about the names of the geysers, as they appear in this book, are needed. There has often been a tendency in the past for geyser gazers (myself included) to invent names for unnamed features in an offhand way. While there is good reason for discouraging this practice, it nevertheless happens and such names become familiar to at least some observers. In the first edition of this book I used such unofficial names in nearly all situations where I had personally accepted the name. This time I take a somewhat different tack.

Nearly any name used in the first edition has been used again unless I have been shown that it is in conflict with an earlier, proper name. For any other geyser that has received a widely recognized but unofficial name in the past few years, a new way of designating this has been adopted. This is a numerical designation followed by the suggested name. An example from the Upper Geyser Basin is listed as: "79. UNNG-CGG-4 ("Bush" Geyser)." The meaning here is:

79. This is the 79th geyser described for the Upper Basin; UNNG–The geyser is officially unnamed;

CGG–The geyser is a member of the Castle-Grand Group of geysers (each group or area has its own three-letter abbreviation);

4–This geyser is the fourth unnamed geyser described as a member of this group;

("Bush" Geyser)–This name has appeared in verbal and/or written reports about the geyser's activity.

By using this technique throughout the book, I hope my system will be helpful for all. It should avoid conflicts regarding naming techniques, while also avoiding the long-standing confusion as to "which unnamed geyser is that?"

The individual who has done the greatest amount of work about Yellowstone's place names, including the thermal features, is Lee H. Whittlesey. Employed for many years by both the park concessions and the National Park Service, Lee has conducted extensive research in places such as the National Archives in Washington, D.C., and the U. S. Board on Geographic Names in Reston, VA. He has communicated much long-forgotten information to me through the years, and many of the name revisions in this book are a result of his efforts.

The extensive numerical revisions of this edition reflect data that has been obtained by the "geyser gazers." When I wrote the first edition of *The Geysers of Yellowstone,* there were few geyser gazers. Now more than 200 have banded together as The Geyser Observation and Study Association. Far too many to thank individually, my greatest thanks go to all of them for their valuable information, stimulating discussions, thoughtful ideas, and enjoyable times.

Dr. Donald E. White of the U.S. Geological Survey is responsible for developing our modern theories of how geysers work. He provided ideas vital to this book and gave a favorable pre-publication review of the first edition, probably assuring its existence.

Dr. George D. Marler was *the* Ranger-Naturalist geyser gazer of Yellowstone for several decades before his death in 1978. Had he not kept extensive and detailed notes about the geysers and their dynamic changes, relatively little would be known about long-term geyser action and its meaning for us today. His numerous publications are indispensible references.

The Ranger-Naturalist staff and Research Geologist of Yellowstone keep the daily logbooks of geyser activity accurate and up-to-date at all times during the visitation seasons, something especially vital during the winter, when geyser gazing is severely limited.

We must remember, too, those who were here during the early surveys of Yellowstone. Geologists such as Drs. Hayden, Hague, Peale, Weed, Allen, Day, Fenner, and many others set the stage for us by helping to create, maintain, and understand what Yellowstone is really all about. And Saxo Grammaticus, an English monk who saw and described Iceland's Geysir, was the first to let scientific thinkers know about geysers and so became the first geyser gazer we know of, more than 700 years ago.

Finally, but foremost, tremendous appreciation is due to my wife, Betty. *The Geysers of Yellowstone* was actually her idea in the first place, and her questions, prodding, and encouragement did a job that might never have happened otherwise.

Thank you, one and all!

Chapter 1

About Geysers

What is a geyser?

According to the simplest possible definition, a geyser is a hot spring that periodically erupts so as to throw water into the air. It sounds simple enough, but it really is not. A hot spring that only occasionally overflows rather quietly is often called a geyser, but it is more properly called an *intermittent spring*. A "geyser" that erupts continuously is properly known as a *perpetual spouter;* strictly speaking it is not a geyser because its eruption never stops. In any of these three cases, however, the cause of the eruption is the same.

What makes a geyser function?

Three things are necessary for a geyser to exist: an abundant supply of water, a potent heat source, and a very special and critical underground plumbing system.

It is the plumbing system that determines whether a spring will be quiet or will erupt. It must be constructed of minerals strong enough to withstand tremendous pressure, and it must be shaped so as to hold the huge amounts of water that are ejected during an eruption.

Nobody really knows what a plumbing system looks like (it is, after all, below ground and filled with hot water and steam), but considerable research drilling has been done in the world's geyser areas. None of this has yet found any large, open water storage cavities, leading many to conclude that a geyser's water reservoir is nothing more complex than the open spaces in the porous rocks that surround the plumbing system. Cracks and channels in these same rocks make up the rest of the plumbing, through which water can flow swiftly and freely. The character and performance of every geyser is determined by its plumbing system and, as in all of nature, no two are alike.

With this, enough information is available for us to reconstruct the plumbing system of a geyser. An example is shown in figure 1. It consists mainly of a tube extending into the ground, containing many sharp bends and constrictions along its length. Connected to this main pipe are small open spaces and, more especially, water-storing sand and gravel of high porosity – the reservoirs. Most of this plumbing is quite near the surface, and even the largest of geysers extend to a depth of only a few hundred feet. Finally, much of the system is coated with a watertight lining of *siliceous sinter* or *geyserite,* commonly known simply as *sinter.* This mineral is also deposited outside the geyser and in and about the quiet hot springs. Of course, the sinter is not magically deposited by the hot water. Its source is the quartz (or silica) in the rocks underlying the geyser basin.

The water that erupts from a geyser arrives there only after a long, arduous journey. Water first falls in Yellowstone as rain and snow, then travels to as much as 8,000 feet below the surface and back again. The round-trip journey takes hundreds, perhaps thousands, of years. This is something that can actually be determined with reasonable accuracy by studying the *tritium,* or "heavy heavy hydrogen," content of the geyser water. Tritium is radioactively unstable and decays with age. So, young water contains considerable amounts of tritium while old water contains little or none. It is absent in most waters from Yellowstone geysers.

At the depth of a mile or more below the surface, the water is heated by contact with the enclosing rocks. Once heated, it dissolves some of the quartz from the rocks. All this takes place at very high temperatures – over 400°F (200°C) in many cases, and 460°F (over 240°C) was found in one research drill hole. This silica will not be deposited by the water until it has approached the surface and cooled to a considerable extent.

Now an interesting and important phenomenon occurs. Although it was the mineral quartz that was dissolved out of the rocks, the deposit of sinter is a form of opal. The mechanisms involved in this process are complex, involving temperature, pressure, acidity or alkalinity of the water, and *time.*

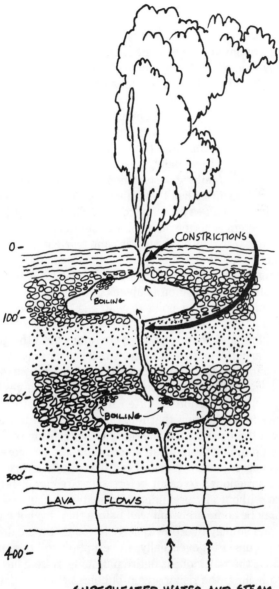

Figure 1. The plumbing system of a geyser

How a geyser erupts

The hot water, circulating up from great depth, flows into the plumbing system of a geyser. Because this water is many degrees above the boiling point, some of it turns to steam instead of forming liquid pools. Meanwhile, additional, cooler water is flowing into the geyser from the porous rocks nearer the surface. The two waters mix as the plumbing system fills.

The steam bubbles formed at depth rise and meet the cooler water. At first, they condense there, but as they do they gradually heat the water. Eventually, these steam bubbles rising from deep within the plumbing system manage to heat the surface water until it also reaches the boiling point. Now the geyser begins to function like a pressure cooker. The water within the plumbing system is hotter than boiling, but "stable" because of the pressure exerted by all the water lying above it. (Remember that the boiling point of a liquid is dependent upon the pressure. The boiling point of pure water is 212°F (100°C) at sea level. In Yellowstone the elevation is about 7,500 feet, the pressure is lower, and the boiling point of water is only about 199°F (93°C).)

The filling and heating process continues until the geyser is full or nearly full of water. A very small geyser may take but a few seconds to fill whereas some of the larger geysers take several days. Once the plumbing system is full the geyser is about ready for an eruption. Often forgotten but of extreme importance is the heating that must occur along with the filling. Only if there is an adequate store of heat within the rocks lining the plumbing system can an eruption last for more than a few seconds. Again, each geyser is different from every other. Some are hot enough to erupt before they are completely full and do so without any preliminary indications of an eruption. Others may be completely full well before they are hot enough to erupt and so may overflow quietly for some time before an eruption occurs. But, eventually, the eruption will take place.

Because the water of the entire plumbing system has been heated to boiling, the rising steam bubbles no longer collapse near the surface. Instead, as more very hot water enters the geyser at depth, even more and larger steam bubbles form and rise toward the surface. At first, they are able to make it all the way to the top of the plumbing system. But a time will come when there are so many steam bubbles that they can no longer simply float upwards. Somewhere they encounter some sort of constriction or bend in the plumbing. To get by they must squirt through the narrow spot. This forces some water ahead of them and up and out of the geyser. This initial loss of water reduces the pressure at depth, lowering the boiling point of water already hot enough to boil. More water boils, forming more steam. Soon there is a virtual explosion as the steam expands to over 1,500 times its original, liquid volume. The boiling rapidly becomes violent and water is ejected so rapidly that it is thrown into the air.

The eruption will continue until either the water is used up or the temperature drops below boiling. Once an eruption has ended, the entire process of filling, heating, and boiling will be repeated, leading to another eruption.

Why are some geysers regular, others irregular?

The inflow of water into a geyser system is constant. Thus it would seem that the activity of any geyser should also be continuous. But only a few are classed as regular geysers. In order to be regular, a geyser must be either isolated from other springs or connected only with springs whose own activity is so steady that they do not affect the geyser. Old Faithful is the famous example of regularity. Its eruptions can be predicted with about 90% accuracy. Several other geysers, including Riverside, Daisy, Echinus, and Plume, are even more regular, sometimes operating with almost stopwatch-like precision.

But most geysers are irregular. The time interval between eruptions is erratic. One time it may be just minutes between the plays, the next several hours. In no way can these geysers be predicted.

The mechanism behind this has been termed *exchange of function,* as first described by G. D. Marler in 1951. What that basically means is that water and energy can be diverted from a geyser to some other hot spring or hot spring group (another geyser is not necessarily involved). This happens because the plumbing systems of most springs and geysers are intertwined with those of others. Indeed, one group of active springs may suddenly stop functioning while a nearby group of insignificant springs becomes animated.

Just what makes exchange of function occur is not known, but the effects can be drastic. Perhaps the best example involved Daisy Geyser and nearby Bonita Pool in the Upper Basin. For years Daisy was one of the largest and most regular geysers in Yellowstone, while Bonita overflowed only slightly. Suddenly the energy shifted toward Bonita. Daisy was drained of the energy necessary for eruptions as Bonita overflowed heavily and underwent frequent small eruptions. The result was that Daisy erupted just three times in over 13 years. During the mid-1970s the energy flow gradually shifted back toward Daisy. Now it erupts as regularly and frequently as ever, and Bonita lies quietly below overflow.

Why are geysers so rare?

There are few places on earth where the three requirements for the existence of geysers are met. The requisite water supply poses no great problem; in fact, a few geysers are able to exist in desert areas, places normally thought of as dry. But the heat source and plumbing systems are tied to one another and are much more restrictive.

Nature's heat source is volcanic activity. The heat is supplied by large bodies of molten rock lying at great depth. Given a proper water supply, geysers become theoretically possible in any area of geologically-recent volcanism. (In geology, "recent" can be as much as several hundred thousand years ago.)

But there is a catch. Not just any volcanism will do. We must still have the pressure-tight plumbing. Therefore, we must have silica-rich rocks to provide the source of the sinter that lines the plumbing systems.

The answer is *rhyolite*. Rhyolite is a volcanic rock very rich in silica; it is the chemical equivalent of granite. Rhyolite itself is rather uncommon, and large recent fields of it are found in few places. Yet virtually all geysers are found in such areas. Most of the few exceptions to this rule are still associated with recent volcanic activity although their rocks – dacite, andesite, and basalt – are somewhat less rich in silica. And as seems to be usual in science, there are a couple of completely anomalous geyser localities, such as Beowawe, Nevada (see Appendix), where the activity is associated neither with recent volcanic action nor even with volcanic rocks.

Not only is Yellowstone a major rhyolite field, but it is of very recent origin. Although the last major volcanic eruption was 600,000 years ago, minor activity continued up to as little as 70,000 years ago. Yellowstone could be the site of further volcanic eruptions, but that is another story entirely.

Chapter 2

Some Background on the Yellowstone Geysers

Geysers are beautiful and rare. Wherever they are found, they have attracted attention for the duration of their known history. Outside of Yellowstone some geysers have been watched for hundreds, even thousands, of years. Within the Park they have been observed for far longer than recorded history. The Indians certainly saw them and wondered about them.

But just *what* the Indians thought about the geysers is uncertain. Few tales have come down to us. At least some of the Shoshoni Indians called the geyser basins "Water-That-Keeps-On-Coming-Out." But, despite popular notions about native religions, the Indians were obviously not afraid of the geysers in any way. Remains of their campsites have been found within nearly every hot spring area of the Park. In some of these places obsidian chips left over from tool-making litter the ground, suggesting that these areas must have been virtual factories for the production of arrow and spear points.

In at least one place in the Park, an unknown native piled logs about the crater of a geyser. Why this was done will always remain a mystery, but it suggests that Indians probably did not fear geysers. Perhaps the Indians did hold a special reverence for the geysers, though; one story claims that geyser eruptions were the result of underground battles between the spirits, but even these wars did not affect mortals. Whatever the Indians thought, they harbored no great myths about either Yellowstone or its geysers.

Their wild stories about the geothermal wonders, however, attracted many early explorers to the Yellowstone Plateau. Probably the first of them all was John Colter. As a member of the Lewis and Clark Expedition, he was so intrigued with the Montana–Wyoming area that he left the main party in 1806 and moved south along the Yellowstone River, where he may have visited the huge terraces of Mammoth Hot Springs.

Colter's reports, though factual, were regarded as pure fancy and were ignored. But other mountain men soon moved into the area and emerged with similar stories, all too fanciful and fantastic to be true.

Mountain man Jim Bridger, already notorious for his tall tales, drifted into the Yellowstone country and confirmed Colter's findings. But when he talked about the towering columns of water and boiling rivers, people listened only for a laugh. Another Yellowstone trapper of the 1830s, Osborne Russell, kept a journal of his travels. His written descriptions of some of the geysers and hot springs were so accurate that the hot springs can be identified from them today, yet even these seemed unbelievable to "civilized" people back east.

The stories didn't stop, though. In time the versions of just what Yellowstone really was had become tremendous. Clearly, there had to be some honest answers.

Several attempts to lead expeditions into the Yellowstone country were made during the 1860s. Because of frequent Indian scares throughout the area or the lack of financing, planned expeditions continually fell through until 1869, when Charles Cook, David Folsom, and William Peterson, all from the mining town of Helena, Montana, decided to go it alone.

They rode down the Yellowstone River, past the Mammoth Hot Springs, and over the plateau to the Mud Volcano area. From there they went due west—straight into the Lower Geyser Basin. They were thrilled by Great Fountain Geyser and amazed at the Midway Basin. Here, figuring that they had seen enough, they moved down the Firehole River and so missed the fantastic Upper Basin by just 4 miles.

But Cook, Folsom, and Peterson kept excellent records of what they saw, and their report renewed the enthusiasm of three men who had thought of making the trip earlier. Big names were involved this time: Henry Washburn, the Surveyor General of Montana Territory; Cornelius Hedges, a judge; and Nathaniel P. Langford, who was later to become the first Superintendent of Yellowstone Park. Along with an Army contingent led by Lt.

Gustavus C. Doane for protection, these men and others set out in the late summer of 1870 on what has become known as the "Discovery Expedition."

It was a long journey, one that saw hardship and tragedy, but eventually the explorers reached the Upper Geyser Basin. One of their first sights is said to have been Old Faithful erupting against a sunset sky. In the next day and a half they saw the eruptions of countless other geysers, large and small. They named several, including Beehive, Giantess, Castle, Grotto, and Old Faithful itself. After recording their findings, they left the basin.

The Washburn Party spent the last night of their expedition in what is now Yellowstone National Park at Madison Junction. Around a campfire they discussed the marvels they had seen. Almost to a man, they wanted others to be able to see what they had seen. But how to do it?

It was there, around the evening fire in the middle of a wilderness, that the national park idea was born. Apparently Judge Hedges said it first: withdraw the entire area as a park, excluded from settlement and protected for all time by the government. The plan was agreed upon and all would work to that end upon their return to Montana. And work they did–some of them, anyway. But most Easterners simply would not believe their reports, despite the integrity of the explorers. In fact, one article submitted to a magazine was returned with the cryptic rejection: "Sorry, we do not print fiction."

But the leader of the Geological and Geographical Survey of the Territories, Dr. Ferdinand V. Hayden, did believe the report. He organized and led a complete survey of the proposed Park area during 1871. The Hayden Survey's report, combined with the excellent photographs of William H. Jackson and paintings by Thomas Moran, convinced the nation, or at least the Congress. On March 1, 1872, quite soon, really, after all those "tall tales" of the mountainmen, President U. S. Grant signed the bill establishing the "Yellowstone Park" into law.

Thanks to the efforts of those early explorers, we are able to visit what is certainly the greatest, most wonderful thermal area on Earth. More than one hundred years later, Old Faithful, Grand, Clepsydra, and all the other geysers continue to spout skyward, just as they always have. The preserve we call Yellowstone has hardly changed. Or has it?

The geysers of Yellowstone often seem to be tremendously permanent features. Time after time, day after day, they go through their eruption cycles, usually with little or no apparent change.

But at 11:42 P.M. on the night of August 17, 1959 the entire Yellowstone area was jarred by a severe earthquake. With a Richter magnitude of 7.2, it ranked as one of America's major tremors of all time. Just outside of the national park twenty-six people were killed by landslides. There were no fatalities in Yellowstone, but structural and road damage was severe.

One of the greatest and longest-lasting reminders of the quake was its effect on the geysers and hot springs. On the night of the tremors and within the next few days, hundreds of geysers erupted, including many hot springs that had not previously been known as geysers.

Exactly what caused these eruptions is difficult to say with certainty. It might have been a twofold event. With some geysers, compression resulting from the quake might have forced a small amount of water out of the plumbing systems, resulting in subsurface boiling and eruptions. In others, especially those that did not erupt before the earthquake, the underground water circulation patterns may have been altered so that more energy was channeled to these springs. Whatever the reasons for the increased activity, most died down quickly. Virtually every spring returned to its pre-quake state within a year. But some new activity continues to this day, and changes such as these are probably permanent.

Geologic study has shown that the surface vent of every hot spring in Yellowstone, be it quiet pool or geyser, probably formed as a result of earthquakes. The shaking of the ground creates cracks in the sinter, and these rifts tap the hot water source and become the sites of new springs. Several are known to have formed as a result of the 1959 earthquake.

One of these, Seismic Geyser, must be considered a major spouter. At first, the new crack steamed quietly. With time the force of the steam grew stronger until a steam explosion opened a large crater at the site during the winter of 1961–62. Within

The 1959 earthquake caused Sapphire Pool to erupt violently, some bursts reaching over 125 feet high. With declining force, the activity persisted for twelve years. (NPS photo by George Marler.)

the crater was a small geyser. Again, as time passed, the activity of the geyser became more powerful; by 1966 Seismic was erupting to as high as 75 feet. But that force was too great. In 1971 another explosion opened a crater known as Seismic's Satellite. Eruptions from the new vent, small as they were, were enough to prevent any further eruptions by Seismic itself. Now, even the activity of the Satellite has declined, and the Seismic group no longer does more than boil.

Seismic Geyser is but one example of this process. Yellowstone is the site of frequent major earthquakes; over the past century there has been one about every 25 years. On June 30, 1975 a quake of magnitude 6.2 shook the Park. No changes as a result of this shock could be found in the Old Faithful area, but one backcountry area was affected. Changes resulting from the Borah Peak, Idaho, earthquake of October 28, 1983 were more dramatic. Even though that tremor was located nearly 200 miles from Yellowstone, its magnitude of 7.9 had effects. Ex-

The entire history of Seismic Geyser—its birth, growth into a major geyser, and decline back to quiescence—was entirely the result of the 1959 earthquake. (NPS photo by George Marler.)

change of function dramatically changed the performance of many springs on Geyser Hill, and related to that was a temporary and very slight slowdown by Old Faithful. Here and there throughout the Park were notable increases in eruptive activity, and most of these have persisted in the two years since.

Every year in the Yellowstone Plateau up to 2,000 tremors are recorded by seismographs. These quakes are normal events. There is little doubt that Yellowstone has been shaken by a great many major shocks over the ages. The resulting thermal changes must be very large in number.

Of course, not all change and variation is due to major earthquakes. Yellowstone can be subtle, too, and perhaps nothing shows this as well as the spectrum of colors seen in the hot springs and their runoff channels. Just as each geyser or pool is different, each geyser basin has its own personality. None of the coloration is ever exactly the same, neither from place to place nor from time to time.

The broad flats and cones of the basins are accented by tones of white and gray. These stark colors are caused by the siliceous sinter that, when underground, is so important to the existence of geysers (see Chapter 1). It forms very slowly, sometimes at the rate of only 1/100 of an inch per year. Most deposits vary from a few inches to a few feet thick. Obviously, such specimens took many, many years to form. Yet they are delicate and beautiful, too. Pause someplace in the basins and take a close look at the lustrous, pearly beads and compare them with the wafer-thin, artistic laminations of other spots. But as you do this remember the tremendous age and rarity of this geyserite. Don't try to take a piece with you. In time it will only dry out and crumble to dust. Please leave the formations untouched for others to see.

Minerals other than sinter are also present, though rarer. Most common are bright yellow sulfur and red-brown iron oxide. These deposits are especially prominent at the Norris Geyser Basin. Here and there throughout Yellowstone sinter is sometimes stained dark gray or black because of small impurities of manganese oxide minerals; interestingly, the same minerals in even smaller amounts cause a fine pink color. Brilliant red and orange-yellow arsenic compounds appear at Norris and Shoshone, curious because apparently at no other place in the world are they deposited right on the surface of the ground. Small popcorn-like aggregates of complex sulfate minerals show up as white and light yellow puffs on gravel in barren, acid flats. The minerals are everywhere, but always with different combinations and compositions.

The hot pools themselves are often deep blue or green, a coloration that led some early explorers of Yellowstone to believe they had found a bonanza. Copper in solution will turn water blue or blue-green, and that is what they thought they had found. But any deep body of water will look blue. Water absorbs most of the colors of the rainbow, but not the blues and blue-greens. Those colors are reflected back, making the water appear bluish. If any other material is present in the water or lining the crater walls, that tint will be added to the blue. Most common is the yellow of either the mineral sulfur or hot water algae. This blending of yellow and blue can produce a green of incredible intensity and richness.

The brilliant oranges, yellows, browns, and greens in the wet runoff channels are due to algae and bacteria. (To be technical, the algae is also bacteria; many microbiologists now call what was "blue-green algae" by a new name, "cyanobacteria.") These microscopic plants have been studied extensively. You can tell the approximate temperature of a stream by the color of its algae; if it's bright yellow the temperature is around 160°F (71°C); brilliant orange, about 145°F (63°C); the dark browns come in at about 130°F (57°C); pure green shows up at around 120°F (50°C) and below. If stringy pale yellow or pink strands of bacteria are visible in a very hot runoff, one can be pretty sure the temperature is over 180°F (82°C). In relatively narrow, fast-flowing channels one often sees a V-shaped pattern to the colors. The stream cools more slowly near the center of the channel. There the algae that thrive at higher temperatures are able to survive farther from the source of the stream; less tolerant plants hug the edges of the stream where the water cools more quickly nearer the source. Some runoffs also support a mixture of algae types, which produce a different color scheme altogether. One of these is a nearly fluorescent chartreuse.

Large or small, obvious or subtle, Yellowstone and its thermal features are constantly changing. But now there is another cause of great change on the scene, one that is able to cause change more extensive than that of Mother Nature's greatest earthquake. It's called PEOPLE.

A century ago some men with vision fought to protect and preserve Yellowstone's unique geysers. It's well that they did so, for we now know that Yellowstone contains fully 60% of all the geysers in the world. Yet the remains of an old slatback chair were recently removed from Old Faithful. Please, let's not let our founders down.

It is destructive, dangerous, *and* illegal to leave the constructed trails and boardwalks or to throw any object into any hot spring or geyser. Obey the signs in the geyser basins. Don't be Man-the-Destroyer. Instead, be Man-the-Protector. Help yourself and others to have safe, enjoyable visits to the greatest geyser field in the world . . . now and in the future.

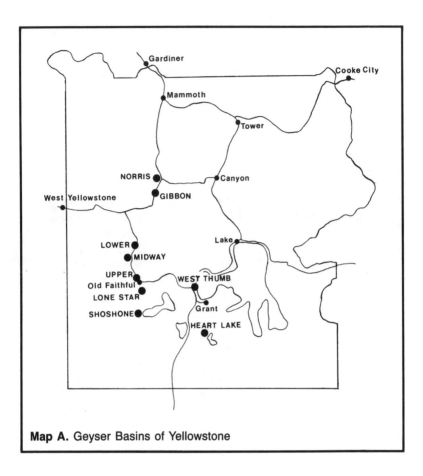

Map A. Geyser Basins of Yellowstone

Chapter 3

Geysers of Yellowstone National Park

Yellowstone National Park, Wyoming, is the home of Steamboat Geyser, the largest active geyser in the world. It is the site of Giant Geyser, which has the greatest water discharge of any geyser when it has one of its rare eruptions. Another geyser here is Bead Geyser, which often erupts with stopwatch precision. And so on. Pick nearly any category you wish and you will probably find the "best" example among the geysers of Yellowstone. This really shouldn't surprise anybody. Yellowstone is by far the largest geyser field in the world. Its more than 300 geysers make up at least 60% of all geysers on the planet.

Geysers have long fascinated mankind. A possible single geyser (Gayzer Suyu) near the site of Troy in Turkey is mentioned in Homer's *Iliad,* written around 800 B.C. The first accurate description of a geyser eruption came from an English monk in A.D. 1294. Anyplace that they have been encountered at any time, they have always been noted. Therefore, for all their rarity, geysers are well-known features of our world. But, aside from Yellowstone, one must do a lot of travelling to see other good examples. The next best geyser fields outside of Yellowstone — those of Iceland, New Zealand, Chile, and Kamchatka — contain no more than about 25 active geysers each. (For more about these localities, see Appendix.)

Within Yellowstone are more than 10,000 hot springs of various types. Overall, fumaroles (steam vents), mud pots, and quietly flowing springs are much more common than geysers. The geysers are found in only a few relatively small areas. These are the "geyser basins" — specifically, Upper, Midway, Lower, Norris, West Thumb, Gibbon, Lone Star, Shoshone, and Heart Lake (see Map A).

These geyser basins are not necessarily true basins, but instead are simply geographical areas within which hot springs, including geysers, are found. The basins are not large. For example, all of the more than 180 geysers of the Upper Basin (which is the biggest) are located within an area just 2 miles long and ½ mile wide.

The Upper Geyser Basin is the most important. There are more geysers here than in any other area of either Yellowstone or the world. This is the home of Old Faithful, Beehive, Grand, Riverside, and a great many more. Interspersed among them are hundreds of other, beautiful hot springs.

The Lower Geyser Basin covers a much larger area – about 5 square miles – but the geyser groups are more widely scattered. Among these geysers are some of the best known, such as Great Fountain, Fountain, White Dome, and Clepsydra.

The Norris Geyser Basin is the third largest, both in area and number of geysers. To many it is the most important because it is different from any other. The water at Norris is acidic; some of it is comparable to battery acid in strength. All other geyser basins discharge alkaline water. Norris is the site of Echinus Geyser, one of the more beautiful and regular geysers in the Park, and Steamboat, the largest anywhere when active.

The Midway, West Thumb, and Gibbon Geyser Basins contain fewer geysers than the rest. They are, however, accessible areas, with relatively little walking necessary to see the geysers. Definitely, each has its own special attractions and is well worth the time it takes to see.

Three other geyser basins lie in the backcountry. The Lone Star Basin is about 2½ miles by trail, and includes two large and several small geysers. The Shoshone and Heart Lake Geyser Basins lie at greater distances. Few people visit them, so they remain virtually untouched by man. Marked trails lead to these basins, but not through them. Although one is free to wander among the hot springs, the hiker should remember that all thermal areas are dangerous and extreme caution is necessary.

In the following descriptive chapters the geysers are detailed according to geyser basin. Each area is further subdivided into groups, and there the geysers are described according to the order in which they lie along the trail. Every set of descriptions is followed by a table summarizing the activity of that group.

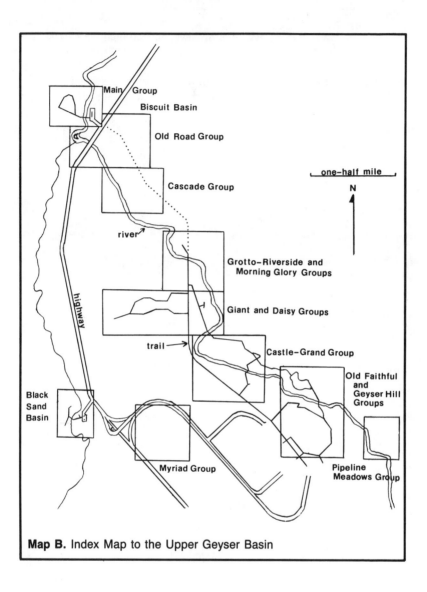

Map B. Index Map to the Upper Geyser Basin

Chapter 4

Upper Geyser Basin

The Upper Geyser Basin is the first area to be described. This is always the case, and it isn't because of habit that it is placed here. The Upper Basin is the home of Old Faithful and many other major spouters. It is the greatest concentration of geysers anywhere.

Over 150 geysers, certainly better than 25% of the world total, are found within this area of about 1 square mile. The hot springs are scattered among several nearly contiguous groups (Map B). Most of them lie within a few hundred feet of the Firehole River, and nowhere is the basin more than ½ mile wide.

The Upper Geyser Basin understandably attracted the greatest attention of the early explorers of Yellowstone. Many of the names given the geysers and pools here were applied during the early 1870s. While it was recognized that all of Yellowstone was worth preserving, it was probably the Upper Basin above all else that provided the greatest wonders and led to the founding of the world's first national park.

With four exceptions, all of the geyser groups are threaded by boardwalks and other trails. The areas that aren't—the Cascade, Old Road, Myriad, and Pipeline Groups—can still be visited to at least some extent. Because of the thermal dangers involved, however, casual wandering through these places is not encouraged. Naturalist tours occasionally explore these groups and, if nothing else, the visitor can walk along more distant roads and trails so as to view these areas from somewhat greater distances than usual.

To properly see the Upper Basin one *must* spend two or three days in order to wait for the large and famous geysers to erupt. There are minor details in the basin to be observed, too—colorations, forest life, hot spring life, and so much more—many of which are found no place else in the world. To spend less time is to cheat oneself.

Old Faithful Group

Only five springs are described as belonging to the Old Faithful Group (Map C, Table 1). In reality, the group is an isolated portion of the Geyser Hill Group, but because of its location on the opposite side of the Firehole River, it seems separate.

Two of the springs are not geysers. Between Old Faithful and Chinaman Spring is a very pretty pool; the origin of Blue Star Spring's name is obvious. Right next to Chinaman is North Chinaman Spring; it boils and overflows but never erupts.

1. OLD FAITHFUL GEYSER is the most famous geyser in America, as it should be. However, it certainly is not the most famous in the world. That distinction belongs to the "Geysir" in Iceland, the namesake of all geysers. But no geyser anywhere can match Old Faithful in terms of size, frequency, and regularity of eruptions. It can be viewed from the many benches near the Visitor Center, Inn, and Lodge. The most scenic view, however, is from Geyser Hill, across the Firehole River. There, at a greater distance and with green hills and blue sky as a background, Old Faithful provides one of the finest sights in Yellowstone.

Old Faithful was discovered by the Washburn Expedition. Rumor has it that as they entered the Upper Geyser Basin at sunset on that day in 1870, the first thing they saw was Old Faithful in full eruption. Unbelievably, here was one of the towering columns of water the mountain men had talked about for so long. Although they spent just 1½ days in the Upper Basin, the Expedition was so impressed with this geyser's frequent activity that they called it Old Faithful. It's well that they did, for it has been true to its name for well over a century now.

A lot of rumors make the rounds about Old Faithful. Many believe that it once erupted "every hour, on the hour." Others swear that it is far smaller than it once was. Following the earthquake at Borah Peak, Idaho, in 1983 dozens of newspaper, radio, and television reports said that Old Faithful was dying. None of these stories are true. Old Faithful is a natural feature, and it is subject to changes. But it is also very much the geyser it has always been.

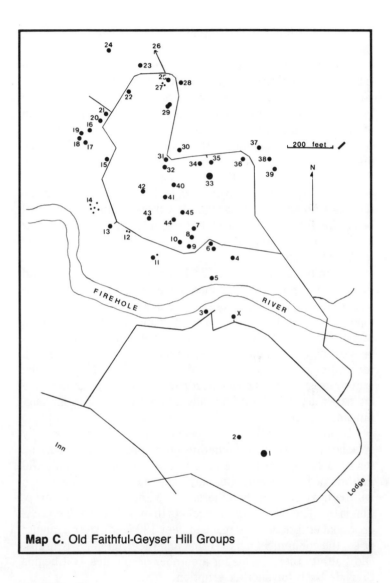

Map C. Old Faithful-Geyser Hill Groups

Over the years a lot of data has been gathered about Old Faithful. The long-run average interval between eruptions is usually near an hour. After over 46,000 eruptions were timed, the actual average was exactly 64.91 minutes, with known extremes of 33 and 120 minutes. During June 1985 the average height of 211 individual eruptions was 123½ feet. As always, the eruptions last anywhere from just 1½ to 5 minutes.

Old Faithful is regular enough to allow the ranger-naturalists—and the Park visitor—to predict the times of eruption with fair accuracy. Only one prediction can be made at a time because the length of the interval is dependent on the duration of the preceding eruption. It's easy to make the prediction yourself. A short eruption means that less water and heat has been discharged, that a shorter time span will be required to regain that water and heat, and therefore that the interval between the eruptions will be shorter than average. For example, if the eruption lasts about 2 minutes, then it will be around 53 minutes before the next one. On the other hand, a long duration (say near 5 minutes) will lead to a longer interval; the prediction will be for 76–80 minutes.

Much of the belief that Old Faithful is slowing down and that it isn't as powerful as it once was probably results from different viewing times. It is possible that such stories arise when a person visited the geyser years ago and happened to see an especially fine eruption; any smaller play will make it seem to be slowing down. Also, a person's memory can play tricks; a remembrance of years past is often magnified. The evidence is in contrast to any such ideas. *Every* bit of information we have indicates that Old Faithful really has not changed to any significant degree.

Shortly before Old Faithful begins to play, water periodically splashes from the vent. Sometimes this "preplay" will continue for 10 to 20 minutes before the eruption begins, but usually Old Faithful begins to spout after only a few such surges. One splash will be heavier than the others, and within seconds the eruption is on. The water rapidly rockets to over 100 feet high. Exceptional eruptions have reached over 180 feet. After a minute or so, the column begins to shrink and the height slowly drops. Old Faithful then steams for a number of minutes as it begins to cycle back for another eruption.

Each of Old Faithful's eruptions is different from every other, and all are magnificent. Old Faithful Geyser *is* one of the natural wonders of the world.

2. UNNG-OFG-1 ("TEAPOT" GEYSER) is located on top of a low geyserite mound only about 150 feet northwest of Old Faithful. Its eruptions are not seen very often, and they aren't very impressive. Although the durations are long, the height is no more than 2 feet.

3. CHINAMAN SPRING. In the early days of Yellowstone Park there were many more concessions than at present. One of these was a Chinese laundry. One day the proprietor was doing some wash when his spring erupted and blew clothes all over the landscape. And so the name. Chinaman Spring rarely erupts, but when it does the water column surges to 20 feet for about 2 minutes.

Geyser Hill Group

On Geyser Hill, the white, sinter-clad area directly across the Firehole River from the Old Faithful Geyser area, are found about 40 geysers (Map C, Table 1). Some of these are among the largest anywhere; many others are almost inconspicuously small. It is certainly worth mentioning that this concentration of geysers would, by itself and with no other geyser anywhere in Yellowstone, be the largest single geyser field in the world!

Geyser Hill is traversed by a loop trail. It connects with other trails leading to Old Faithful, the Grand Geyser area, and Solitary Geyser-Observation Point.

4. LITTLE SQUIRT GEYSER was so named because of the squirting nature of its eruptions. Unless it is playing, its location goes completely unnoticed, being little more than a 3-inch hole in the geyserite. Before the 1959 earthquake Little Squirt was very irregular in its action. Since then it has been active during most seasons, and it was especially so during 1985. The periods of activity and quiet are of about the same length and can last from several hours to days. Throughout the eruption the squirting is about 4 feet high.

5. CASCADE GEYSER was very active during the early days of the Park, but it became dormant around 1900. The only known activity since then has come following both the 1959 and 1983 earthquakes. Spurred to life, eruptions reach 25 feet high. The lack of any well-defined runoff channels indicates that Cascade is almost always dormant. It has been dormant since early 1984.

6. THE ANEMONE GEYSERS. Anemone is a double spring. Two vents about 10 feet apart are the sites of semi-independent geysers. Most of the time the two act separately with little apparent relationship between them, but during some periods an eruption of one will invariably follow that of the other. The geysers rarely play simultaneously. Both craters are shallow basins lined with pearly beads of sinter; the larger is tinted pinkish-gray, the smaller pale yellow.

"Big" Anemone, nearest the boardwalk and the larger of the two, normally shows the greater activity. During most seasons it erupts every 5 to 8 minutes. Some of the spray reaches over 8 feet high, while other bursts may reach the boardwalk. Most eruptions last about 40 seconds. If "Little" Anemone erupts, then the interval before "Big" does so again may be as long as 15 minutes.

"Little" Anemone plays from the vent farther from the boardwalk. Its eruptions are smaller than those of its neighbor, but they generally last considerably longer. On rare occasions near-constant activity by "Little" will render "Big" dormant for days at a time.

7. SURGE GEYSER is an old spring or geyser rejuvenated by the 1959 earthquake. Before then the crater was there, but no eruptions had ever been recorded. Following the earthquake, Surge erupted frequently until 1963. Since then it has *sometimes* been active in concert with Giantess Geyser (33), proving an underground connection between the two. Such eruptions, lasting as long as 1 minute and reaching 8 feet high, were last seen in 1984.

8. UNNG-GHG-1 had its first recorded activity following the earthquake of 1983. The ragged crater was considerably enlarged by these eruptions, which burst powerfully to at least 10 feet high. The activity rapidly died down, and the spring now does little more than periodically boil.

9. PLUME GEYSER is of fairly recent origin. In 1922 a small steam explosion created its surface vent. Following a short period of activity, it was dormant until 1941. Since then it has been continuously active, often with an extreme degree of regularity. For a long time, Plume really did seem to erupt "every hour, on the hour." Its average interval was almost exactly 60 minutes. However, as time went on it gradually became more irregular until, just after the 1959 earthquake, it seldom erupted. Plume was not to be done in, though. By 1962 it was again highly regular, but the new average interval was only 27 minutes. Such was the case until 1973.

Plume is a good example of how geysers may change themselves. In December of 1972 another steam explosion added an extension to the vent. Much of the eruption now issues from this new opening. Plume is still quite regular, but less so than before, and the eruptions are massive bursts to 25 or 30 feet rather than the slender 40-foot jettings of old.

Detailed observations since 1982 have shown that Plume's action varies according to the current activity in Giantess Geyser (33). The overall average interval remains about 27 to 30 minutes. This may decrease to as little as 23 minutes when Giantess starts and can then briefly increase to as high as 55 minutes following a Giantess eruption.

10. UNNG-GHG-2 ("BALLCAP" GEYSER) is a ragged hole just a few feet to the left of Plume Geyser (9). It seems to have increased the strength of its eruptions in the past few years. Activity is frequent, the eruptions reaching about 2 feet high. (For years, under the proper lighting conditions, a green ballcap could be seen within this crater, but it has now disappeared.)

11. BEEHIVE GEYSER is presently the second or third largest in Yellowstone and, therefore, in the world. Unfortunately, it has been an infrequent performer during most of its known history. Eruptions are several days apart. Starting in the early 1970s and continuing into 1985 it erupted with almost unprecedented frequency, with average intervals as short as 11 hours. During 1984, for the first and only time, predictions of Beehive's

Beehive Geyser, on Geyser Hill, is among the largest cone-type geysers in the world. The steady jetting reaches over 170 feet high.

eruptions were posted in the Visitor Center. All that has changed now; during July 1985 Beehive suddenly became more erratic and infrequent, with intervals the more usual 3 to 10 days in length.

The eruptions issue through a cone 4 feet high and shaped like an old-fashioned straw beehive. The vent within the cone is very narrow and acts like a nozzle so that a slender column of water is shot under great pressure to as much as 200 feet high. To observe an eruption of Beehive from the boardwalk near its cone is a unique experience. The awesome display combined with the dull roar of escaping steam is completely unforgettable. Viewed at a distance, the impression is very different. Then the slenderness of the water jet becomes apparent – almost like a needle of water towering above the surroundings. The entire eruption, including a short, concluding steam phase, lasts about 5 minutes.

It is difficult to tell just when Beehive might erupt. Water splashes out of the cone throughout most of the quiet interval. Shortly before the eruption these surges become larger and more frequent. It is one of these that finally triggers the full display.

Sometimes, especially when Beehive is relatively frequent and regular, a spouting vent known as *Beehive's Indicator* can be used. It plays from a crack a few feet to the front-left of Beehive's cone. If it is active, then the 6- to 10-foot eruption normally indicates that an eruption of Beehive is very near, probably within 20 minutes. Unfortunately, the use of the Indicator is not always reliable. It may begin spouting as much as 45 minutes before Beehive's activity. It may start and stop several times without subsequent eruptions by Beehive. And, in fact, during most of its recorded history, Beehive's Indicator has not been active at all.

12. SCISSORS SPRINGS. These two small springs used to flow steadily. The two rivulets converged a short distance from the springs, then split again so that the whole formation resembled a pair of shears. By 1950 one spring had stopped flowing; shortly, the other also stopped. In 1974, they suddenly sprang to life again, not only overflowing, but erupting to a few feet high. Since then the activity has waxed and waned several times, and in 1985 there was little discharge.

13. DEPRESSION GEYSER is yet another spring dramatically affected by earthquakes. Both that of 1959 and that of 1983 caused considerable change in its activity. Before the time of the 1959 earthquake, Depression was so seldom active that it hadn't even been given a name. Now the pale blue-green pool plays often and regularly. Intervals average about 3½ hours. The eruptions, 6 to 10 feet high, last about 3 minutes.

14. UNNG-GHG-3. In the flat area a short distance to the right (northwest) of Depression Geyser (13) are a number of small spouters and geysers. The largest of these erupts up to 8 feet high, but most are very small. These geysers have been dormant for most of their known history. Previously active only during 1947, 1959, and 1962, they have now been playing continuously since 1972.

On the opposite side of the boardwalk in this vicinity are several explosion craters. Although all were formed in prehistoric times, several of these had eruptions as a result of the 1983 earthquake. None were regular or frequent in their performances, but some eruptions reached 10 feet high.

15. UNNG-GHG-4 ("POT-O-GOLD" SPRING) is immediately next to the boardwalk midway between Arrowhead Spring and Heart Spring. A cool, quiet, and very small spring before 1980, it has since had several eruptions that have enlarged the crater. Most, if not all, of these were simultaneous with eruptions by Giantess Geyser (33). About 12 feet to the right of Pot-O-Gold is another vent; this similarly has erupted and enlarged the crater. These happened during 1985, when the boardwalk was found littered with geyserite fragments on several occasions.

THE LION GEYSER COMPLEX. Situated on a high sinter mound rising abruptly from the Firehole River at the far northwestern end of Geyser Hill are four geyserite cones. These are the Lion family. Related to them are other springs below and to the north of the mound. They make up one of the most active sets of geysers in Yellowstone.

16. LION GEYSER itself issues from the largest cone, the one nearest to the boardwalk. Lion is also the largest geyser of the pride. During an active period, eruptions recur every 1 to 3 hours. They last from 2 to 7 minutes. Most eruptions reach only 50 feet high, but a record of 98 feet was measured in 1988. Following an active phase, which lasts from 1 to 36 hours (usually 2 to 5), it will be anything from a few hours to 9 days before another episode begins. This is a classic example of cyclic activity.

Lion was originally known as Niobe Geyser, who in Greek mythology was turned to stone and remained forever wet with tears. It was renamed because of periodic loud bursts of steam that come from the vent during an active cycle.

17. LITTLE CUB GEYSER is the only other member of the Lion Complex to be frequently active year after year. It is the small cone on the far left of the mound, farthest from Lion. Little Cub normally erupts every 1 to 1 ‰ hours, sending some spurts up to 10 feet high for about 10 minutes. Notable is that most of Lion's active cycles begin at about the time of a Little Cub eruption.

18–19. LIONESS GEYSER and BIG CUB GEYSER are the center cones, on the left and right, respectively. These two geysers seldom erupt, but when they do they often erupt together. Lioness can reach 30 feet and Big Cub about 40 feet.

The geysers of the Lion Complex clearly show the effects of exchange of function. When Lion is in an active cycle, Lioness and Big Cub normally are not. Because of this, these geysers have been barely active during recorded history. Lion was dormant during 1984, and when it reactivated there were frequent heavy splashes from Lioness and Big Cub. But only one eruption — that by Big Cub alone on August 6, 1987 — was ever triggered, the first since 1952.

20. GOGGLE SPRING is the irregular vent a few feet north of Lion's mound. It was probably active during the 1920s and before, but modern eruptions were not seen until 1985. Following the rejuvenation of Lion from its 1984 dormancy, there was an increase in the overall activity by all the rest of the complex. Goggles shared in this by having several eruptions in concert with those of nearby North Goggles Geyser (21) and Lion. The eruptions were brief and not more than 6 feet high, but the bursts were jetted with enough force and at such a low angle as to reach the boardwalk. Such action has been extremely rare since 1985.

21. **NORTH GOGGLE GEYSER** was evidently the site of frequent action before recorded times, as it has large runoff channels leading away from the site. Historically, though, it was rarely seen prior to the time of the 1959 earthquake. Since then it has been active during every year except 1963. North Goggle has both major and minor eruptions. During most years the minors are the more common. These are very brief and seldom reach more than 10 feet high. Unlike most seasons, 1985 saw most eruptions to be majors. These eruptions are spectacular, especially so since one can stand within 10 feet of the vent. The major play may reach more than 50 feet high. The water jet pulsates throughout the eruption and only begins to decline near the end of the 4-minute duration. These eruptions are followed by a short but briefly powerful steam phase.

Immediately beyond North Goggle, a paved trail takes off to the left. After a pleasant walk through the forest, it leads you to the Castle-Grand Group of geysers. Straight ahead on the boardwalk takes in the rest of Geyser Hill.

22. **EAR SPRING** is a prominent, small pool. It is superheated — the water temperature is above the boiling point. The water overflows slightly as it sizzles and boils about the rim of the crater. The only known eruption of Ear Spring was a result of the 1959 earthquake. It is believed, however, to have undergone at least heavy surges during some eruptions of Giantess Geyser (33).

23. **PENDANT GEYSER** is something of a mystery. There seems to be no record of when it was named or what sort of activity it has had in the past. The first known record of eruptions dates to the late 1960s. Since then it has normally been dormant, but for a while during 1984, as a result of the 1983 earthquake, Pendant played frequently as much as 6 feet high. It now undergoes small, irregular splashes.

24. **UNNG-GHG-5** lies near the woods beyond Pendant Geyser (23). While it was always a small, perpetual spouter prior to the Borah Peak earthquake, those shocks triggered significant eruptions during 1984. These were frequent and up to 5 feet high. It has since relapsed to its previous minimal activity.

25. BEACH SPRING is technically not a geyser but a cyclically boiling intermittent spring. Much of the time the water lies low within the crater, but at times it fills so that the outer platform of sinter is covered. Only then does the pool undergo periods of boiling. The duration is only a few seconds.

Across the boardwalk from Beach Spring a trail leads up the hill 0.3 mile to Solitary Geyser (26). Continuing along the trail from there will take one to Observation Point and then back to the starting point of the Geyser Hill Loop.

26. SOLITARY GEYSER is, in effect, a man-made geyser. It is, at least, man-caused, the only one in Yellowstone. It was a quiet pool until 1915. In that year permission was given to use the water of the seldom visited spring for a swimming pool. Immediately, Solitary Spring became Solitary Geyser. A deepened runoff channel had lowered the water level enough to allow boiling to take place at depth – and, consequently, eruptions began. The play was frequent and powerful, reaching 25 feet high. The Old Faithful Geyser Bath was closed around 1950 and the runoff channel was repaired, but eruptions continue despite the renewed high water level, a good illustration of just how delicate these hot spring systems are. The eruptions recur every 4 to 8 minutes, last less than 1 minute, and usually reach less than 4 feet high.

27. UNNG-GHG-6&7. These two small geysers lie a few feet beyond Beach Spring. Related to one another, they are frequently active. GHG-6 is the larger of the two, lying to the north of the other. It plays up to 4 feet high, while GHG-7 seldom exceeds 2 feet.

28. AURUM GEYSER was so named because of the golden color of iron oxide staining within the little cone. Aurum is cyclic in its activity. During most years it is nearly dormant. In others, and continuously since the 1983 earthquake, eruptions are common and regular. Never have eruptions been stronger than those of 1985. Recurring every 3 to 4 hours, the 1-minute play often exceeded 20 feet. On rare occasions a seemingly normal but short eruption will be followed by another within only a few minutes.

29. DOUBLET POOL is one of the most beautiful pools in the Old Faithful area. Very deep and of rich azure color, it overflows lightly but steadily. Doublet Pool has been classed as a geyser, but most, if not all, eruptions are nothing more than a heavy boiling with consequently heavier overflow. Even these are rare. On two occasions associated with eruptions by Giantess Geyser (33) and once following the 1959 earthquake, Doublet apparently had larger eruptions, reaching perhaps 2 feet high.

30. PUMP GEYSER seems to be nearly unchangeable. A perpetual spouter, its activity was completely unaffected by any earthquake. Although steady, the eruption waxes and wanes considerably so that it nearly stops every few minutes. The fan-shaped spray reaches 2 to 3 feet high at the peak of play.

31. SPONGE GEYSER is the smallest officially named geyser in Yellowstone. It gets its name because the geyserite beadwork on the outside of the cone resembles a sponge. Also, the entire eruption could be soaked up by a large sponge. The size of the cone belies this and makes it seem that Sponge was once a larger, more important spring or geyser. But it probably never was. Water stands near the top of the cone since Sponge recovered from a long dormancy during 1984. Eruptions recur every minute or so and involve minor boiling and splashing to a maximum height of about 9 inches.

32. PLATE GEYSER, lying on the sinter platform behind Sponge Geyser (31), is probably a delayed result of the 1959 earthquake. Its formation did not come until the late 1960s, however, so there might be no relationship at all. In any case, Plate has mostly been an infrequent performer. Sometimes it is active only during activity in Giantess Geyser (33), such eruptions being brief and only a few feet high. The best year on record was 1985, when Plate erupted regularly every 2½ hours, each eruption lasting up to 10 minutes and reaching 10 to 15 feet high.

33. GIANTESS GEYSER is one of the largest and most powerful in Yellowstone. You must be very lucky to see it erupt, though. Over the last 50 years it has averaged only 2 to 3 eruptions per year. Recently it has had some better years. The all-time record for activity was set in 1983 (before the earthquake), with 41 eruptive episodes. Given the infrequent performances, it is amazing that the Washburn Expedition saw an eruption during their 1½-day visit in 1870. They described it as "the grandest wonder" of their trip.

During the long quiet phase, the large, clear pool periodically boils around the edge of the crater. An eruption begins during one of these "hot periods." Suddenly, surging begins to spill a tremendous flood of water over the surrounding sinter. After several minutes this ceases briefly, and the water level drops several inches within the crater. But then the eruption begins in earnest, jets of water being rocketed to as much as 200 feet in height.

The entire active phase may last anywhere from 1 to 43 hours; the 1959 earthquake caused one of over 100 hours. Each of these phases consists of a number of separate eruptions, which can be classified into types. The water phase type will jet water for 5 minutes every 25 to 60 minutes, for a total of about 24 hours. In the steam phase type, the water gives way to power-fully roaring steam after 20 to 50 minutes; this will then last about 12 hours. First observed in 1969 and very often since is the mixed phase type eruption, which begins like the steam phase but reverts to water phase after 3 to 6 hours; these last as long as 43 hours total. Finally, first observed in 1981, is the short, or aborted, eruption; this is a water or a mixed type phase that ends after a very short and weak duration. Following any of these varieties, the crater will refill in anything from a few hours to 3 days. There is then absolutely no indication of an erup-tion until the next actually begins.

A geyser as great as Giantess would be expected to have an effect on other springs in the area, and indeed it does. Vault Geyser (35), Infant Geyser (36), Teakettle Spring (34), Plate Geyser (32), Doublet Pool (29), Ear Spring (22), Pot-O-Gold Spring (15), Beehive Geyser (11), Plume Geyser (9), and Surge Geyser (7) are all definitely and rather directly connected with Giantess. These facts are known because of the reactions of these springs to the eruptions of Giantess. In fact, it is probable that every spring on Geyser Hill is in some way related to Giantess; even Old Faithful is probably affected. It is these con-nections that make Giantess an infrequent and irregular performer. All its many relations relieve some of Giantess's pressure and prevent its eruptions.

34. TEAKETTLE SPRING is not a geyser and likely never was. It is mentioned here because it does have a geyser-like cone. The water level is now deep within this crater, where it can be heard boiling and splashing. The pool was full until 1946; in that year Vault Geyser (35) began erupting after a long dormancy. The water immediately began ebbing in Teakettle.

35. VAULT GEYSER was hardly known until 1946. Before then it was either dormant or active very infrequently. By 1947 it had become very active, with eruptive periods lasting several hours and separated by 1 or 2 days. During the active phases, eruptions recur every hour or so. Water surges in great masses, often reaching over 20 feet.

36. INFANT GEYSER is closely tied to Giantess (33) but seems to be on the wane. Before the 1959 earthquake, it erupted only when Giantess did, and the water constantly stood below overflow. After the tremors, Infant began having eruptions on its own several times per day. Gradually the water level rose, and when the crater began to overflow in 1964 all eruptions ceased. The water level has since dropped back within the crater, but Infant no longer erupts, evidently not even with Giantess.

37. MOTTLED POOL lies uphill, across the boardwalk from Infant Geyser (36). Nothing of it can be seen from the boardwalk (and, of course, you must stay on the boardwalk). Deep within the crater are eruptions, frequent and lasting a few seconds. Some reach about 5 feet high. Evidently, Mottled had some rather large eruptions during the 1800s, but virtually nothing is known about them.

38. BUTTERFLY SPRING, named for the shape of the crater, is a perpetual spouter. The steady play is generally 1 to 3 feet high, but occasional surges to over 6 feet have been reported.

39. DOME GEYSER erupted rarely prior to 1927. From then until the 1959 earthquake it was completely dormant. It rejuvenated in November 1959, possibly as a delayed response to the August tremors. From then through 1960 there were occasional periods of activity. The major part of the eruption, as much as 30 feet high, was in the first minute; the entire play lasted 5 minutes. From 1960 through 1969 Dome was rarely seen in action, and then no further activity was observed until 1972. Dome has been active ever since, but on a much changed pattern. Active episodes recur every several days to weeks; then Dome's eruptions are usually no more than violent boiling with jetting to about 3 feet. On one occasion during 1985 a single burst estimated at 20 feet high was seen, but generally Dome is very unimpressive.

OTHER GEYSERS OF THE GEYSER HILL GROUP. Six other geysers of this group are worthy of mention. Because of their mostly small sizes and locations away from the boardwalk, they are not viewed easily.

40. MODEL GEYSER is a small spouter of frequent activity, regular at times and very irregular at others. Viewed from between Sponge Geyser (31) and Teakettle Spring (34), this is the most obvious geyser in the central portion of Geyser Hill. The eruptions reach about 4 feet high.

41. DRAGON SPRING is a beautiful blue pool and is again best seen from the vicinity of Sponge Geyser (31). Dragon apparently erupted the night of the 1959 earthquake. Though not seen because of the darkness, it is estimated to have been 20 feet high.

42. ROOF GEYSER cannot be seen — it lies completely below the ground. In a deep hole, over which is a "roof" of sinter, a small pool erupts every few minutes for a few seconds. This activity began with the 1959 earthquake.

43. UNNG-GHG-8 is but one of many craters atop the hill above Scissors Springs (12) that erupted following the 1983 earthquake. This, however, is the only one to have persisted in its activity. Eruptions, though irregular, are quite common and reach over 20 feet high.

44. UNNG-GHG-9 showed up before the time of the Borah Peak earthquake of 1983, but it has been much more active since then. The eruptions recur every few minutes. Minor plays last but seconds while majors may have durations in excess of 20 minutes. In either type of eruption, the height is 3 to 4 feet.

45. BENCH GEYSER, formerly very active, had its crater filled in by runoff from Giantess (33), and the site can no longer be found.

Table 1. Geysers of the Old Faithful and Geyser Hill Groups

Name and Number	Interval	Duration	Height (ft)
Anemone Geysers (6)	5–20 min	40 sec–min	3–8
Aurum Geyser (28)	3–4 hrs	1 min	10–25
Beach Spring (25)	irregular	secs–min	boil
Beehive Geyser (11)	hrs–days	5 min	150–200
Bench Geyser (45)	min (extinct?)	seconds	6
Big Cub Geyser (19)	rare	4–8 min	30–40
Butterfly Spring (38)	steady	steady	1–3
Cascade Geyser (5)	rare	2–3 min	25
Chinaman Spring (3)	rare	2 min	20
Depression Geyser (13)	3–4 hrs	3 min	6–10
Dome Geyser (39)	infrequent	5–10 min	3–20
Doublet Pool (29)	rare	3 min	boil–2
Dragon Spring (41)	rare	unknown	20
Ear Spring (22)	rare	1–2 min	boil
Giantess Geyser (33)	0–41/year	1–43 hrs	100–200
Goggle Spring (20)	rare	seconds	6
Infant Geyser (36)	rare	hours	2
Lion Geyser (16)	1–3 hrs	2–5 min	30–50
Lioness Geyser (18)	rare	5–10 min	30
Little Cub Geyser (17)	½–4 hrs	5–30 min	10
Little Squirt Geyser (4)	hrs–days	hrs–days	3–5
Model Geyser (40)	minutes	2–10 min	3–5
Mottled Pool (37)	frequent	seconds	3–5
North Goggle Geyser (21)	hrs–rare	sec–5 min	10–50
Old Faithful Geyser (1)	33–120 min	1½–5 min	100–186
Pendant Geyser (23)	irregular	seconds	1–6
Plate Geyser (32)	2–3 hrs	5–12 min	8–15
Plume Geyser (9)	26–48 min	1 min	10–30
Pump Geyser (30)	steady	steady	2–3
Roof Geyser (42)	3–5 min	seconds	3
Scissors Springs (12)	freq–rare	sec–min	2
Solitary Geyser (26)	4–8 min	1 min	2–6
Sponge Geyser (31)	1 min	seconds	9 inches
Surge Geyser (7)	infrequent	1 min	8
Vault Geyser (35)	45 min–1½ hrs	4–5 min	10–20
UNNG-GHG-1 (8)	rare	seconds	2–10
UNNG-GHG-2 ("Ballcap") (10)	frequent	minutes	2

Table 1. Continued.

Name and Number	Interval	Duration	Height (ft)
UNNG-GHG-3 (14)	frequent	sec–min	1–8
UNNG-GHG-4 ("Pot-O-Gold") (15)	infrequent	unknown	2–4
UNNG-GHG-5 (24)	frequent	1–3 min	3–5
UNNG-GHG-6 (27)	frequent	minutes	2–4
UNNG-GHG-7 (27)	frequent	minutes	1–2
UNNG-GHG-8 (43)	infrequent	minutes	10–20
UNNG-GHG-9 (44)	minutes	sec–20 min	3–4
UNNG-OFG-1 ("Teapot") (2)	unknown	min–hrs	1–2

Castle-Grand Group

The Castle-Grand Group of geysers (Map D, Table 2) is the most extensive in the Upper Basin. It includes over forty geysers, most of which are active to some degree all of the time. Four of the geysers are very large, and if there is any area in Yellowstone where one can be assured of seeing major geysers erupt, this is it. Besides the numerous spouters, the group contains several beautiful pools.

The Castle-Grand Group can be approached in two ways. A paved trail leads directly from the Visitor Center, past the Inn and lower store, to Castle Geyser. The other route leaves the Geyser Hill loop near North Goggle Geyser and leads more directly to Grand Geyser.

46. SPRINKLER GEYSER is difficult to see well; the best viewing spot is from the boardwalk across the river, near Liberty Pool. Because of this inconvenient location, Sprinkler has not received the study it deserves. It was named in the 1870s and has probably been continuously active since then. All eruptions involve spurts up to 10 feet high. The durations range from just 5 minutes to several hours, but long or short, the intervals are consistently 20 to 40 minutes long.

47. SPATTER GEYSER is directly across the Firehole River from Sprinkler Geyser (46). Its only known activity was a result of the 1959 earthquake, when its behavior made it a near twin of

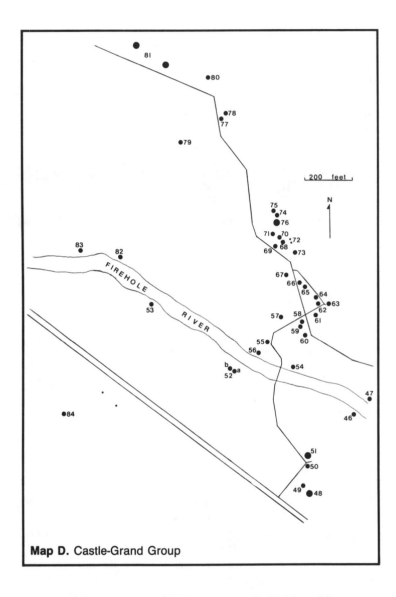

Map D. Castle-Grand Group

Sprinkler. Spatter returned to dormancy in 1962, and its crater is now nearly filled by slumped material from the slope above.

48. CASTLE GEYSER always attracts a lot of interest. It was so named by N. P. Langford of the 1870 Washburn Expedition because the cone resembles the ruined tower of an old castle. The huge geyserite cone, over 12 feet high, is one of the landmarks of the Upper Basin, striking even when the geyser isn't erupting.

Castle must be a very old geyser. The massive cone itself required several thousand years to form; the estimates of its age run all the way from 5,000 to 50,000 years. The lower figure is probably more accurate, but to consider that it has probably been continuously active during that entire time makes it even more amazing. However, the history of Castle itself isn't the whole story. The cone is built atop a huge sloping geyserite mound that was formed by an earlier hot spring over thousands of years. Put simply, Castle and its predecessor have been around for a very long time, and it shows no signs of becoming inactive.

When talking about the personalities of geysers, Castle heads the list. It has been known to undergo at least four different types of eruptions. Probably the most common through the first century of the Park has been a steady steaming, punctuated every few minutes by jets of water 40 feet high. When this type of action takes place, Castle will have an extremely powerful eruption once every several weeks. Well over 100 feet high, the 10-minute water eruption is followed by a steam phase lasting several hours.

At other times Castle will not give off such frequent splashes of water. Instead, following a relatively short interval, an eruption lasting 4 minutes will ensue. Also very powerful, it is not followed by the steam phase, but ends very suddenly. On still other occasions this same activity takes place but lasts just 2 minutes. More recently, these minor eruptions have lost their limited durations and have ranged between about 2 and 7 minutes in length. As a general rule, this duration in minutes is nearly equal to the expected following interval in hours. About a dozen of these minor eruptions are seen during a typical year.

Much more typical of Castle over the past 20 years has been a fourth kind of eruption. Steam wells quietly from the crater, then about 3 hours before the time of eruption water begins to splash a few feet above the rim. The surges increase in size until an especially heavy one initiates the eruption. For about 20 minutes water is thrown into the air as an almost continuous column. Sometimes the jets are only 30 feet high, but more commonly they reach 80 feet. A rare burst may even exceed 100 feet. As the eruption progresses water is slowly lost from the system and the steam phase begins. At first it is very powerful, producing a deep, thunderous roar. Then over the next hour or so, Castle slowly calms down. Around 10 hours will then pass before the next predictable eruption occurs.

This changeable tendency makes Castle one of the most interesting geysers in all of Yellowstone. At any time it could initiate activity that was typical of its behavior at some time in the past. Who knows? It might have yet another new trick to spring on us, too.

49. TORTOISE SHELL SPRING is located right at the base of Castle's (48) huge cone, yet there seems to be little, if any, connection between the two. Even the most powerful eruptions of Castle do not visibly affect Tortoise Shell. This spring is the hottest in Yellowstone, highly superheated with temperatures as great as 207°F (97°C) having been recorded. The result is a constant, violent boiling, strong enough to throw considerable water out of the open, bowl-like crater. Rarely, brief eruptive bursts send water up to 6 feet.

50. TILT GEYSER nearly always manages to catch someone by surprise — when it is active. The vents attract little notice even though they are located very close to the boardwalk. Thus, the people gathered around Crested Pool (51) and waiting for Castle Geyser (48) are often startled by the sudden gushes of steam near their feet. Tilt Geyser itself is the right-hand one of the vents here; angled away from the boardwalk, its spraying eruption is about 6 feet high. The left-hand collection of vents is sometimes referred to as "Tilt's Baby." It formed as the result of a steam explosion on July 6, 1976. Since this development, most of the eruption comes from the new vents. They splash just 2 feet high but seem to produce greater discharge than Tilt alone ever did. In concert with these, Tilt itself undergoes powerful steam phase eruptions. Intervals range from just ½ to 3 hours and durations from 2 to 3 minutes, but Tilt is dormant during most years.

51. CRESTED POOL is 42 feet deep and intensely blue. Like Tortoise Shell Spring (49), the water is superheated. Boiling around the lip of the crater is constant. On frequent occasions a sudden surge of hot water will rise to the surface, causing a violent boiling that may dome the water up as much as 6 feet.

Crested Pool is not only very beautiful, it is also very dangerous. The spring is surrounded by a railing because this is one of the pools that has taken human life. Yet now you often see people climbing this railing and trying to balance themselves on the top—a very foolhardy practice.

52. TERRA COTTA SPRING is the official name for what is really a number of separate hot springs, two of which are geysers. In practice, these have come to be called Terra Cotta "A" and Terra Cotta "B" Geysers.

Terra Cotta "A" Geyser, closer to the boardwalk, is by far the more active of the two. Spouting from at least four vents, the major part of the play reaches between 5 and 10 feet high. Intervals here are hours in length—usually, however, just about 2—with durations of a few minutes.

Terra Cotta "B" Geyser is much less active than "A," with no eruptions seen at all during some seasons. It plays from a beautiful, symmetrical vent a few feet beyond "A." Also lasting for a few minutes, these eruptions are about 6 feet high.

53. SPANKER GEYSER has been remarkably constant in its activity. Rising from the left bank of the Firehole River, it is located far downstream from the boardwalk bridge which, nevertheless, provides as good a view as any. It is a perpetual spouter, and most bursts are considerably less than 6 feet high so that steam is often all that is visible of Spanker.

54. CHIMNEY GEYSER, though marked with a sign, is not a geyser as such and never has been during the recorded history of the Park. Perhaps it once was a geyser, but its vent has been all but sealed by internal deposits of silica. A small spring at the base of the cone bubbles and occasionally splashes a few inches high, enough for it to be technically considered a geyser.

55. SCALLOPED SPRING has probably never been a natural geyser. There are ways of making some springs erupt unnaturally, and Scalloped was a victim of such activity. The induced eruption was quite powerful with a heavy discharge of water. No details about the play were ever recorded, of course, for the people who caused it certainly did not report their illegal act. The pool never recovered, and the water level now lies several feet below the ground surface. The Scalloped Spring incident is another example of just how fragile these springs are; induced eruptions were not meant to be and often destroy the spring.

56. DELETED TEAKETTLE GEYSER got its name when it was decided that too many springs in Yellowstone had been named "Teakettle." Apparently the intention was that this particular geyser would have its name deleted from the records; instead, the "deleted" notation became added as an official part of the name! The geyser erupts from a small cone right on the brink of the Firehole River. The cone indicates that Deleted Teakettle was a geyser in the past, but no eruptions were recorded until the 1959 earthquake. For several days thereafter it underwent frequent, 15-foot-high eruptions. Then the activity declined; by 1964 it would only boil up about 1 foot high. These small eruptions continue, recurring every few minutes and lasting several minutes.

SAWMILL GEYSER COMPLEX (numbers 57 to 67). The Sawmill Geyser Complex is one of the more active groups of geysers in all of Yellowstone. It is generally difficult to visit the area without seeing at least something in eruption, and often you'll find yourself surrounded by activity. The nature of activity in the group is cyclic. Usually the only significant eruptions are by Sawmill, Tardy, and Spasmodic Geysers; when they quit (nearly simultaneously in most cases), the water of every spring in the group drops from a few inches to several feet below the full level. Then every spring refills simultaneously. The eruptive activity, whatever it may turn out to be, normally starts at about the time of first overflow from Sawmill Geyser. Also, no place better represents exchange of function; because of this, what is "normal" at one time might be replaced by completely different performances at other times.

Generally speaking, one can expect to see Sawmill, Tardy, and Spasmodic Geysers in eruption. Play by Old Tardy and Bulger is not unusual, but to see eruptions in any among Twilight, Uncertain, Penta, Oval, Crystal, or Churn is a rare treat.

57. CHURN GEYSER is the least active member of the Sawmill Complex. It was named at a time when the only known activity was little more than a surface commotion of the water. After the 1959 earthquake it would sometimes boil up a foot or two high and overflow, but no actual eruptions were ever seen until 1971. During that summer Churn played several times. Churn is a cyclic geyser; active periods last about 2 hours, during which there may be between 5 and 10 eruptions. Each eruption lasts less than 1 minute, but some bursts reach over 20 feet high. Since 1971, Churn has continued this sort of action, but only very rarely. The 3-foot-high eruptions of August 1985 were the best in years.

58. SAWMILL GEYSER is the namesake of and largest geyser in its complex. During an eruption the water spins about in the crater, resembling a large, circular lumbermill blade. Sawmill is a very interesting and typical fountain-type geyser. The eruptions are a series of separate bursts of water; some are not more than 3 feet high, but others easily exceed 35 feet. Throughout the eruption there is a copious discharge of water.

Detailed studies during the past few years have shown that Sawmill has eruptions of three distinctly different lengths. By far the most common are durations of near 45 minutes; others last between 12 and 20 minutes, or more than 80 minutes. Essentially no eruptions have durations of other lengths, making it evident that these three different types must involve progressively greater portions of the plumbing system. Whatever the case, Sawmill is in eruption around 30% of the time, so that a typical interval is between 1 and 3 hours in length.

59. UNCERTAIN GEYSER is very much that. Not only does it seem unsure as to whether it should erupt or not, but its relationships to other springs of the Sawmill Complex are uncertain, too. The small, round vent lies hidden within the deep sinter shoulders on the far side of Sawmill Geyser's (58) crater; hence a second name, "Sawmill's Satellite Vent." It appears that Uncertain can erupt *only* when every other member of the complex is quiet—something that is not at all common. Also, it may begin eruption just as Penta Geyser (62) is apparently about to begin, stopping that spectacular play. In any case, the activity of Uncertain is normally preceded by a few minutes of light overflow. The eruption is a steady jet of mixed spray and steam reaching 15 feet high. It can last anywhere from 2 to 5 minutes and is often abruptly terminated by the start of action in Sawmill.

60. TARDY GEYSER looks and acts like the far more impressive Sawmill Geyser (58), and indeed it was once known as "Little Sawmill." The origin of the present name is unknown, but this is not the first geyser to have had the name. Eruptions by Tardy are usually about 10 feet high, considerably more if the eruption is in concert with Sawmill. Should Tardy's activity last for several hours, Sawmill may fall dormant.

61. UNNG-CGG-1 ("TWILIGHT" GEYSER) lies to the right of the boardwalk as one walks from Sawmill Geyser (58) toward Penta Geyser (62). Water is constantly rocking about in the crater, occasionally splashing over the edge. When the crater partially drains following the activity of other geysers within the Sawmill Group, Twilight sometimes erupts, the splashes reaching 2 to 3 feet above the ground and, therefore, fully 5 feet above the pool level.

62. PENTA GEYSER is a very enjoyable geyser; it is also the most complex member of the Sawmill Group, and its activity is always highly irregular. During most years only two or three eruptions are observed; during other years it may be seen almost daily, and briefly during 1984 it played as often as every 6 hours. Most eruptions of Penta begin before any other member of the group has begun eruption after refilling; Tardy Geyser (60) may be having a weak eruption, causing a water level decline in the other springs of the area. Penta's eruptions begin abruptly, with a pulsing main jet reaching over 25 feet high. Four other vents spaced around the low gray geyserite cone splash to much lower heights. The play usually lasts around 45 minutes and does not seem to be affected by subsequent eruptions in other geysers.

During 1984 a second type of eruption was noted in Penta, one which might explain the relatively large geyserite cone at a geyser normally very inactive. This can best be described as a steam phase eruption. Beginning at most any point in the Sawmill Group cycle, this brief eruption sprays mixed water and steam sufficient to do no more than wet the cone.

63. SPASMODIC GEYSER plays from about twenty separate vents. While erupting, the activity is constant from most of the openings. Every few seconds to minutes there will be a momentary increase in intensity, and then all vents spout, sometimes accompanied by bursting from the two blue pools. A last vent is located on the far side of the crater, between the two pools. It is truly periodic. When Spasmodic as a whole is erupting, this geyser plays every 1 to 2 minutes to 10 feet, the action lasting a few seconds. The intervals and durations of Spasmodic as a whole are both hours in length.

64. OVAL SPRING was a quiet, greenish pool before the 1959 earthquake. Those tremors induced eruptions, and for the next several weeks it continued to boil heavily. By 1960, Oval had resumed its pre-quake state, and no further activity was seen until the 1980s. Oval is a member of the Sawmill Complex, and its two vents are actually separate geysers. Most eruptions come from the east vent when the pool has dropped to a low level along with the other members of the group. These typically come in a series of brief plays about 10 minutes apart and up to 12 feet high. The other vent erupts through a full pool; though rare, it has sometimes soaked the boardwalk.

65. OLD TARDY GEYSER became so called after the name Tardy was inadvertently moved from and then returned to its rightful location. Old Tardy is quite irregular in its activity. Although some dormant periods have been recorded, it is normally active. The intervals are known to range from just a few minutes to many hours. During an eruption, which lasts 1 minute to more than an hour, water jets to as much as 15 feet.

Between Old Tardy Geyser and Oval Spring (64) is a small spot in the sinter gravel that sizzles steam and a small amount of water on irregular occasions. Sometimes this seems to be a precursor to eruptions by Old Tardy, because its play ceases just as Old Tardy begins. Many times, though, this activity seems to be independent of anything else.

66. CRYSTAL SPRING is a shallow, nearly colorless pool near Old Tardy (65). The water constantly rocks in the crater, and every few minutes it temporarily rises to cause overflow. Thus, Crystal

Spring is a good example of the intermittent spring. When this overflow occurs, most of the runoff drains into a small hole. This is Crystal Spring Geyser. The irregular, rather rare eruptions last many minutes and are 1 foot high.

67. BULGER GEYSER (the sign here once read "Bugler" and may again, since such signs are still on hand) may not be a member of the Sawmill Group, but its activity does show at least some response to that group's cycles. Prior to the 1959 earthquake, Bulger was a relatively infrequent performer. Now the action is quite frequent. Minor eruptions are common, sometimes recurring every few minutes but lasting just a few seconds. Major eruptions are less common, but they may have durations approaching 10 minutes. Each kind of eruption sends bulging bursts of water about 6 feet high.

THE GRAND GEYSER COMPLEX (numbers 68 to 76). The Grand Geyser Complex is just that—complex. It includes at least ten springs, all geysers, as members of the group itself. Known connections add to the complexity. To the north, Grand is known to be related to the Economic Geysers, more than 400 feet away, and is probably connected with others even more distant. To the south, activity in the Sawmill Complex is certainly related to that of the Grand Complex. Taken as a whole, the total number of springs involved exceeds thirty and is probably much greater than that. No wonder Grand Geyser has been unpredictable for most of its history!

68. EAST TRIPLET GEYSER is certainly, now, the least important existing member of the Grand Complex. Prior to 1947 it erupted quite often. Since then, however, most seasons have seen no activity at all. Occasional minor eruptions, such as those of 1974, were themselves infrequent and only 5 feet high.

69. WEST TRIPLET GEYSER lies in a symmetrical funnel-shaped vent right next to the boardwalk. In the years before 1947 it erupted regularly about every 3 hours, nearly always in concert with East and North Triplets. Since then it has been more irregular, the nature of the activity being directly related to that of Grand Geyser (76). Periods of complete dormancy have rarely occurred, these always being times when Grand is exceptionally

The combination of Grand (right), Turban (left-center), and Vent (left) Geysers is unmatched by any of the world's natural spectacles.

regular *and* frequent. More often it plays two or three times during Grand's interval, and there is evidence that such activity will delay eruptions by Grand by as much as 2½ hours. Eruptions of West Triplet involve distinctly separate bursts of water, ranging from 1 to 10 feet high. Accompanied by a heavy discharge of boiling water, these may last anywhere from 15 to 90 minutes.

70. NORTH TRIPLET GEYSER was the closest of the Triplets to Grand Geyser (76). Before the advent of boardwalks, Park visitors were free to wander about in the geyser basins. As a result, a great number of rocks were thrown into the crater of Grand. Had such acts continued, Grand's vent might have become plugged, robbing us of what is now the largest frequently active geyser in the world. To prevent this destruction the Park Service removed many rocks from within and about Grand's crater. Grand was saved, but this removal allowed the water from Grand's eruptions to wash gravel into the crater of North Triplet Geyser. Filled in, it ceased activity so completely that the site is no longer visible.

71. PERCOLATOR GEYSER'S small, orange vent is near the site of the old North Triplet Geyser (70), and it may be an expression of that geyser's thermal energy. Percolator is active only for a period of time before Grand (76) erupts. Just how long before depends on the frequency of Grand. In years when Grand is frequent, Percolator's play usually begins about 2 hours before Grand's eruption; in other years it may precede Grand by more than 12 hours. So, while Percolator's eruption is a sure sign of building pressure within the Grand system, it cannot be used as a reliable predictor. The 1- to 2-foot eruptions will stop shortly after Grand begins its play. Overall, it is not a significant member of the Grand Complex.

72. UNNG-CGG-2&3 are very informally known as "Sput" and "Sputnik." These small geysers first appeared during the early 1980s. Although they do not seem to play an important role in the activity of the Grand Complex, the fact that they are closely related to Rift Geyser (73) indicates a potential for greater status in the future. Both geysers are small, Sput reaching perhaps 3 feet high and Sputnik not more than 2 feet high.

73. RIFT GEYSER is a very important geyser, yet one would little suspect that a geyser of any sort lies at this site. The crater is a slightly depressed, sandy area at the base of some rhyolite boulders. The vents, which may total more than two dozen, are actually nothing more than cracks in the rocks beneath the sand. Most of the water jets are just a few inches high, but two of the central vents jet to about 4 feet. Throughout the eruption about twenty-five gallons of boiling water are given off every minute. Given that the activity can last as long as 4 hours, that's a big volume.

And this is the trouble with Rift. Most eruptions begin at about the time that Grand Geyser (76) is expected to erupt. But, instead, because of the great loss of water and heat through Rift, Grand is delayed. The amount of delay is highly variable, but as a general rule it amounts to about 2 hours for every 1 hour of Rift's eruption. Therefore, although Rift is a very interesting geyser, any geyser gazer wishes it ill luck.

If you are very lucky, you might see a shorter eruption from Rift, with a duration of only around 15 minutes, which has a minimal effect on Grand. Also, some eruptions begin during or shortly after Grand has started, in this case with no evident effect at all. But such situations are rare at best. Seasons in which Rift is active are almost surely those when Grand is erratic and unpredictable. These have been all too common in the last decade.

74. TURBAN GEYSER, lying as it does in a raised sinter bowl, is mistaken by most would-be Grand (76) watchers as being Grand itself. Grand is the large pool with no rim just to the right of Turban. Because of this it is often thought that Grand is starting to play when it is actually only Turban undergoing its normal small eruption.

Turban is very important to Grand, however. It normally erupts on a 17- to 22-minute interval. The duration is about 5 minutes, throughout which the water bursts unimpressively to about 5 feet. But, except for rare occasions, Grand will begin erupting *only* at the time of the start of Turban's action. The rising water level in Turban acts as a trigger, sending Grand into play. Turban then erupts constantly and more powerfully during and for about an hour after Grand's eruption before it returns to its normal intervals.

75. VENT GEYSER is an unexpected bonus to an eruption of Grand (76). It issues from a small crack-like vent on the left side of Turban's massive sinter shoulder. Except for very rare plays, Vent erupts only in concert with Grand, starting 2 or 3 minutes after Grand begins. At the beginning of the eruption the slightly-angled water column slowly builds in force until it is fully 70 feet high—a major geyser in its own right. Thereafter, it dies down to about 35 feet. Vent continues to erupt in company with Turban for an hour or more after Grand has stopped.

On seven known occasions during the 1960s, once in 1978, and once in 1982, Vent began erupting 1½ to 2 hours *before* Grand. During these eruptions the water levels in both Grand and Turban slowly dropped about 1 foot. Then Grand went into a normal eruption. Even rarer have been the three or four times when Vent erupted weakly and briefly in a strictly independent fashion.

76. GRAND GEYSER. If any geyser anywhere is worth seeing, it is Grand. Countless people have waited for hours, commenting later that it was certainly well worth the time. With its massive water column sparkling in the sun, a rainbow captured in its steam, and accompanied by the slender arching jet of Vent Geyser, Grand is unlike any other sight in the world.

During its long quiet period, Grand slowly fills with water so that the first overflow is about 5 hours following an eruption. From then until the time of its next activity the water slowly rises and falls in sympathy with the eruptions of Turban Geyser (74). Each cycle, from high water through low water as Turban plays and back to high water, takes about 20 minutes to complete. It is this water level that enables the geyser gazer to tell how near Grand is to an eruption.

Stand where you can see the outermost part of the basin where small pieces of sinter project through the water. Use these to gauge the level of the pool. If the water level drops rapidly and far enough to stop almost all overflow when the time for Turban to play is approaching, then you'll know it will be at least one more cycle of Turban, and maybe longer, before Grand erupts. As Grand gets closer and closer to the time of eruption, the water level generally drops less, and more slowly. Finally will come a cycle when the water level doesn't appear to drop at all. Now is the time to watch closely. Very small at first, waves begin to wash across the surface of the pool. Soon they become obvious as the water level continues to rise and discharge becomes heavy. Only rarely will the wave action start without a consequent eruption; if that does happen it will probably be at least another three cycles before there is another chance for an eruption. Remember, though, that any prediction is only guesswork; anything might happen and appearances can be deceiving.

The eruption begins when the water of the pool suddenly domes over the vent. This bubbling, frothing, and surging will continue for several seconds. It may even stop an agonizing time or two. But soon the geyser rockets forth, sending massive columns of water to tremendous heights. Some of the early bursts can reach 150 feet, but the best is yet to come.

Grand's eruption consists of a series of "bursts." The first one normally lasts around 9 minutes. During this time Grand averages "only" about 100 feet high, but the activity is continuous and a great amount of water is discharged. Suddenly this burst ends and the geyser is quiet. After a few seconds of refilling the crater, Grand jets forth again. This and any succeeding bursts may be over 200 feet high. If the second burst is short, there may be another pause leading to a third burst, and so on. Grand most often has two to four bursts; sometimes there is only one, but there may be as many as six. An exceptional eruption in 1983 had 11 bursts!

During most years since 1950, Grand's intervals have been very regular considering its many connections with other geysers. At these times the average is often near 8 hours, and the eruptions can be predicted with a great degree of accuracy. However, in some years, such as 1981 and 1983–85, Grand is erratic and much less frequent. These are the years of vigorous action in other members of the Grand Complex, and Grand is then nearly unpredictable.

Whatever the nature of its current activity, Grand is the largest frequently active geyser in the world. No geyser anywhere has ever approached it in terms of size, frequency, and predictability. And the consensus never changes; no geyser can match Grand in beauty, either.

77. ECONOMIC GEYSER was once a geyser of considerable interest and importance. It erupted frequently and became one of those spouters that could always be counted on to perform. So it continued until sometime in the 1920s. Since then the only activity was during the five weeks following the 1959 earthquake. Now its water temperature is only 130°F (54°C), and the crater is lined with dark orange-brown algae. Economic is probably connected with Grand Geyser (76), more than 450 feet away. When Economic was active in 1959, Grand was dormant for the first and only time in decades. Grand reactivated within a short while of Economic's renewed dormancy.

78. EAST ECONOMIC GEYSER, located just 20 feet to the back left of Economic (77), was not known as a geyser until the shocks of the 1959 earthquake. Its activity then was closely tied to that of Economic – an eruption of one would result in a lowering water level in the other, and both returned to dormancy on the same day. The eruptions of East Economic were considerably more powerful than those of its neighbor, sometimes reaching 35 or 40 feet high. The lodgepole pines just behind East Economic were killed by these eruptions, proving that any previous activity (if any) was long ago.

79. UNNG-CGG-4 ("BUSH" GEYSER) is only one of a number of small, infrequently active geysers in the open flat across the boardwalk from Economic Geyser. Bush is the largest of these. Eruptions have not been observed in several years, but, when active, Bush can reach up to 4 feet high.

80. CRACK GEYSER became active on September 21, 1959, the same day that the Economic Geysers went dormant, showing that connections from there extend both north and south. The eruptions came from an earthquake-caused crack in the sinter platform. Through 1961 there were frequent eruptions from Crack. The 6-foot-high spout would last for several minutes. Except for slight occasional bubbling, there has been no activity since 1962.

81. BEAUTY AND CHROMATIC POOLS are not geysers, but no springs provide a better example of exchange of function than these. A periodic energy shift from one pool to the other causes one to overflow while the other declines, then the reverse. The time interval between such shifts ranged from a few weeks to a year or more before the 1959 earthquake. Since then the flow has almost always been from Chromatic Pool, with only brief shifts to Beauty Pool on the order of years apart. Aside from this interesting relationship, Beauty and Chromatic are among the most beautiful pools in the Upper Geyser Basin.

82. WITCHES CAULDRON lies right beside the Firehole River at such a level that high water will cover it. At low water it roils and boils, seemingly toiling for the proverbial trouble, but the highest surges are only 2 feet tall. Witches Cauldron is all but invisible from any trail, but it can be seen from the paved trail on the opposite side of the river.

83. LIME KILN SPRING is a small perpetual spouter. Its small cone is perched atop a large sinter mound, which indicates a very long period of activity. Like Witches Cauldron, it is best seen from the paved trail running between Castle (48) and Grotto (111) Geysers. Lime Kiln's eruption is 1 foot high.

84. UNNG-CGG-5 ("PULSAR" SPOUTER) is the only spring to have erupted within the Orange Spring Group since the early 1970s. Its steady bursting play reaches about 4 feet high. Other springs in this group have been active as geysers, and one, informally known as "UNNGOSG" (unnamed geyser, Orange Spring Group), played as much as 15 feet high during a brief episode in the early 1970s.

Table 2. Geysers of the Castle-Grand Group

Name and Number	Interval	Duration	Height (ft)
Bulger Geyser (67)	5 min–hrs	sec–10 min	6–8
Castle Geyser (48)	8–12 hrs	1 hr	30–100
Chimney Geyser (54)	inactive	–	–
Churn Geyser (57)	seldom	1 min	3–20
Crack Geyser (80)	rare	minutes	6
Crested Pool (51)	frequent	seconds	boil–6
Crystal Spring Geyser (66)	infrequent	minutes	1
Deleted Teakettle Geyser (56)	frequent	2–5 min	1–2
Economic Geyser (77)	rare	seconds	8–25

Table 2. Continued

Name and Number	Interval	Duration	Height (ft)
East Economic Geyser (78)	rare	2–3 min	35–40
East Triplet Geyser (68)	rare	minutes	5
Grand Geyser (76)	5–18 hrs	9–13 min	150–200
Lime Kiln Spring (83)	steady	steady	1
North Triplet Geyser (70)	dead?	–	–
Old Tardy Geyser (65)	min–hrs	1–90 min	12–15
Oval Spring (64)	infrequent	unrecorded	2–12
Penta Geyser (62)	infrequent	15–120 min	25
Percolator Geyser (71)	min–hrs	hrs	1–3
Rift Geyser (73)	irregular	15–90 min	4
Sawmill Geyser (58)	½–3 hrs	12–90 min	30–40
Scalloped Spring (55)	rare	unrecorded	unrecorded
Spanker Geyser (53)	steady	steady	2–6
Spasmodic Geyser (63)	hours	hours	2–10
Spatter Geyser (47)	rare	unrecorded	10
Sprinkler Geyser (46)	20–40 min	min–hrs	10
Tardy Geyser (60)	1–many hrs	min–hrs	10–25
Terra Cotta "A" Geyser (52a)	1–4 hrs	5–10 min	10
Terra Cotta "B" Geyser (52b)	infrequent	minutes	6
Tilt Geyser (50)	½–3 hrs	2–3 min	2–6
Tortoise Shell Spring (49)	steady	steady	boil–6
Turban Geyser (74)	14–30 min	4–5 min	5–10
Uncertain Geyser (59)	hrs–days	2–5 min	15
UNNG-CGG-1 ("Twilight") (61)	infrequent	minutes	2–3
UNNG-CGG-2 ("Sput") (72a)	irregular	min–hrs	3
UNNG-CGG-3 ("Sputnik") (72b)	irregular	min–hrs	2
UNNG-CGG-4 ("Bush") (79)	seldom	minutes	4
UNNG-CGG-5 ("Pulsar") (84)	steady	steady	4
Vent Geyser (75)	5–18 hrs	30–60 min	35–70
West Triplet Geyser (69)	hours	8–90 min	1–10
Witches Cauldron (82)	steady	steady	2

Giant Group

The Giant Group (Map E, Table 3) as handled here includes the hot springs of a number of independent smaller groups. Everything near the river between the Grand Group and the Grotto

Group is included. The area actually contains few geysers, but those present are some of the largest in Yellowstone. Giant Geyser (94), when active, is apt to be the largest geyser not only in Yellowstone but in the world; it has been essentially dormant since 1955. Oblong Geyser (86), while not very high, discharges a tremendous amount of water and has, therefore, always been considered a major spouter.

The Giant Group lies in the area where the two Upper Basin trails begin to merge into one. The best views are from the boardwalk, but all springs can also be seen from the paved trail that runs directly between Castle Geyser (48) and Grotto Geyser (111).

85. INKWELL SPRING sits on a small mound immediately next to the Firehole River. There are several craters that constantly discharge water, and two of them spout to about 2 feet. Though this is nearly a perpetual spouter, there is some variation to the play along with infrequent brief pauses.

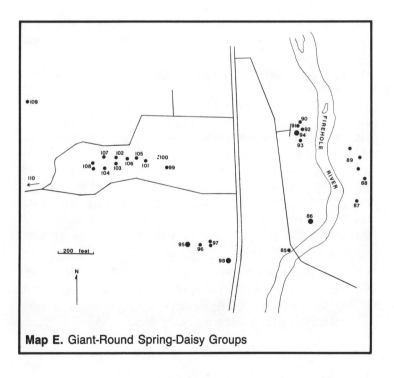

Map E. Giant-Round Spring-Daisy Groups

86. OBLONG GEYSER cannot be considered a major geyser in terms of the size of eruption, but because of its tremendous water discharge it has always been high on the list of important geysers. The actual amount discharged has never been determined because it spreads out across a broad sinter platform and almost immediately cascades into the Firehole River, but it certainly amounts to several tens of thousands of gallons.

During many seasons, Oblong is regular enough to be predicted, with intervals close to 8 hours. Often, however, it is highly irregular, and these episodes might be related to active phases by nearby Giant Geyser (94).The intervals at such times range from as little as 4 hours to as long as 2 or 3 days. There may then be a series of two or three eruptions, with intervals of around 2 ½ hours and then 30 minutes following the initial play.

Whatever the interval, during the quiet phase the water periodically rises and falls within the crater, resulting in intermittent overflow. Near the time of an eruption such cycles last about 20 minutes. Eruptions always begin during the overflow. Suddenly there is a flood of water leaving the crater, and the ground begins to pound as steam bubbles form and collapse deep within the plumbing system. The pool begins to boil, and soon the entire volume is domed upward in massive surges that reach 20 to 40 feet high. The entire play lasts 5 to 7 minutes.

87. NEW GEYSER didn't last long, but it certainly may become active again. The first known eruption was on September 1, 1970 and lasted several minutes. Pieces of jagged sinter strewn about the vent indicated that an old vent had been enlarged by a small steam explosion. In the succeeding two months several other eruptions were seen. The intervals could not be determined, but they may have been several days long. The maximum height of the eruption was about 15 feet. No eruptions have occurred since 1970, but the vent did overflow on occasion throughout the 1970s.

88. UNNG-GNT-1 broke out in eruption on May 1, 1970, exactly four months before the first activity by nearby New Geyser (89). These two events are certainly related. This geyser played from a small pool about 30 feet from South Purple Pool (89). It may have also been active during the early 1950s, but the records kept about that activity were insufficient to determine its exact site. When first active, GNT-1 had continuous eruptions; after a short early-summer dormancy, the play resumed on a periodic basis. During both periods, the eruptions were about 15 feet high. The 1970 eruptions by this geyser are believed to have ceased on the same day that New Geyser began to play.

THE GIANT GEYSER COMPLEX. The Giant Complex contains many springs. Most are small perforations in the sinter mound that is capped by Giant Geyser's massive cone. It also includes the Purple Pools, 300 feet across the Firehole River, and is positively known to be connected with the Oblong Geyser area to the south, the Grotto Group to the northwest, and the Daisy Group to the west. Although largely inactive at present, the Giant Complex is a pivotal and highly important group of hot springs.

89. THE PURPLE POOLS, South, East, and North, are all connected with Giant Geyser (94). As an eruption of Giant progresses, the water level in these pools subsides until it is about 3 feet below overflow. The only known eruptions among the cluster occurred during 1971; then both East and North Purple Pools erupted frequently to about 2 feet high and South Purple Pool boiled heavily. Some thought that this activity might have been a precursor to renewed activity by Giant, but the activity soon stopped without anything out of the ordinary happening, and no such eruptions have been seen since 1971.

90. BIJOU GEYSER used to be called Young Faithful Geyser; just who changed its name is uncertain, but in ways the new name does fit with the definition of "a charming, delicately made thing." Bijou is by far the most active member of the Giant Complex. For most of its history it has played nearly constantly to 5 to 15 feet high, the water wetting all sides of a symmetrical, algae-covered cone quite unlike any other. The only known lengthy pauses in the activity are just after eruptions by Giant (94). Also, during Giant's hot periods Bijou enters a loud steam phase, which is converted to water jets 30 feet high at the start of Giant's eruption.

91. CATFISH GEYSER is very closely related to Giant (94). At the time of the latter's hot periods, Catfish would erupt violently to 15 feet for several minutes. During 1951, the thermal energy of the Giant Complex shifted to the north, toward Catfish, Mastiff (92), and Bijou (90) Geysers. During this activity, known as the *Mastiff Function,* Catfish became a major geyser, erupting for many minutes to heights ranging between 75 and 100 feet. Such activity ended in January 1952 when the energy shifted back to the south, and Catfish resumed its pre-shift behavior.

92. MASTIFF GEYSER was known to be active just preceding eruptions of Giant during the 1870s, when it ejected large amounts of water to about 35 feet. Thereafter, though, Mastiff was so inactive that it was all but forgotten; some even listed the crater just behind and to the left of Giant (94) as extinct. But in 1951 an exchange of function shifted energy to the north portion of the Giant Complex. Catfish (91) erupted to 75 feet. And, quite unexpectedly, Mastiff joined in with a massive column of water reaching well over 100 feet. Such action was totally without precedent, for just a few minutes later Giant itself began playing. Catfish stopped, but Mastiff continued on equal terms with Giant for fully 5 minutes; only when Mastiff stopped would Giant assume its usual stupendous eruption. When the Giant Complex behaves in this way it is called the *Mastiff Function.* Since the energy shifted away in early 1952, Mastiff has had nothing more than frequent weakly splashing eruptions.

93. TURTLE GEYSER is little known. It possesses the highly eroded and somewhat detached cone on the far right side of Giant's (94) mound. Turtle is apparently active only at the time of one of Giant's eruptions, and usually not even then. It has been known to erupt to greater than 20 feet high. Turtle might be an example of a geyser that has nearly sealed itself in by the deposition of geyserite within the vent.

94. GIANT GEYSER was appropriately named. When in eruption there is nothing quite like it. A huge tower of water is thrown far into the air, and being a cone-type geyser, this is a steady column rather than the intermittent bursts seen in most of the other large, but fountain-type, geysers. In the early references to Yellowstone, Giant is listed as erupting to 250 to 300 feet. During most of the more recent active cycles it has not approached that kind of height, with many eruptions perhaps not even 150 feet high. It is possible that Giant has two distinctly different modes of activity – the *Normal Function,* when it may reach near 200 feet, and the *Mastiff Function,* when, in concert with Catfish (91) and Mastiff (92) Geysers, the play reaches well over 200 feet high. In the first decade of Park history, Giant might have been on the *Mastiff Function,* leading to the tall figures of those years. Such activity has been the exception since then, occurring only during the latter half of 1951.

When active, Giant is characterized by well-defined "hot periods." At these times the surging within the crater becomes more violent and numerous little vents in front of the cone undergo small eruptions. When on the *Mastiff Function,* this action is added to by the powerful steam phase of Bijou (90) and minor eruptions by Catfish and Mastiff Geysers. Eventually, one hot period will culminate with an eruption. The water within Giant suddenly lifts. The maximum height comes within the first few seconds of activity. A single eruption lasts between 1 and 1½ hours and expels over 1 million gallons of water. During the active period of 1951–55, the eruptions recurred every 2 to 14 days. The average interval, though, was only 54 hours and Giant was nearly predictable for much of those four years.

It is highly unfortunate that the Giant Complex has been adversely affected by exchange of function. The energy has always been known to shift back and forth between the Giant and Grotto complexes. When Grotto is highly active, Giant is dormant; when Giant is active, Grotto remains active but plays far less frequently. Prior to 1955 it seemed that the time required for a complete cycle of shifting from Giant to Grotto and back to Giant required about 5 years. Thus, when Giant went dormant during 1955 it was anticipated that its next active episode would begin by 1960. It seemed, in fact, that the switch was beginning to take place when the 1959 earthquake struck. The energy then shifted back to Grotto, and there it remained, at least for the most part, until 1987 (see Addenda).

It seems that this shift involves water volume more than

it does heat. When too much water is lost from the system via Grotto, Giant isn't properly primed. Isolated eruptions took place in 1963, 1978, 1982, 1984, and 1986, but with none of these did Giant show signs of true reactivation. However, the eruption of September 12, 1987, was followed by the first series of hot periods since 1955, and Giant responded. Eruptions on June 28, September 12, and December 18, 1988, are hoped to be the start of a new active phase . . . but only time will tell.

Any geyser gazer prays for the reactivation of Giant, yet alone for the geyser to play on the *Mastiff Function*. Imagine the sight. Bijou goes into a violent steam phase. Catfish begins splashing, then explodes to over 75 feet. Then comes Mastiff, its steady column of water reaching over 100 feet high. And finally the Giant, reaching up to 200 feet and higher. All of this happening at once within a complex less than 100 feet long. What a sight it must be!

THE ROUND SPRING GROUP is a small cluster of springs of little overall significance. Several of them have, however, records of geyser activity. The group is closest to the paved Upper Basin Trail and is best viewed from there.

95. WEST ROUND SPRING, along with North Round Spring and several small, unnamed features within the group, erupted the night of the 1959 earthquake. Nothing more is known about any of that activity, and of all these springs only West Round is known to have erupted at any time since. For a brief period during August 1971 West Round played frequently. Some eruptions reached more than 15 feet high.

96. PEAR GEYSER is known to have been active only during 1961. For that one year it was highly regular, erupting every 5 minutes to a height of about 12 feet. No further activity has been recorded, and the site is now a partially dry, rather decayed looking crater that one would never suspect of having been a significant geyser.

97. UNNG-RSG-1&2 are located about midway between Pear Geyser (96) and North Round Spring. First active during 1956, they reactivated during 1982 and now play frequently up to 8 feet high. The geyser to the north is the more active and larger of the two. The other plays only after an exceptionally long interval by the other and, in fact, may be triggering the start of a new episode of short-term cyclic action.

98. ROUND SPRING is the member of the Round Spring Group closest to the paved trail. It is also just about the least important member of the group. Round is not a geyser, but it is an intermittent spring. With the nearby unnamed geysers (97) active, Round Spring spends most of its time in an ebbed state, and overflow, though briefly heavy, is a rarity.

Table 3. Geysers of the Giant and Round Spring Groups

Name and Number	Interval	Duration	Height (ft)
Bijou Geyser (90)*	near steady	near steady	5–15
Catfish Geyser (91)*	frequent	seconds	2–20
Giant Geyser (94)*	2–14 days	1–1½ hrs	150–300
Inkwell Spring (85)	steady	steady	2
Mastiff Geyser (92)*	frequent	seconds	2–35
New Geyser (87)	rare	minutes	15
Oblong Geyser (86)	5–11 hrs	5–7 min	25
Pear Geyser (96)	rare	2–3 min	12
Purple Pools (89)	rare	minutes	2–3
Round Spring (98)	infrequent	unrecorded	overflow
Turtle Geyser (93)*	rare	unrecorded	20
UNNG-GNT-1 (88)	rare	minutes	10–20
UNNG-RSG-1&2 (97)	sec–min	seconds	2–8
West Round Spring (95)	rare	sec–min	12–20

*Members of the Giant Complex, dormant since 1955.

Daisy Group

The terms "Daisy Group" (Map E, Table 4) and "Daisy Geyser Complex" are nearly synonymous. Of all the geysers here, only two—Bank and Pyramid—are not certainly known to be connected with Daisy. Aside from the geysers, the group includes only three cool, quiet pools.

The Daisy Group lies to the west of the Firehole River and the Giant Group, up on a low hill and thoroughly separated from other hot spring clusters. There are two approaches to the area. From the paved Upper Basin Trail are two smaller paved trails leading up the hill; passing on opposite sides of the springs, they then merge and head toward the Punchbowl Group. The alternate route is from the Punchbowl Group, which may be reached from Black Sand Basin on the main highway.

Daisy and Splendid Geysers are very large, always among the favorites. Splendid is seldom active, but when so it may rival Grand Geyser in size and beauty. When Splendid is not active, then Daisy usually is. During some years it has been the most regular major geyser in Yellowstone.

99. BANK GEYSER is one of those believed to be unconnected with the Daisy Group, even though it lies within a few feet of springs that certainly are members of the group. Lying within a small alcove down the hill toward the Giant Group, Bank is a petite, blue pool. It erupts every minute or so. The play is a series of bursts, some of which may reach about 4 feet high. During some years the eruptions degenerate to periods of mild boiling. The runoff from Bank supports a fine growth of orange algae.

THE DAISY COMPLEX. The Daisy Complex is a very interesting group of springs. It includes at least ten geysers, two of which are among the largest in the Park, and almost no other springs. All of the geysers are rather directly connected to one another, and exchange of function leads to great overall irregularity among them all. Any description of one geyser almost demands mention of the others.

Daisy is, in spite of her many relatives, a highly predictable geyser most of the time. A sign for the predictions is maintained both at the Visitor Center and at the start of the southernmost of the two trails leading to the group.

100. UNNG-DSG-1 is a set of several vents near Radiator Geyser (101), all of which erupt simultaneously. Most of the vents sputter only a few inches high, but the largest may play up to 2 feet. These vents are most active during active episodes of Splendid Geyser (107), when short intervals separate durations of several hours. At other times, although still active, this geyser plays rather infrequently and briefly.

101. RADIATOR GEYSER is a geyser of historical origin; it sprang to life within the old Daisy Area parking lot, beneath a car, so

Daisy Geyser can erupt as often as and more regularly than any other major geyser in the Upper Basin, including Old Faithful.

that people in the area thought the car's radiator was boiling. These eruptions were never more than gentle boiling until the time of the 1959 earthquake. It has been active in company with Daisy (106) and Splendid (107) Geysers ever since. Most eruptions come following the activity of one of the larger neighbors. These may reach over 10 feet high. Otherwise, Radiator's eruptions are much weaker, being infrequent and no more than 2 feet high.

102. COMET GEYSER is located between Daisy (106) and Splendid (107) Geysers. Its cone is the largest in the complex, yet the geyser is one of the smallest. The cone has been built to its size by the nearly constant splashing of Comet over a long period of time. At best, this play reaches 6 feet high. Every few minutes the surging becomes heavier and large amounts of water are ejected. Even this discharge is never sufficient to form a runoff channel. The only time that Comet seems to stop erupting is following eruptions by Splendid. Even then, though, the play has not quit; instead, the water level has been drawn down so far that the eruption is entirely confined to the subsurface.

103. BRILLIANT POOL was evidently never more than a very calm spring prior to 1950. Until then it had ebbed at the time of Daisy's eruptions; refilling was simultaneous with that of Daisy (106). In 1950 Brilliant began to overflow heavily, but only on occasion. Whenever this happened, though, eruptive action in Daisy would stop. This interplay happened many times during 1950 and was probably a prelude to renewed activity by Splendid (107) in 1951.

The response of Brilliant Pool to eruptions by Splendid is quite different. Following each eruption, the water level may drop by as much as 4 feet. After several eruptions by Splendid the crater may be completely empty. Then, and only then, can Brilliant commence its own eruptive activity. This play, lasting as long as 2 minutes, is characterized by explosive jets of water 20 feet high and angled sharply away from Splendid. Brilliant has continued to play in the same fashion following eruptions by Splendid, except that the eruptions now come in a series, each lasting less than 10 seconds.

104. DAISY'S THIEF GEYSER was first seen in eruption in 1942. Just moments before Daisy Geyser (106) was due to begin spouting, the Thief began jetting a steady column of water to 15 feet. The eruption lasted about 25 minutes without pause. Throughout, the water level in Daisy dropped slowly; at the end of the Thief's activity it had been lowered to the same point as following a normal eruption of Daisy. And, because Daisy finally did erupt after a normal interval following the eruption of Daisy's Thief, it appeared that the latter had discharged an amount of water and energy exactly equivalent to that of one eruption of Daisy. The origin of the name should now be obvious.

Daisy's Thief continued to be occasionally active throughout the 1940s, but then, in 1953, the manner of action changed. Instead of the 25-minute eruption, the spouting lasted many hours. It was less forceful than before, and when it ended Daisy erupted immediately. This type of function continued until the time of the 1959 earthquake. Since then there have been few eruptions. The last was in 1968. That one lasted over 7 hours, during which time Daisy erupted weakly three times. Except for these 1968 eruptions in company with the Thief, Daisy was dormant for nearly 11 years.

This sparse record of activity is all we have for Daisy's Thief, but the size of its cone and the nature of erosion in its surroundings indicate that the past has seen a great deal of activity. There seems to be little question that if it should begin frequent action, it would be the dominant member of the Daisy Complex.

105. BONITA POOL was used as an indicator of Daisy's (106) eruptions until 1937. In that year the water level rose higher than ever before, and whenever overflow was achieved all eruptions by Daisy were stopped. On one occasion the high water persisted for several months. Daisy was dormant for that entire period of time to the extent that orange algae was able to grow in the crater. This happened several other times until the 1959 earthquake.

At first, following the big shock, Daisy continued with normal activity. Then, early in 1960, Bonita Pool became very active, overflowing steadily and experiencing frequent small eruptions. Daisy went dormant, and Bonita did not stop overflowing until 1967. At that time it would sometimes stop. Immediately, Daisy began filling and heating, but just when an eruption seemed imminent, Bonita would refill. Except for one occasion in 1968 when activity was initiated by Daisy's Thief Geyser (104), Bonita's action was enough to bring about complete dormancy in Daisy until 1971. Only then did Bonita again stop overflowing. And this time Daisy managed to erupt all by herself. The time required for a complete energy shift back to Daisy was long, but by 1978 Daisy could finally be predicted with confidence. Bonita is again quiet and low. A little spray plays from some sputs next to its vent, usually near the time of Daisy's eruption, but Bonita seems finished for the time being.

106. DAISY GEYSER is the most important in the Daisy Complex. Although Splendid Geyser (107) is larger, Daisy is far more active. That this has been the case for a long time is shown by the runoff channels of the two geysers. Those of Daisy are wide and deep; Splendid's are almost non-existent.

Daisy erupts from a crater partially surrounded by a heavy sinter rim. At two points this margin is perforated by small vents, which have formed cones; these begin to spout shortly before an eruption. There are also several small vents within the main crater. When Daisy is being very regular and highly predictable, the activity in these small vents can be used to give an accurate time of eruption. Usually, the larger of the two cones begins to splash about 20 minutes before the eruption; the smaller begins 10 to 12 minutes beforehand. Meanwhile, the water in the crater boils and surges constantly over the vent. The eruption begins when this splashing suddenly begins to get heavy; it becomes higher and stronger until Daisy rockets forth. The maximum height of 75 feet is quickly reached, with the water column sharply angled from the vertical. When in concert with Splendid, the height may approach 120, even 150, feet, and the normal duration of 3½ to 4½ minutes may extend to 6 minutes.

When the activity of Bonita Pool (105) is such that it does not erupt and overflow, Daisy can be extremely regular. During most seasons Daisy is the most predictable of the major geysers. The average interval is quite variable, but during the

1980s it has ranged between 85 and 100 minutes. If Daisy is giving this sort of activity, then only two things can throw it off. One is strong south winds; common especially when summer thunderstorms are in the area, they may delay Daisy's eruption by as much as ½ hour. The other is Splendid Geyser (107).

During recorded history, Daisy has been much more active than Splendid. But Splendid has been active, and these times are always periods of great irregularity by Daisy. The longest such period was during the years before 1900, and others occurred during the 1950s and the 1970s. One of Splendid's best years ever was 1985; at times, that was one of Daisy's worst. Yet Splendid plays a beneficial role in Daisy's activity, too. All this can best be shown with the story of events during the 1970s.

Following the 1959 earthquake, Daisy was as active as before. Indeed, as time passed, it became more active until the average interval had shortened to only 48 minutes! Then in February 1960, Bonita Pool (105) began to overflow and erupt. Daisy rapidly declined and was soon dormant. Except for one day in 1968, Daisy remained dormant until July 22, 1971. With a couple of eruptions on that day came the first signs of a shift back to Daisy, away from Bonita. By 1972 Daisy would have two or three eruptions during the course of a few hours, then lapse back into dormancy lasting for several days. It soon became evident that these brief active phases were often initiated by eruptions of Splendid Geyser. By 1973 it became clear that not only did active phases begin with Splendid, but that action by Splendid was occasionally required to keep Daisy going. So it was until 1978. By then there had been such a complete shift of energy to Daisy that not only was Splendid not needed, but Splendid couldn't erupt at all.

From this it seems that maybe eruptions by Splendid do not so much occur because of energy shifts to it, but rather because of energy shifts away from Daisy. The two certainly are not the same thing. In any case, it is only at such times that Daisy and Splendid can erupt simultaneously. Such plays, known as concerted eruptions, were first seen during the 1890s, again on occasion during the 1950s, and then starting in 1972. Never have they been seen with such frequency as during 1985, when single active phases of Splendid included as many as four concerted eruptions. When in concert, Daisy is usually much stronger than normal. Some such eruptions may reach 150 feet, and nearly all exceed 100 feet (this opposed to the normal 75 feet or so). In duration Daisy is increased, too, playing for as long as 6 minutes instead of the usual 3½ minutes. All in all, then, Daisy owes a lot to the existence of Splendid.

Situated on a hill as it is, Daisy can be seen from much of the Upper Geyser Basin. It is always spectacular. It is best to see it erupt close at hand from a position where the sharp angle of the column is visible. There is no other geyser like Daisy.

107. SPLENDID GEYSER has seldom been active. It was erupting during the early days of the Park and continued to do so until around 1900. Then it was dormant until 1951. From then until 1959 there were several short periods of activity, but it again returned to dormancy after the 1959 earthquake. Another active period began in 1971. One of Splendid's best years ever was 1985.

Splendid is always on a hair trigger, requiring little to set off a series of eruptions. For years it has been known that eruptions would most likely begin during a storm, when the barometric pressure has dropped far and fast. It appears that such falling pressure is always a requirement for Splendid to be active, but surely it is not the only one. Nobody has yet found a way to predict active episodes.

The water in Splendid's large crater is constantly agitated, frequently boiling up several feet. The strongest action is at about the time of one of Daisy's (106) eruptions, and the quietest period is that immediately following Daisy. If an eruption by Splendid is to occur, the surging will abruptly build to as much as 30 feet. It would seem that such tremendous surging would have to trigger an eruption, but not so. It is at times like these that Daisy frequently begins playing, eliminating any of Splendid's hopes. But sometimes Splendid does manage. The heavy action will hold its height for several seconds, then suddenly and rapidly build to the full height. Few eruptions are less than 150 feet high, and nearly all this small will be in concert with Daisy. Most eruptions approach 200 feet high, and one was measured at 218 feet, making Splendid one of the five largest geysers in

Yellowstone. Once started, an eruption may last anywhere from 2 to 10 minutes and, if it is a series of eruptions, the intervals range from just over 1 to more than 12 hours.

At times the activity of the 1970s and 1980s has been almost without precedent. Most of the time, if Daisy or Splendid has been active, then the other has been dormant. Starting in 1972 there have been perhaps as many concerted eruptions as in all the years that passed before. During 1985, when Splendid had a total of at least 37 eruptions, 11 were in concert with Daisy. Concerted eruptions always (with just two exceptions) begin with Splendid. Within the first two minutes of its eruption Daisy will join in. Then the two geysers nearly match one another, each reaching between 100 and 150 feet high. The spectacle is truly magnificent. The refilling of the craters is rapid, and Daisy will sometimes erupt alone scarcely an hour following the concerted play.

That Splendid has not been frequently active is shown by the surrounding sinter platform. The recent cycles of activity have caused much erosion in the area, yet the sinter otherwise seems almost untouched. Very many eruptions would cause a considerable change in the crater and its surroundings. It may be that Splendid is of relatively recent origin and that much more can be expected from it in the future. For now, it is a rare treat.

Table 4. Geysers of the Daisy and Punch Bowl Groups

Name and Number	Interval	Duration	Height (ft)
Bank Geyser (99)	1–2 min	seconds	1–4
Bonita Pool (105)	rare	days–years	2
Brilliant Pool (103)	w/Splendid	10 sec–2 min	5–20
Comet Geyser (102)	steady	steady	1–10
Daisy Geyser (106)	1¼–5 hrs	3½–4½ min	75–150
Daisy's Thief Geyser (104)	rare	min–hrs	8–15
Pyramid Geyser (109)	3–8 min	seconds	8
Radiator Geyser (101)	irregular	sec–min	2–10
Splendid Geyser (107)	infrequent	2–10 min	100–218
UNNG-DSG-1 (100)	irregular	hours	2
UNNG-DSG-2 ("Murky") (108)	rare	10–15 min	2–15
UNNG-PBG-1 (110)	unrecorded	hours?	4–5

108. UNNG-DSG-2 ("MURKY" SPRING), somewhere west of Daisy's Thief Geyser (104), was active during the 1950s and again during the 1960s. Descriptions do not allow a positive identification as to just which spring is Murky. Near Splendid (107), northwest of Thief, are two sinter-lined craters that show evidence of having erupted in the past. These are definitely a part of the Daisy Complex, as shown by their dropping water levels whenever Splendid erupts. These, however, contain clear water. In the woods, to the southwest of the Thief, are two additional pools, both of which contain murky water but show no evidence of connection with the Daisy Complex. It is one of these two pools that has been erupting since 1982, the steady play being only 1 to 2 feet high. During the 1950s, Murky played every 6 to 8 hours, lasted 10 to 15 minutes, and reached 15 feet high. It was probably one of the two sinter-lined vents, but probably none alive can now say which.

109. PYRAMID GEYSER is located at the base of the White Pyramid, also known as White Throne, across the meadow from the Daisy Complex. Before the 1959 earthquake Pyramid erupted every few hours, each play lasting 5 minutes. The quake brought on a dormancy, and Pyramid was not seen again until 1971. Since then it has been continuously active, but now on a cyclic pattern. During most years, an inactive period of several hours duration is followed by an eruptive episode consisting of several closely-spaced eruptions. Most active periods consist of six eruptions with intervals of 3 to 8 minutes. The maximum height is 8 feet.

THE PUNCH BOWL SPRING GROUP is a small collection of springs in the immediate vicinity of Punch Bowl Spring. Punch Bowl itself is an intermittent, boiling spring. Vague reports have it as a geyser during the 1870s and 1880s, but it certainly has not been since. The spring immediately at the eastern (right-hand) base of the cone is also an intermittent spring, with periods showing no evident relationship to those of Punch Bowl.

110. UNNG-PBG-1 is the nearest and largest of the pools to the west of Punch Bowl Spring. Eruptions have been recorded for only 1976 and 1985. On each occasion the activity was in progress when first seen and was still going on when last seen. Thus, the play of 4 feet may last for hours.

The two other small pools beyond this geyser have also been recorded as geysers, and their activity may be related to that of PBG-1.

Grotto-Riverside Group

The Grotto-Riverside Group (Map F, Table 5) consists of three functional hot spring groups–the Grotto Geyser Complex, Riverside Geyser, and the Chain Lakes Complex. Riverside is the only major geyser in the group. Grotto Geyser, because of its frequent activity and heavy water discharge, and Link Geyser, which rarely erupts, are also important members of the cluster.

The two main trails through the Upper Geyser Basin merge into one at Grotto Geyser. This point is about 0.9 mile from the Old Faithful Visitor Center and about 0.2 mile from the end of the developed trail at Morning Glory Pool.

THE GROTTO GEYSER COMPLEX. The Grotto Complex includes six geysers and several small sputs. Four of these are in closely related pairs; the others are more separated. Grotto Geyser is an almost never-ending source of pleasure for its visitors. Geologically, it is important in that it serves as a sort of pressure release for the Giant Complex. Any frequent activity by Grotto results in the dormancy of Giant (94), as has been the case since 1955. Should Grotto decline, then perhaps Giant would reactivate. Grotto would then be less active than now, but we would be afforded both geysers.

111. GROTTO GEYSER was given its name by the Washburn Expedition in 1870. The interesting projections and caverns of the cone were formed as siliceous sinter was deposited about a stand of dead trees. The remaining stumps are now thoroughly coated and petrified by the geyserite. An early-day picture shows a man sitting in one of the openings of the cone. One look at the steam that steadily issues from that hole would discourage anyone from doing that today. Obviously, Grotto was not as active then as it is now, and in fact, that photograph was taken when Giant (94) was active, that is, during a time when exchange of function had shifted energy away from Grotto.

The eruption of Grotto resembles a series of large splashes.

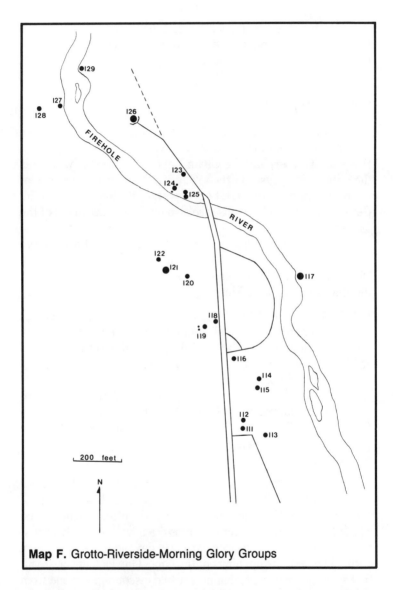

Map F. Grotto-Riverside-Morning Glory Groups

At the very beginning of activity these may reach over 40 feet high, but the play quickly dies down to 15 feet. Both the duration and interval can vary from as little as a few tens of minutes to 36 hours.

The discharge of water by Grotto is very high. An 8-hour eruption by the complex will spill over 225,000 gallons of boiling water. In any typical 24-hour period, the Grotto's total output is more than three times greater than Old Faithful's. Because of this high rate of water loss, Grotto has always been numbered among the most important geysers.

112. ROCKET GEYSER always erupts in concert with Grotto (111). During most of Grotto's activity, Rocket steadily churns and splashes about in its crater, most bursts reaching no more than 3 feet above the crater rim. On occasion, however, Rocket will take over the entire activity. Water jets in a steady stream to as much as 50 feet high while Grotto falls completely silent. These major eruptions last from 2 to 9 minutes, after which Grotto resumes its normal splashing action. Major eruptions by Rocket have been rare during most years, but of late it has been active during nearly every eruption of Grotto, usually occurring about 2 to 2½ hours after Grotto's start.

113. UNNG-GRG-1 is the first pool to the east of both Grotto and the boardwalk leading toward Giant. Rather infrequently this spring has had eruptions in the past, but they seem to be more common since the 1983 earthquake. Eruptions are always associated with murky water, which splashes about 2 feet high.

114 & 115. GROTTO FOUNTAIN and SOUTH GROTTO FOUNTAIN GEYSERS are very closely related both to each other and to Grotto (111). Although they have been active for most of the past twenty years, such activity might actually be exceptional. Long dormant periods have been recorded. It was the shock of seeing eruptions from these long "dead" craters during the 1950s that led to the original name of "Surprise" Geysers.

The small cone of Grotto Fountain certainly does not look like the source of a major geyser. Only a few inches high, it sits in the center of a broad, depressed runoff channel leading from Grotto and Rocket. Yet when Grotto Fountain plays, the play will reach between 30 and 50 feet for most of the 17-minute duration. The steady spout is very beautiful, especially when joined by South Grotto Fountain.

South Grotto Fountain's crater is about 30 feet to the right of the other. When the two geysers are active it is usually Grotto

Fountain that plays first, closely followed by its southern brother. If the reverse is true, then Grotto Fountain may not play at all. South Grotto Fountain usually does not exceed 10 feet high, but may play for more than 30 minutes.

When active, these geysers will play only *immediately* before the start of Grotto. The longer the headstart, which ranges from 2 to 8 minutes, the bigger the eruption by Grotto Fountain.

116. SPA GEYSER looks like a large, oval bathing pool, but nearly every eruption by Grotto (111) results in overflow at near boiling temperatures in Spa. During most years eruptions are infrequent, but 1985 saw a great deal of activity; Spa erupted nearly every time Grotto lasted more than 2½ hours. The activity consists of a series of eruptions. Very explosive, the eruption jets large masses of water between 6 and 45 feet high. These recur every 2 to 5 minutes during a 3-hour eruptive episode. Although not seen in several years now, exceptionally vigorous eruptions by Spa have been known to visibly weaken Grotto. Also, Spa erupted powerfully after every eruption by Giant (94) during the 1950s.

117. RIVERSIDE GEYSER is one of the favorites. It is highly regular, even more so than Old Faithful (1). Somehow, the first discovery expedition to Yellowstone missed seeing an eruption of Riverside, but it was studied by the Hayden Survey of 1871. Even though it was then known to be a very regular spouter, it was seldom seen by Park visitors. The area is out of sight from most of the Upper Basin; consequently, less frequent geysers received much more fame and attention. In fact, it was many years before the majority of visitors were positive about just which geyser was the one called Riverside.

Riverside is an isolated spring, not connected with any other so far as is known. As a result, the flow of water and heat into its plumbing system is constant, resulting in extreme regularity. Only changes in the flow rate can vary Riverside's performance. Over the years, intervals have ranged from about 5½ to 8½ hours.

Unlike those of most regular geysers, very few of Riverside's eruptions occur at the time of average interval. Instead, nearly all take place either about 25 minutes before or 20 minutes after the average time. It is the combination of this bimodal distribution of intervals that gives the average time. The predictions that the ranger-naturalists make are based on the simple average, because one never knows whether the next will be a long or short interval; beyond that, though, eruptions almost never occur more than 30 minutes off of the average.

The setting of Riverside is superb. The crater rises directly out of the far bank of the Firehole River against a background of grassy meadowland and tall lodgepole pines. The cone is shaped somewhat like a chair. The main vent is a shallow basin near the front part of the "seat." On the far side of the seat are two minor vents. The large hole on the chair "back" may once have been the main vent, and some play still issues from it during the beginning stages of an eruption.

Between 1½ and 2 hours before an eruption, the main vent begins to overflow. The discharge is periodic and punctuated by boiling spells. Starting about an hour before the play, the minor vents behind the main vent begin to bubble, spouting to a few inches. During this preplay, the old vent will occasionally splash directly into the river. It is a particularly heavy splash that initiates the eruption. Boiling over the main vent becomes heavy, and within a few seconds Riverside is arching out over the river, sometimes nearly spanning it. The maximum height of 75 feet is held for several minutes. Then the geyser slowly dies down. It doesn't stop spouting for about 21 minutes, and that is followed by a short, weak steam phase.

The average interval of Riverside is practically the same as it was in the 1870s. The present activity has probably been the same for several centuries and will continue for many more. With its column arching over the river and a rainbow in its spray, Riverside Geyser is one of the beauties of Yellowstone.

THE CHAIN LAKES COMPLEX. The Chain Lakes and surrounding springs are all interconnected. Geyser activity in the complex is rare, but major in size at times. Only two geysers have had notable activity – Link and North Chain Lakes Geysers.

118. CULVERT GEYSER was hurt, then helped, by the hand of man. When the road was built through the Upper Basin, a number of small springs blocked the engineer's plans. Therefore, they were buried and forgotten. At this time a spring near Spa Geyser (116) was buried while another had a retaining wall built around its crater. Now known as Culvert Geyser, the latter was certainly not the boiling pool of today. Apparently, the energy of the buried spring was diverted here. Culvert Geyser rapidly enlarged its crater and began spouting to 2 feet. Such play is uncommon now, but Culvert still boils and behaves as an intermittent spring.

119. SQUARE SPRING, and the two smaller springs beyond, had an episode of eruptions during the 1950s, but no details were written about this activity. Square alone was active again following the 1959 earthquake. These eruptions reached perhaps 10 feet high.

120. LINK GEYSER, so named when it proved to be an important link in the Chain Lakes, is a truly major geyser. But it rarely erupts, much to the disappointment of the geyser gazers but to the great delight of maintenance crews. The tremendous eruptions discharge so much water that very much activity would wash away the trail.

Link has had minor eruptions throughout recorded Park history. Even these 4-footers have been unusual much of the time. Such play lasts around 15 minutes and is really nothing more than slightly more vigorous boiling than normal. Major eruptions probably begin during the minor play.

The signs left by a major eruption are unmistakable, making it unlikely that any had occurred for many years before recorded history and certain that none have gone unnoticed during recent years. In 1936, signs of activity were observed during the spring months, but no eruption was seen until early summer. Throughout the course of that season eruptions were reported to the rangers with fair frequency. Sixty feet high and lasting less than 1 minute, they continued into 1937. No further major activity was reported until 1954, and during the next three years it erupted a total of 15 times.

It was in 1957 that Link first showed that it could erupt in series, many eruptions occurring in the course of a day. During such a series, the intervals would lengthen. This sort of activity continued periodically through 1958. Then Link became dormant, and no further eruptions were seen until 1968.

Link has had two modern active episodes, both involving series of eruptions. During the single day of August 8, 1974 there were eight eruptions. The first interval was 70 minutes, the last 197. Each play lasted less than a minute, but so much water was discharged that the Firehole River flowed muddy for a considerable time after each eruption. The play began with a doming of the water in the crater, sending a flood across the surroundings. Then the geyser literally exploded with jets of water reaching over 100 feet and carrying rocks along with them. The next active episode occurred during the winter of early 1984 and consisted of several series of eruptions. Very similar to those of 1974, they answered the question as to whether or not the rocks thrown at that time had damaged the plumbing system.

Link is directly connected with the other members of the Chain Lakes Complex, several of which have also erupted (though rarely). After the 1984 eruptions, energy shifted to North Chain Lakes Geyser (121); that geyser did not erupt this time, but the shift cooled Link to only about 120°F (49°C). What a change from the powerhouse of such a short time before. Now the energy has returned to Link, but no one knows how much time must pass before another spectacle takes place.

121. NORTH CHAIN LAKES GEYSER was not known to erupt until the late 1940s; it then had a very few eruptions up until the time of the 1959 earthquake. It has not played since.

122. UNNG-CLC-1 ("CLASP" GEYSER) is the northernmost of the Chain Lakes, somewhat separated from the others. It was seen to have a single, 20-foot eruption during 1974. Although that lasted but seconds, it seems to have thoroughly upset the system, as overflow, once common, now almost never occurs.

Morning Glory Group

Lying at the northwestern limit of the Upper Geyser Basin proper is the Morning Glory Group (Map F, Table 5). Named for Morning Glory Pool, the area contains seven geysers. Downstream from here it is about ⅓ mile to the next cluster of hot springs, the Cascade Group. Between the two groups are a narrowing of the Firehole River canyon and a hill, marking the

Table 5. Geysers of the Grotto-Riverside and Morning Glory Groups

Name and Number	Interval	Duration	Height (ft)
Culvert Geyser (118)	steady	steady	boil–2
Fan Geyser (124)	days–rare	15–90 min	125
Grotto Geyser (111)	1–36 hrs	1–36 hrs	15–40
Grotto Fountain Geyser (114)	1–36 hrs	8–25 min	30–50
Link Geyser (120)	rare	1 min	4–100
Morning Glory Pool (126)	rare	unrecorded	40?
Mortar Geyser (125)	days–rare	15–90 min	40–80
North Chain Lakes Geyser (121)	rare	2 min	20
Riverside Geyser (117)	5½–8½ hrs	21 min	75
Rocket Geyser (112)	1–36 hrs	1–36 hrs	3–50
Sentinel Geyser (129)	seldom	minutes	10–40
Serpent's Tongue (128)	steady	steady	1–5
South Grotto Fountain Geyser (115)	1–36 hrs	2–30 min	5–10
Spa Geyser (116)	irregular	sec–hrs	6–45
Spiteful Geyser (123)	irregular	minutes	10–30
Square Spring (119)	rare	unrecorded	10
UNNG-CLC-1 ("Clasp") (122)	rare	seconds	20
UNNG-GRG-1 (113)	infrequent	unrecorded	2
West Sentinel Geyser (127)	steady	steady	2–3

lower end of the continuous, open valley of the Upper Basin proper. Although the more northerly spring groups are included within the Upper Basin, they have been relatively ignored until recently.

The developed Upper Basin Trail ends at Morning Glory Pool. Beyond is the route of the old highway, which traversed the Upper Basin until 1971. Now designated as an unimproved trail, this old road leads on to the Cascade and Biscuit Basin groups.

123. SPITEFUL GEYSER occupies a deep and jagged crater right next to the trail. Formed by a steam explosion long before the discovery of the Park, it lies on a prominent fracture in the sinter. This crack probably owes its origin to an earthquake of considerable size. Though eruptions were observed during the early years of Yellowstone, it was then dormant until 1964. The new activity was very regular, with eruptions recurring every 15 minutes and reaching 10 feet high. The crater always remained empty between the plays. Following a brief dormancy, Spiteful rejuvenated in the early 1970s. The renewed activity was much more irregular than before. Always starting with the crater full, the geyser would abruptly rocket thin jets of water to as much as 30 feet. By 1974, progressively smaller eruptions gradually led into another dormant period which, except for a single eruption in 1984, continues to the present.

124. & 125. FAN GEYSER and MORTAR GEYSER cannot be discussed separately. With but few exceptions, these two large geysers erupt in concert. Fan, with not less than nine separate vents, lies along the same fracture that contains the crater of Spiteful Geyser (123). The two cones to the left, very near the Firehole River, are Mortar.

Although not active very often, Fan Geyser's seventeen vents sometimes put on tremendous displays that reach 125 feet high.

The large size of the cones and the great amount of erosion in the surrounding sinter platform prove that these geysers have been very active in the past. But during recorded history, eruptions have occurred infrequently, at best, and Fan and Mortar have been dormant during most years. For a time during the 1870s and 1880s they played about every 8 hours. But from that time on there were no further major eruptions until 1938.

Minor activity, eruptions just a few feet high, occurs often. Even periods considered dormant can be punctuated by such play. At these times, Fan will spout to about 3 feet, generally *not* accompanied by Mortar. At other times Mortar, too, has had its own episodes of minor activity. During 1915 these eruptions were both frequent and regular, recurring every 2 hours and reaching a height of 30 feet. During these phases, Fan normally shows no activity.

The first-known modern major eruption was seen in 1938. From then through 1968, only 15 more were seen. But a marked rejuvenation took place in 1969, and in the years since, more than 450 eruptions have been recorded. Throughout this period there seem to have been clear-cut cycles to the performances. Following two years of rather frequent eruptions will be one or two years with few to none. Why this should be so is entirely unclear, but a dormancy in 1989 was right on schedule, as was the reactivation of 1989–90.

When Fan and Mortar are active, they pass through a series of "hot cycles" prior to an eruption. Lasting between 40 and 120 minutes, these involve a quiet period, then surging in Mortar's lower vent, followed by jetting from Fan, and finally a return toward Mortar and another quiet spell. It is during the middle portion of a hot period, when Fan's jetting becomes steady, that a major eruption begins. Words cannot describe the scene. With little warning the water suddenly lifts above all of Fan's vents while at the same moment jetting begins from Mortar. Then the geysers simultaneously explode into the air. The main vent of Fan arches up and out to not less than 125 feet high, the spray arching over the trail. Some of the other vents play to 60 feet, each at its own angle, so that the entire display does indeed look like a fan. Meanwhile, Mortar is striving for its share of the attention. At first, both of its vents shoot vertically to more than 50 feet. Then, first the upper vent and later the lower run out of water. As they enter powerful steam phase eruptions some spray may reach over 80 feet.

The most impressive part of an eruption takes place during the first 10 to 15 minutes. During that time the eruptions are steady, without any pause or diminishing size. Then the play stops almost without warning, only to begin again an instant later. After a few more minutes comes another pause. With each of these, the eruptions become gradually weaker. Most eruptions continue in this manner for about 45 minutes, after which periodic steam bursts may persist for another 45 minutes, giving a total duration of about 1½ hours.

When performing at their best, Fan and Mortar may average as little as about 3 days between eruptions. Since they are not known to be connected with any other geyser except Spiteful, the question as to why they are not more regular has no answer. One thought is that the fracture system including Fan and Spiteful extends into the river where an inflow of cold water may quench potential eruptions. But then that must happen when the geysers are highly active as well as when they are not. In any case, there are no more impressive geysers anywhere. As Dr. Marler, long-time geyser expert, wrote: "To see an eruption of Fan and Mortar is to view some of the most spectacular activity in the Park. The infernal region would seem to have broken loose in full fury."

126. MORNING GLORY POOL is one of Yellowstone's most famous hot springs. Before the highway was removed from the area in 1971, it was visited by more people than any other spring or geyser except Old Faithful. There are many more beautiful pools, but this one, lying as it does at the very entrance to the Upper Geyser Basin and right next to the only road through the area, became a natural candidate for popularity.

That Morning Glory once was, and perhaps is, a geyser is evidenced by the deep runoff channels leading down to the Firehole River. Only one natural eruption has been recorded, and that occurred in 1944. The duration of the play could not be timed, but the height was 40 feet and a tremendous amount of water was thrown out.

It is its popularity that may have spelled the demise of Morning Glory Pool. In the past it was usually hot enough to prevent any growth of algae into the crater. The color of the pool was a delicate pale blue, quite unlike that of any other. But people have thrown so much debris into the crater that the vent is becoming plugged. Hot water has smaller egress into the crater and the temperature has dropped. Now algae can grow down into the crater and the color is far less beautiful than it used to be.

Because it was known to possess geyser potential, Morning Glory was induced to erupt in 1950. The purpose was to empty the crater so it could be cleaned. The list of material disgorged by the eruption is amazing. It included: $86.27 in pennies, $8.10 in other coins, tax tokens from 9 states, logs, bottles, tin cans, 76 handkerchiefs, towels, socks, shirts, and "delicate items of underclothing." Overall, 112 different kinds of items were recovered. Since 1950 several additional attempts to induce eruptions have been made, all without success. Many coins can be seen lining small benches on the crater walls. But Morning Glory was not created to be used as a wishing well, and if such action by Park visitors continues very much longer Morning Glory will die. It would be a tragic loss.

127. WEST SENTINEL GEYSER and its companion across the river (129) were named because they seemed to guard the entrance to the Upper Geyser Basin. Now other, more northerly hot spring groups are included in the basin, and the two Sentinels go nearly unnoticed.

West Sentinel is a perpetual spouter. The eruption is a heavy boiling of the water to a height of about 2 feet. For a brief while following the 1959 earthquake the action was more vigorous, reaching 4 feet.

128. SERPENT'S TONGUE is a small, somewhat cavernous spring up against the hillside behind West Sentinel Geyser (127). Serpent's Tongue is another perpetual spouter, playing about 2 feet high. The origin of the name comes from the eruptive steam bubbles, which enter the crater in a darting fashion.

129. SENTINEL GEYSER, also known as East Sentinel, has a large crater, which forms an island in the Firehole River at times of high water. Some of the time the river water pours directly into the crater, certainly thoroughly stifling any eruptions. When the river is lower, Sentinel constantly boils. True eruptions are very rare. Playing at a low angle, the water jet may reach up 25 feet and out more than 40 feet. Because of the location, eruptions are seen by very few people even when they do occur, and perhaps not more than a dozen have happened during recorded Park history.

Cascade Group

The Cascade Group (Map G, Table 6) has always been virtually ignored. It includes Artemisia and Atomizer Geysers, both of which must be listed among the most important geysers of the Upper Basin. But because these springs lie over a hill from the Morning Glory Group and are hidden by dense stands of pines on the other sides, they simply have not been observed very often.

No trail proceeds directly through the Cascade Group. The route of the old highway between Morning Glory Pool and Biscuit Basin is a designated trail, though it is not maintained in any way, and it affords the best views of the area. Also, an established trail across the river, running from the vicinity of Daisy Geyser to Biscuit Basin, gives views of Seismic and Hillside Geysers. In addition to seeing the area on your own, the National Park Service ranger-naturalists often lead guided walks through the area; check at the Old Faithful Visitor Center for schedules. It's a very interesting area, but given the hazards of thermal areas, please don't leave the trails to wander at will through the group.

130. ARTEMISIA GEYSER was so named because the coloration of some of the geyserite surrounding the crater resembles the grayish blue-green of sagebrush leaves (scientific name *Artemisia*). It has one of the largest craters of any hot spring in Yellowstone and is one of the more beautiful blue pools, in addition to being a major geyser. During its long quiet period there is a steady overflow. Eruptions begin without warning when the water level suddenly rises to cause a copious overflow. Surging then gradually builds into the full eruption. A massive boiling rather than a true bursting play, some of the eruptive surges can reach over 30 feet high. Most eruptions last between 16 and 20 minutes, and while most large bursts occur near the middle of the duration, some often take place at the

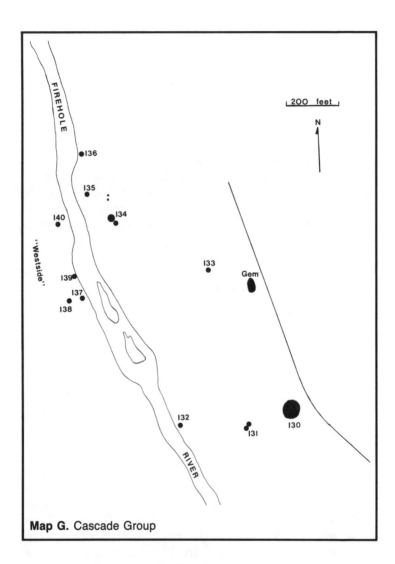

Map G. Cascade Group

very end of the activity. Following the eruption, the water level drops very slowly, requiring at least ½ hour to drop 18 inches. The first overflow comes after another 2 hours. In most seasons, the intervals average between 9 and 11 hours, although the known range is from 5½ to 16 hours. Also, 1985 was the first year in which a number of minor eruptions were observed, although a few were observed previously. Lasting only about 5 minutes, they resemble normal activity and cause slight delays in the onset of the next full eruption.

131. ATOMIZER GEYSER plays from two interesting small cones. About 3 feet tall, they lie directly between Artemisia Geyser (130) and the Firehole River. Atomizer shows an interesting progression of activity through the cycle leading to the major eruptions. As an indication of how little this area has been studied, it was only in 1985 that we finally obtained accurate information about what Atomizer really does. Following one major eruption, it will apparently be about 8 hours before anything of note happens. By then there have been a number of episodes of brief overflow from the main vent, these recurring every few minutes and inspiring the original name for the geyser, "Restless." One of these overflows leads into an eruption. Once started, these minor eruptions normally recur every hour. Lasting a minute or less, they may reach 25 feet high. There are probably six such minor eruptions during a typical cycle. Finally, following a normal minor interval, an eruption merges into the major activity. This resembles the minors at first, except that the play continues beyond 1 minute. The play builds in height to as much as 40 feet when, after about 8 minutes of steady water jetting, the water begins to give out. The concluding steam phase will persist for another 25 minutes. These major eruptions recur about every 15 hours. It is only at the time of the major eruption that the cone nearest Artemisia plays. Nearly sealed in by internal deposits of geyserite, this cone, the actual "atomizer," then jets steam and fine spray a few feet high.

132. SLIDE GEYSER is located on the high bank of the Firehole River below Atomizer Geyser (131). There is no record of activity from this vent prior to 1974. The crater opens directly onto the precipitous slope. Slide is quite regular in its performances. Intervals range from 5 to 12 minutes, with little variation at any given time. The water bursts out of the cavernous vent so that the play is mostly horizontal, sometimes reaching out as far as 10 feet.

133. CALTHOS GEYSER was surely very active in the distant past. The deep crater sits in the middle of an extensive but highly eroded sinter platform, which is drained by a single, very prominent runoff channel. The present quiet pool is intensely blue in color. The only recorded activity was triggered by the 1959 earthquake. For a few weeks Calthos underwent short, irregular eruptions, some of which reached 10 to 15 feet high. Though brief, the water discharged by these eruptions was prodigious, easily filling the drainage channel. During this active phase was the only known time when the water level in nearby Gem Pool was down several inches. For the next few years the two springs would alternately ebb and flow. Then Gem Pool resumed the steady discharge that had characterized it since the discovery of the Park. The only further flow from Calthos occurred during 1970 and 1981–82 and was extremely slight.

134. SEISMIC GEYSER is famous for having been a direct creation of the 1959 earthquake. A crack formed in the sinter and became the site of a small steam vent. Activity increased over the next 3½ years until a steam explosion formed the crater. The activity increased even then, and the newly-formed geyser became stronger and more explosive with every year. By 1966 the eruptions were reaching anywhere from 50 to 75 feet, and some might have been higher. But as the strength of the play grew stronger, the intervals between them increased. When a small satellite crater was developed by a new steam explosion in 1971, most of the eruptive energy shifted to the new vent. Eruptions became more constant but smaller in size. Ever so slowly, Seismic continues to decline in force. By the mid-1980s, even small eruptions by the satellite were uncommon.

Seismic Geyser is unquestionably connected with several other hot springs. The more important of these are Hillside Geyser (135) and the Pulcher Springs, a short distance up the slope. As Seismic increased in vigor, these other springs declined dramatically. Now that Seismic itself has declined, these related features have recovered to some degree. From all appearances, the area is finally approaching stability more than 2½ decades after the earthquake.

135. HILLSIDE GEYSER was never seen in eruption before 1948. It was active throughout that year but then had few additional eruptions before a new cycle was initiated by the 1959 earthquake. The major eruptions, 30 feet high, occurred every 20 minutes and lasted 4 minutes. Such activity lasted into 1961, then only minor eruptions were seen again. These were just 3 feet high, and even they stopped in 1964, just about the time that nearby Seismic Geyser (134) began having its large, explosive eruptions.

Just up the slope from Hillside Geyser, two small geysers made their appearance during 1982. After a year of action, they ceased to erupt. There is no other record of activity by them, either before or since.

136. UNNG-CDG-1 ("OCHEROUS" GEYSER) plays from an iron-colored vent immediately adjacent to the river, a short distance downstream from Hillside Geyser (135). Modern eruptions, the first on record, have been seen throughout the 1980s. They prove to be very irregular. At times the intervals are as short as 5 minutes, at others as long as an hour or more. The height ranges from just 3 feet to at least 25 feet. Regardless of any such variations, though, the duration is never more than a few seconds.

Table 6. Geysers of the Cascade Group

Name and Number	Interval	Duration	Height (ft)
Artemisia Geyser (130)	5½–16 hrs	5–22 min	30
Atomizer Geyser (131), major	13½–15½ hrs	31–33 min	40
Atomizer Geyser (131), minor	49–90 min	1 min	25
Calthos Geyser (133)	rare	1 min	10–15
Hillside Geyser (135)	rare	3–4 min	3–20
Seismic Geyser (134)	infrequent	minutes	3–10
Slide Geyser (132)	5–12 min	1 min	10
UNNG-CDG-1 ("Ocherous") (136)	irregular	seconds	3–25

"Westside" Group

The name "Westside" Group has been devised specifically for this edition of this book. The area (Map G, Table 7) contains a number of small hot springs and at least four geysers, yet evidently none have ever been independently described.

The Westside Group is located directly across the Firehole River from the Cascade Group, and the springs are rightly members of that group. They are handled separately here because of the clear topographic division caused by the river. The springs are accessible via the paved trail leading between the Daisy Group and Biscuit Basin, although that trail does not approach any of the hot springs closely.

Aside from the geysers and other hot springs of this area, a portion of ground to the northwest began to heat up during 1984. By mid-summer 1985, ground temperatures were as high as 205°F (95°C), hot enough to cause a distillation of organic matter in and on the ground. When the breeze is right, the sickeningly sweet odor of burnt sugar can be smelled many feet away.

137. UNNG-WSG-1 is a slit-like vent at the top of the Firehole River bank. More forceful than it looks at first, the eruption does not seem impressive because its horizontal nature confines it almost entirely to within the slit itself. This geyser is in eruption most of the time, periods of complete quiet never lasting more than a few seconds while the durations can exceed 5 minutes.

138. UNNG-WSG-2 is the most impressive geyser of the group. Playing from an oblong crater, the vent at the south end may send bursts as high as 6 feet. The regular intervals are about 1½ minutes long, and durations range from 30 to 40 seconds. This activity apparently began with the 1959 earthquake.

139. UNNG-WSG-3 ("CARAPACE" GEYSER) is a cyclic and usually inactive geyser that can be very impressive in its time. Located immediately above the river, the cone's overall shape vaguely resembles the carapace of a tortoise. When active, Carapace can erupt as often as every 15 to 20 minutes; more typical are intervals approaching 6 hours in length. The eruptions, which last from 2½ to 5 minutes, can burst water as high as 10 feet. Most of the time Carapace is dormant, with only a slight overflow leaving the crater.

140-140a. FANTAIL GEYSER, previously described as UNNG-WSG-4, and nearby OUZEL GEYSER were boiling springs that showed occasional signs of eruptive activity during the early 1980s. No eruptions were actually seen until April 1986. Both geysers were spectacular from the start, but the major activity was mostly confined to that first season. For more about this episode, see the Addenda.

Table 7. Geysers of the "Westside" Group

Name and Number	Interval	Duration	Height (ft)
UNNG-WSG-1 (137)	seconds	sec–5 min	1
UNNG-WSG-2 (138)	1–2 min	30–40 sec	4–6
UNNG-WSG-3 ("Carapace") (139)	irregular	2½–5 min	1–10
Fantail Geyser (140)	6 hrs–rare	10–45 min	30–75
Ouzel Geyser (140a)	irregular	sec–min	2–50

Biscuit Basin

The area traditionally included within the Biscuit Basin is more than ½ mile long. This span covers two distinct groups of hot springs. One group lies parallel to the route of the old highway through the Upper Geyser Basin; that right-of-way does not enter among the springs, but it does provide the only reasonably near view of them. This group is referred to as the "Old Road Group of Biscuit Basin." The "Main Group of Biscuit Basin" is that on the west side of the highway and river. It is traversed by a boardwalk, and a parking lot provides easy access.

Old Road Group of Biscuit Basin

The Old Road Group (Map H, Table 8) occupies an old sinter platform. It is a wide open area of little relief. It can be reached only by following the unimproved trail along the old highway route. Many hot springs perforate this expanse, but the group contains only ten, mostly small, geysers.

141. BABY DAISY GEYSER has been observed to erupt only during 1952 and 1959. Along with it, seven other nearby springs also erupted. None of them had ever exhibited any sort of pre-

vious animation. Baby Daisy was so named because its eruptions were strongly reminiscent of those of the much larger Daisy
Geyser (106). The eruptions, 30 feet tall, recurred every 105
minutes and were remarkably regular. Each eruption lasted 2
minutes. The activity of 1959, following the earthquake, was

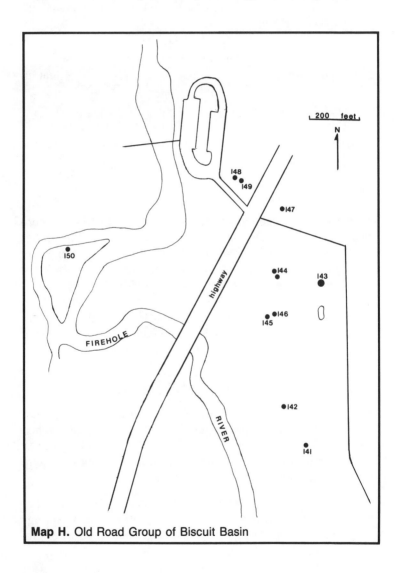

Map H. Old Road Group of Biscuit Basin

identical to that of before, except that eruptions occurred considerably more often. Baby Daisy has been dormant since early 1960, except that new runoff channels indicate that a few small, unobserved eruptions probably occurred during 1980.

142. BISCUIT BASIN GEYSER was one of those springs activated at the same time as Baby Daisy Geyser (141). It was much larger, with eruptions sometimes reaching 75 feet. During 1952, it would play very irregularly with several eruptions on some days, none on others. Every eruption lasted only 1 to 1½ minutes, but they were extremely impressive. Because the crater possesses no runoff channels to speak of other than those formed during the 1952 activity, it is believed that this has been the spring's only geyser activity. It has been totally dormant since 1952; not even the 1959 earthquake caused any noticeable change in its appearance.

143. CAULIFLOWER GEYSER has a large crater lined with cauliflower-like nodules of geyserite. Water continuously stands several inches below overflow in this aquamarine spring. The eruption begins with a sudden rise in the water level, accompanied by heavy boiling and copious discharge. The duration is 1 to 3 minutes, with intervals usually (and interestingly) about 20 *or* 40 minutes long. Beginning in 1980 and in every season since, Cauliflower has infrequently had large bursts during its eruptions, far above the normal vigorous but low boiling. Some of these reach an estimated 30 feet high, but there is absolutely no way to tell when such a burst might occur.

The large pool south of Cauliflower is Mirror Pool. It is one of the most stable features, without the slightest change in water level having been recorded.

144. UNNG-ORG-1 lies at the eastern corner of a shallow crater about 200 feet west of Cauliflower Geyser (143). Active starting with the 1959 earthquake, the geyser continued to play until sometime in the late 1970s. The eruptions were about 5 feet high.

At the northwest edge of this same crater, another vent has been active since 1983. Its eruptions do little more than cause a surface turbulence and heavier overflow. Recurring about every 5 minutes, the duration is 1 minute.

145. UNNG-ORG-2 is nearly hidden in some trees about 200 feet south of ORG-1. The crater of this spring is solidly lined with beautifully beaded geyserite, much of which is stained a pale orange by iron oxides. The eruptions, about 3 feet high, are small enough to be entirely confined to the crater. The play recurs about every 2 or 3 minutes and lasts 10 seconds. Like so many others, this geyser apparently began its current activity with the 1959 earthquake.

146. UNNG-ORG-3, just a few feet from ORG-2, is erratic and infrequently active, but at present it is the largest geyser in the Old Road Group. Eruptions come from a vent deep within an old, extremely weathered crater. Some soil washes into the vent with every eruption, producing muddy water. The jetting play is up to 30 feet high. Evidently cyclic, once started this geyser may erupt every few minutes over a stretch of several hours; such active episodes are, however, probably weeks apart.

147. UNNG-ORG-4 is located very near the highway. Its first known eruptions were in 1980. On irregular intervals it played as high as 6 feet for several minutes. Following a dormancy, the geyser was again active during 1985; this time the play was infrequent and comparatively weak and brief.

148. RUSTY GEYSER is one of the most visible geysers in all of the Upper Basin. It is located just to the right of the roadway as one enters the Biscuit Basin parking lot. Before the 1959 earthquake this geyser was cyclic in its activity, with dormant periods the rule. At such times the rusty-colored basin would pass almost unnoticed. But since the quake, Rusty has been almost continuously active, the only dormancy lasting from 1964 until 1967. The eruptions recur every 1 to 1½ minutes, last 10 to 30 seconds, and are fully 10 feet high.

149. DUSTY GEYSER erupts from a low sinter cone just north of Rusty Geyser. Because its geyserite lacks the iron oxide staining of Rusty, the duller appearance led to the name "Dusty." When active, Dusty erupted several times per day. Each eruption lasted about 3 minutes and was up to 15 feet high. Because there was no evident connection between this and Rusty, the two could often be seen together, providing an impressive pair of eruptions. Unfortunately, Dusty has been dormant for several years, and only infrequent small splashes are seen from it.

150. ISLAND GEYSER is somewhat separated from the other geysers of the group. Its crater is on a low, marshy island in the Firehole River. After the 1959 earthquake, several small springs developed on the island. About a dozen of them were small geysers. In 1966 one of them took over the major function and began spouting to 6 feet. Island Geyser hasn't quit since and is really a perpetual spouter. Following the 1983 earthquake it got stronger still, and some jets now exceed 20 feet.

Table 8. Geysers of the Old Road Group

Name and Number	Interval	Duration	Height (ft)
Baby Daisy Geyser (141)	rare	2 min	35
Biscuit Basin Geyser (142)	rare	1–1½ min	75
Cauliflower Geyser (143)	20/40 min	1–3 min	boil–30
Dusty Geyser (149)	infrequent	3 min	15
Island Geyser (150)	steady	steady	6–20
Rusty Geyser (148)	1–1½ min	10–30 sec	10
UNNG-ORG-1 (144)	5 min	seconds	5
UNNG-ORG-2 (145)	1–2 min	10 sec	3
UNNG-ORG-3 (146)	irregular	sec–min	10–30
UNNG-ORG-4 (147)	infrequent	30 sec–5 min	6

Main Group of Biscuit Basin

Lying on the west side of the Firehole River is the Biscuit Basin proper. It was named after delicately formed pieces of sinter that resembled biscuits. The best examples were at Sapphire Pool, but they no longer exist, having been blown away by powerful post-earthquake eruptions.

The Main Group (Map I, Table 9) is traversed by a boardwalk. From that trail every spring and geyser of the group is easily visible. A trail leading up the Little Firehole River to Mystic Falls departs from the boardwalk at the far side of Biscuit Basin; this trail can be followed farther, to an overlook with a fantastic view from the top of the bluff towering over the area.

151. SAPPHIRE POOL gained early notoriety as one of the more beautiful pools in the Park. The crater is of great depth, giving

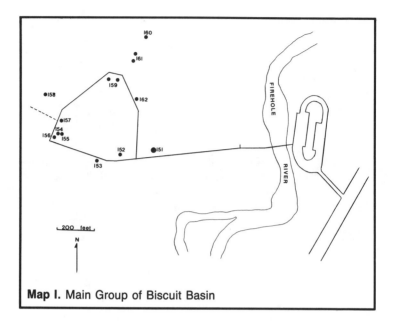

Map I. Main Group of Biscuit Basin

the water an incredibly rich sapphire-blue color. Since discovery, Sapphire has been known as a geyser. Minor eruptive activity occurred every few minutes, doming the water to about 6 feet with resultant heavy overflow.

No spring in Yellowstone was more greatly affected by the 1959 earthquake than Sapphire. A day after the shocks the crater was filled with muddy water, constantly boiling with vigor. Four weeks later Sapphire began having tremendous eruptions. Fully 125 feet high and almost equally as wide, these eruptions were among the most powerful ever known in Yellowstone. At first, the intervals were as short as 2 hours and each play lasted 5 minutes.

Unfortunately, the huge eruptions were short-lived. In time, Sapphire underwent dormant periods; active periods grew shorter while inactive periods became longer. When active, the intervals between eruptions shortened, but with that the force of play subsided. By 1964 no eruptions were more than 20 feet high. It wasn't until 1971 that Sapphire finally cleared all muddiness from its water, and it was just about then that true eruptive activity stopped. The only trace of periodicity now is a slight variation in the rate of boiling.

Whether Sapphire will ever again undergo eruptions, major or otherwise, only time will tell, but there is evidence that the geyser may have damaged its plumbing system. The muddy water indicates that subsurface erosion was taking place. Even the surface area was greatly affected. Before 1959 the crater was circular and about 15 feet in diameter; today it is oval, measuring 18 by 30 feet. The major activity by Sapphire might well be an example of a geyser being too powerful for its size, for its eruptions literally tore it apart.

152. JEWEL GEYSER is appropriately named, whether the term came from the beads of pearly sinter about the vent or the sparkling droplets of water that appear during its eruption. It was originally called Soda Geyser by the early Hayden Survey, who considered this to be the most important geyser of their Soda Group, now called Biscuit Basin.

Eruptions of Jewel are very regular. The average interval is just about 10 minutes, with the known range being from 5 to 12 minutes. Each eruption consists of a series of bursts, anywhere from 1 to 6 but normally 2 or 3, separated from one another by about 30 seconds. The bursts are 15 to 20 feet high. Jewel geyser was greatly but temporarily altered by the 1959 earthquake; the 1983 earthquake evidently had a greater effect, as Jewel now occasionally has bursts fully 40 feet high, strong enough to sometimes reach the boardwalk.

153. SHELL SPRING lies within a yellowish crater that someone felt looked like a clam shell. Shell is a cyclic geyser that has a period not yet accurately determined. When it is in an active phase, each eruption tends to last a little longer and raises the water a little higher within the crater. The highest bursts reach 6 feet above the pool level, however high it is. Near the end of a cycle the crater begins to overflow while one last eruption, with a duration of as much as an hour, fully drains the system. Shell then requires several hours to recover and begin the first weak eruptions of a new cycle.

THE AVOCA-SILVER GLOBE COMPLEX was only recognized as a functional group in 1984; during 1985 something of the very complex nature of its activity was learned from extended observations and interval-duration timings. Perhaps no group of springs anywhere shows such extensive cyclic behavior compounded by exchange of function. Additionally, few groups of geysers were more dramatically affected by the 1983 earthquake than this. A few minutes spent here is bound to be rewarding.

154. SILVER GLOBE SPRING is a pretty blue pool, but nothing of it can be seen from the boardwalk except when it is in eruption. Eruptions are known in three varieties: minors, majors, and "supers." Most activity is of the first two types, which differ mainly in strength, the majors sometimes sending bursts as high as 8 feet. Super eruptions are rare but may propel bursts as high as 30 feet for as long as 30 seconds. Such activity apparently was known during the 1890s but was not seen again until after the 1983 quake.

155. SILVER GLOBE GEYSER plays from a cavernous opening in the cliff just to the right of Silver Globe Spring (154). Its eruptions are closely related to those of the spring, and it shows the same three varieties of eruption. Most of the play is confined to the immediate crater area, but super eruptions may send thin jets of water at a low angle nearly to the boardwalk about 50 feet away.

156. UNNG-BBG-1 ("SILVER GLOBE SLIT" GEYSER) plays from a narrow rift in the geyserite beside a sealed-in pool. It is the closest of the complex to the boardwalk and one of the prettiest of geysers. Slit is most active when the other Silver Globes (154 and 155) are not. Intervals vary from 11 to 45 minutes and at any given time are extremely regular. Throughout the 1½- to 2½-minute eruption a fan-shaped spray of water is sent 10 feet high.

157. AVOCA SPRING was a steadily boiling and overflowing, nonerupting spring prior to the 1959 earthquake. After those shocks it became a powerful steam vent, but by the end of 1959 it had become a geyser. Except for some possible increase in force following the 1983 earthquake, it hasn't changed since. Avoca is

most active at those times when Silver Globe Slit (156) is most active and, therefore, when Silver Globe Spring and Geyser (154 and 155) are least active. Eruptions recur every minute or so during an active cycle, and some are strong enough to send bursts 25 feet high at an angle so as to soak the boardwalk. Active cycles last 10 to 20 minutes and are separated by 6 to 25 minutes of quiet.

158. WEST GEYSER is the blue pool near the trail leading to Mystic Falls, about 150 feet from Avoca Spring (157). Its only known eruptions took place within two weeks after the 1959 earthquake. None was ever seen by a Park Service observer, but the eruptions may have reached 30 feet.

159. MUSTARD SPRINGS, East and West, are separated by 50 feet. Before the 1959 earthquake both craters were lined with brilliant yellow algae, and the activity of the two was always similar until the present. Beginning in early 1983, the water level rose in East Mustard and fell in the other. Now East Mustard is a true geyser. Eruptions reach 6 feet, with occasional bursts to 10 feet; the duration of 5 minutes is longer than the normal interval. West Mustard now lies at a low level with occasional boiling and small splashing nearly out of sight.

160. NORTH GEYSER was so named because it is the most northerly geyser in the Upper Basin. The vent lies slightly over the hill beyond the boardwalk. When active, North is a vigorous geyser with eruptions up to 15 feet high. It has been dormant since 1963.

161. UNNG-BBG-2 is the small spouter visible north of the boardwalk in a position to be confused with North Geyser (160). This perpetual spouter began playing during the late 1970s; before then another vent a few feet away was having nearly identical eruptions. The play reaches 3 feet.

162. BLACK PEARL GEYSER'S crater was coated with dark gray, beaded sinter, but most of it has weathered away during the long and current dormant period. Black Pearl has always been cyclic on long periods, however, so it will undoubtedly resume activity in the future. Then its eruptions will be constant, or nearly so, sending water jets 2 to 4 feet high.

Table 9. Geysers of the Main Group of Biscuit Basin

Name and Number	Interval	Duration	Height (ft)
Avoca Spring (157)	sec–20 min	seconds	3–25
Black Pearl Geyser (162)	dormant	steady	2–4
Jewel Geyser (152)	5–12 min	30–90 sec	15–40
Mustard Springs (159)	2–5 min	5 min	6–10
North Geyser (160)	rare	2 min	15
Sapphire Pool (151)	rare	5 min	6–125
Shell Spring (153)	min–hrs	sec–min	6
Silver Globe Geyser (155)	minutes	seconds	2–50
Silver Globe Spring (154)	minutes	seconds	3–30
UNNG-BBG-1 ("Slit" Geyser) (156)	11–45 min	1½–2½ min	8–12
UNNG-BBG-2 (161)	steady	steady	3
West Geyser (158)	rare	unrecorded	30

Black Sand Basin Group

Black Sand Basin (Map J, Table 10) is named for the obsidian gravel that is found in many areas of this group. It is a small cluster of hot springs, well to the west of the rest of the Upper Geyser Basin. Black Sand Basin is easy to reach and explore. A parking lot gives easy access to boardwalks that approach all of the important springs. Most famous of all in the group is Emerald Pool (at "X" on Map J). Not a geyser, Emerald is of a green color due to the combination of the blue of its water with the orange-brown of algae lining the crater. The color was once much richer, but over the years the temperature has dropped several degrees, allowing darker algae to live.

163. WHISTLE GEYSER is very rarely active, with eruptions known for only six seasons. The best year was 1957, when seven eruptions were recorded. The last known eruption was in 1968. It is only during the first few seconds of the eruption that any water is discharged, in the form of a slender jet 35 feet high. The following steam phase is very powerful, roaring loudly and sometimes whistling a bit. With diminishing force, the entire eruption lasts between 2 and 3 hours. Whistle is probably an example of a geyser that has nearly sealed itself in with internal deposits; judging by the size of its mound it has certainly seen better days.

164. CUCUMBER SPRING was always a quietly flowing spring. The 1959 earthquake created a small steam vent on one shoulder of the crater, and it soon became a perpetual spouter a few feet high. Another explosion in 1969 enlarged the crater and merged it with Cucumber's. The combination now discharges a heavy stream of water as the spouter continues to play 2 feet high.

165. SPOUTER GEYSER was believed to be a perpetual spouter for many years, and perhaps it was so for a time. Now, however, it is periodic. Most eruptions have a duration of around

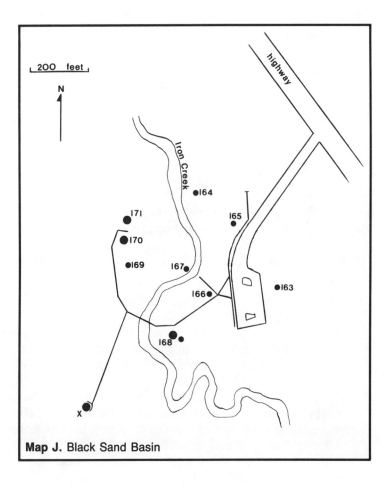

Map J. Black Sand Basin

10 hours, while the quiet interval is less than 2 hours. The play is about 6 feet high.

166. UNNG-BSB-1 is near the head of the boardwalk, next to the spur leading toward Cliff Geyser (167). This spring lies within an old collapsed crater, which in turn developed along a prominent crack in the sinter. This crack was probably formed by an earthquake in the distant past. There was no activity in the crater until 1941, but there have been no dormant periods since. The geyser is in eruption most of the time, with no interval longer than a few seconds. Most of the splashing play is only 3 feet high, but momentarily vigorous episodes may send some jets to 12 feet. In spite of this geyser's obvious location and great activity, no name has even been suggested for it. Perhaps you'd like to give it one of your own.

167. CLIFF GEYSER is the most important in Black Sand Basin. Situated in a wide crater right beside Iron Creek, it seems to be cyclic on long terms. During some years the intervals may be as short as 30 minutes, as was the case in 1985. At other times it is nearly dormant, and for most of the 1960s it was very regular at 12 hours. The eruptions begin with the crater empty. At this time, although the water jets have no pool in their way, they are not as high as those later in the play because they spread out more. The crater slowly fills as the eruption progresses; if this is a time of long intervals and correspondingly long durations, then it will fill completely, well before the eruption ends. Then the water of the pool serves to focus the bursts, and some may reach over 40 feet.

168. GREEN SPRING had its first recorded eruption in 1941, just about the same time that BSB-1 (166) began to play. Eruptions during 1941 were frequent. Since then there were a few eruptions, but no other episode of frequent action until 1975. In that year, for a brief period, eruptions regularly recurred every 30 minutes. Each lasted 3 to 5 minutes and was about 12 feet high. Evidently typical of Green, that active period lasted less than one month. The only further activity occurred during early 1985. Those eruptions were irregular, and while they lasted as long as 7 minutes, no burst was more than 3 feet high.

During 1980, a small geyser appeared just beyond the left side of Green Spring's pool. Very regular, its intervals were about 40 minutes, durations 5 minutes, and heights 5 feet. Although it persisted throughout that summer, this geyser had disappeared by 1981 and not a trace of its vent remains visible.

169. HANDKERCHIEF POOL is the famous spring that once attracted nearly as many visitors as any other single hot spring. It was possible to place a handkerchief at one end of the spring and have convection pull it down a vent and out of sight. A few moments later it would reappear in another vent. Handkerchief Pool continued to work until 1929, when somebody jammed logs into one vent. Later, eruptions by Rainbow Pool (170) washed gravel into the spring, completely obliterating its site. However, in 1950 it began to reappear as bubbling in the gravel. Handkerchief Pool was shoveled out. It no longer functions as it once did and is not even accessible because of thick beds of algae about its crater, but Handkerchief Pool is now a small perpetual spouter about 3 feet high. Two other spouters lie in the same area.

170. RAINBOW POOL has a crater nearly 100 feet across. It is ordinarily a quiet spring with light overflow. Not until 1938 was it known to possess powerful eruption potential. During that summer it erupted several times per day, the play often reaching 80 feet high. By 1939, though weaker, Rainbow was still active. No further play was seen until 1947 and 1948, when most eruptions were only 25 feet high. Beyond that the only other eruption was a single burst in 1973. The fact that it occurred at night, yet was seen by several people, indicates that this eruption might have been artificially induced. It was reported to be more than 100 feet high. For the next several days the water was very murky, an indication that the pool damaged its plumbing with the eruption. Very many such eruptions and Rainbow Pool would probably destroy itself.

171. SUNSET LAKE, even larger than Rainbow Pool (170), has undergone small eruptions for many years. Because the high temperature of the spring causes dense steam clouds to form, it is always difficult to observe the play. Eruptions during 1985 recurred every 20 seconds to 5 minutes and consisted of a single burst ranging from 2 to 8 feet high.

Table 10. Geysers of the Black Sand Basin Group

Name and Number	Interval	Duration	Height (ft)
Cliff Geyser (167)	30 min–12 hrs	7 min–2 hrs	15–40
Cucumber Spring (164)	steady	steady	2
Green Spring (168)	rare	minutes	boil–12
Handkerchief Pool (169)	steady	steady	3
Rainbow Pool (170)	rare	6–8 min	25–100
Spouter Geyser (165)	1–2 hrs	10 hrs	6
Sunset Lake (171)	sec–min	seconds	2–8
UNNG-BSB-1 (166)	seconds	sec–min	3–12
Whistle Geyser (163)	rare	2–3 hrs	35

Myriad Group

The Myriad Group (Map K, Table 11) is generally noticed by very few people. Only the Three Sisters Springs lie close to the road. The remainder of the springs are hidden behind the Old Faithful Inn. True to its name, the area contains thousands of hot spring vents. It is closed to public exploration, and rightly so because of the extreme thermal hazards. No trail leads through the area, but views can be obtained from the service road that runs behind the Inn.

The Myriad Group is the site of several important geysers. One of them, Round Geyser, is among the largest in Yellowstone. Located within the group are a number of mud pots, too. Rare features in the Upper Geyser Basin, these are the largest and best in the area. Very close to the service road, they are easily viewed.

172. BASIN SPRING underwent its only known period of eruptions during 1984, undoubtedly as a result of the 1983 earthquake. The activity was somewhat erratic. Most intervals were only a few minutes long, but others extended for hours. There were also several brief dormant periods. When active, the eruptions lasted 3 to 10 minutes, during which a violent boiling domed the water as high as 6 feet.

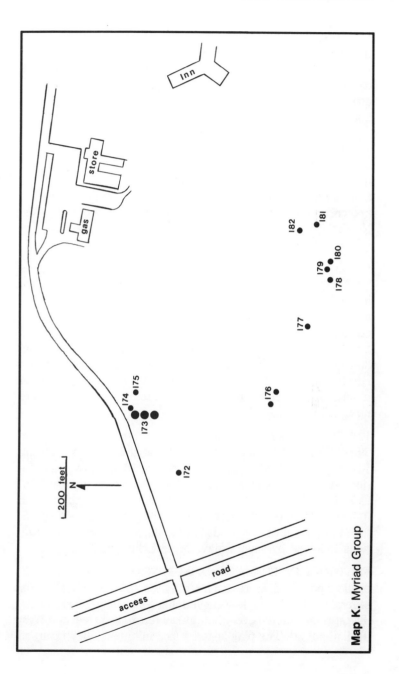

Map **K.** Myriad Group

173. THREE SISTERS SPRINGS sit next to the road leading from the Upper Basin access route to the front of the Old Faithful Inn. These three craters, filled with pale greenish water, are connected both above and below ground. Before the 1959 earthquake, only the North Three Sister, that closest to the road, was known to erupt. The earthquake initiated activity in the other two craters as well. The Middle Sister was the most powerful, with bursts reaching 15 feet high. The following year the major activity shifted back to North Sister, and it began playing to 30 feet. In time, this activity died down, and by 1968 the Three Sisters resembled their pre-quake state. Dormant periods are known, and the Three Sisters were so during most of the 1970s. North Sister rejuvenated during 1983, and it now erupts frequently to about 3 feet.

174. LITTLE BROTHER GEYSER is closely related to the Three Sisters (173). Its first known eruption was during 1950, when it briefly splashed every 5 minutes to 3 feet. The next year of activity was 1957, with eruptions to 12 feet. Following the earthquake, Little Brother rejuvenated along with the Middle and South Sisters, and these more erratic eruptions reached fully 30 feet. The most recent period of activity was 1983–84. Little Brother was then very regular, most intervals being about 14 minutes in length. Eruptions lasted 40 to 80 seconds and were up to 25 feet high.

175. COUSIN GEYSER is an even more distant relative of the Three Sisters. It underwent its first known active spell during July and August 1980. Lasting as long as 12 minutes, the eruptions shot a steady stream of murky water at an angle as high as 25 feet. At first the play recurred every 1½ to 3 hours, then it slowly declined into dormancy. During 1985 Cousin reactivated to a slight extent, evidently having a few very weak eruptions followed by several days of periodic overflow.

176. TRAIL GEYSER and nearby **WEST TRAIL GEYSER** are small, shallow pools that were activated by the 1959 earthquake. For several weeks they underwent simultaneous, powerful eruptions. The springs erupted every hour, Trail reaching 50 feet and West Trail about 20. The play lasted 1 to 2 minutes. They returned to dormancy in December 1959 and are again cool, scarcely noticeable springs.

177. MYRIAD GEYSER was so named because during its brief activity it was the largest geyser ever known in the Myriad Group. The only recorded eruptions were during 1954. That summer it erupted daily, the intervals ranging from 5 to 13 hours. The eruptions were between 80 and 100 feet high; shot out at an angle, they strongly resembled those of Daisy Geyser (106) during the 5 minutes of play. Exchange of function was in force during the activity of Myriad. While it and four other small spouters were active, the Three Sisters, over 450 feet away, were completely dormant for the first time in history. It is interesting to note, however, that succeeding dormancies of the Three Sisters have not resulted in the animation of Myriad and its neighbors.

178. ROUND GEYSER, not to be confused with the Round Spring Group elsewhere in the Upper Basin, is the largest geyser ever known in the Myriad Group and one of the largest in Yellowstone. It erupts from an impressively deep crater, 4 feet in diameter and almost perfectly round.

The first known eruptions were just after the 1959 earthquake. These were just 10 feet high. Following this brief period, Round was dormant until 1966. During the renewed activity the eruptions were more powerful, sometimes reaching 50 feet. With time they gradually gained in strength so that by the mid-1970s some eruptions were fully 150 feet high. The intervals during an active period are usually quite regular, averaging around 14 hours, with a 9- to 18-hour range.

During the quiet period the small pool periodically boils around the edges. It is during one of these perturbations that the water level suddenly rises. Heavy overflow is accompanied by a vigorous boiling up of the water to 2 feet. There will always be three such surges, separated by about 10 seconds, immediately before the eruption. A fourth surge suddenly rockets the water, needing only a few seconds to reach the maximum height. The eruption itself lasts less than 1 minute, but it is followed by a series of equally short but impressive steam phase eruptions. Unfortunately, although still boiling, Round has been dormant since 1981.

179. ABUSE SPRING was so named because of the vast amount of debris that was thrown into the crater by early Park concessioner employees. It was also once a source of hot water for the employee kitchens at the Old Faithful Inn. The crater still shows the abuse it received over the years. The first known eruption by Abuse was a result of the 1959 earthquake. Though the eruption was not observed, the amount of debris thrown out indicated that it was very powerful. Further play did not occur again until 1974, when nearby Spectacle Geyser (180) activated. At first there was an exchange of function between these two springs. Abuse would have one or two eruptions, then Spectacle would play over a period of several days. The eruptions by Abuse were massive domes of water about 15 feet high. In May 1976 unprecedented activity took place in the two geysers. Abuse and Spectacle became truly major geysers, with intervals as short as 90 minutes. In Abuse the height was not less than 90 feet and at times certainly exceeded 100 feet. While such eruptions were taking place, concerted activity in Spectacle reached as high as 75 feet. For this one-week period, Abuse and Spectacle were among the most powerful geysers in the world. But it was nearly the end of the show. During June 1976, Abuse had only a few more small eruptions, and it has been inactive since.

180. SPECTACLE GEYSER has had an uncertain history. During one construction episode at the Old Faithful Inn during 1928, a small spring was used as a hot water source by the workers' camp cook. The resultant lowering of the water level caused eruptions. To stop them the crater was filled with sand. Spectacle Geyser may be this small spring, but if so its crater is now much larger than it was in 1928.

The first recorded eruptions of what is definitely Spectacle occurred during 1974, at the same time that nearby Abuse Spring (179) began erupting. Of the two, Spectacle was the larger and more active. During its active periods it erupted about every 20 minutes. Each play lasted 1 to 3 minutes and was 25 feet high. The eruptions were vigorous and, jetting at an angle, very beautiful. After several months of activity, Spectacle and Abuse were dormant until May of 1976. Over a period of a few days both Spectacle and Abuse became tremendous geysers. Erupting as often as every 1½ hours, Spectacle would play at least 75 feet high, while Abuse joined the concert at up to 90 feet. Following the major eruptions, which ended on May 31, Spectacle continued having minor activity through most of that summer. Since then Spectacle has been dormant most of the time. It would sometimes erupt shortly after eruptions by Round Geyser (178), but those 10-foot plays ended with Round's dormancy in 1981. Occasional weak eruptions still occur.

181. WHITE GEYSER is the most visible geyser in the Myriad Group. Usually active, eruptions recur every 2 to 15 minutes and last about 30 seconds. The 1959 earthquake caused White to become more frequently but less powerfully active. The maximum height is now about 12 feet. Dormant periods have been recorded. Usually these are infrequent and brief, but a series of dormancies occurred during 1985 so that White was active only about half the time. When the usual case is the rule, White is the only geyser apt to be seen in the Myriad Group. It is so frequent that it can hardly be missed.

182. LACTOSE POOL is a muddy, milky white spring near White Geyser. It spends most of its time bubbling gently from a water level deep within its crater. On infrequent occasions, seemingly always in late summer, it begins frequent eruptions, which may persist for several days. Some bursts of the muddy water may reach 20 feet.

Table 11. Geysers of the Myriad Group

Name and Number	Interval	Duration	Height (ft)
Abuse Spring (179)	rare	1 min	15–90
Basin Spring (172)	rare	3–10 min	6
Cousin Geyser (175)	seldom	12 min	25
Lactose Pool (182)	infrequent	minutes	5–20
Little Brother Geyser (174)	irregular	40–80 sec	3–30
Myriad Geyser (177)	rare	4–5 min	80–100
Round Geyser (178)	rare	1 min	10–150
Spectacle Geyser (180)	infrequent	sec–3 min	5–75
Three Sisters Springs (173)	frequent	minutes	3–30
Trail Geyser (176)	rare	1–2 min	50
West Trail Geyser (176)	rare	1–2 min	20
White Geyser (181)	2–15 min	30 sec	12

Pipeline Meadows Group

No trail leads into the Pipeline Meadows Group (Map L, Table 12). The area is located upstream from the main portion of the Upper Geyser Basin; these are the springs visible from the cabin area of the Old Faithful Lodge. Only a small number of hot springs are located here, but four of them are geysers, two of which can be impressive at times. To get to the area, remembering as always that a thermal area is dangerous, leave the established Observation Point trail from near its start between Old Faithful and Geyser Hill.

183. UNNG-PMG-1 ("DILAPIDATED" GEYSER) is the first Pipeline Meadows spring encountered when walking upstream along the Firehole River. It plays from a badly weathered cone next to a deep crater with a considerable overhang. Dilapidated has been listed as a geyser since the early days of the Park, but no eruptions were ever seen until the late winter of 1980. It was then active for the next year or so. Cyclic in its activity, Dilapidated would experience a series of eruptions followed by a day or more without eruptions. Intervals were about 2 hours long. Throughout the 2- to 5-minute duration the geyser would burst from the cone, some spray reaching 30 feet high. The size of Dilapidated's cone and runoff channels indicate a great deal of activity in its past, but the water level is now lower than it was before 1980. Dilapidated is probably finished for a long time to come.

184. UNNG-PMG-2 erupts from a small vent surrounded by a round geyserite platform. Leading from the platform are several deeply cut runoff channels that owe their existence to activity since 1981. There is no certain record of activity for any time before then. This geyser is erratic in its performances. Intervals evidently range from only a few minutes to several hours, while the eruptions last little more than 1 minute. The play is a squirting action reaching about 10 feet high. This geyser activated at about the same time that Dilapidated Geyser (183) quit, indicating a possible connection between the two.

185. UNNG-PMG-3 ("PIPELINE MEADOWS" GEYSER) is the most active geyser of the group, playing every 3 to 8 minutes. Mentioned in some early reports on the Upper Basin, it is not known to have ever had a dormant period. So, although the 30-second

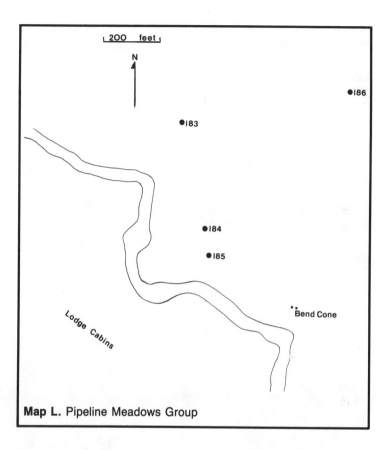

Map L. Pipeline Meadows Group

eruptions are not impressive, never being more than 2 feet high, this is a remarkable feature. Simple math shows that it has probably had at least 12,000,000 eruptions since it was first seen!

186. UNNG-PMG-4. There is no known report about this geyser from any time in Park history. It was first observed during 1985, yet the deposits of sinter in and about the crater prove it to have been active for many years. It is known to have both major and minor eruptions, both types occurring in erratic fashion. The minor eruptions are far the more common, lasting a few seconds and bursting about 3 feet high. Major eruptions may recur as often as every 20 minutes but are normally hours apart. They last more than 2 minutes and may reach 7 feet high. Separate from the rest of the Pipeline Meadows Group, this geyser is most easily found on a cold day, when steam will guide one to the spot.

Table 12. Geysers of the Pipeline Meadows Group

Name and Number	Interval	Duration	Height (ft)
UNNG-PMG-1 ("Dilapidated")			
(183)	rare	2–5 min	10–30
UNNG-PMG-2 (184)	min–hrs	1 min	10
UNNG-PMG-3 ("Pipeline			
Meadows") (185)	2–8 min	30–45 sec	2
UNNG-PMG-4 (186)	minutes	sec–2½ min	3–7

Chapter 5

Midway Geyser Basin

The Midway Geyser Basin (Map M, Table 13) is a small area. Its hot springs are almost totally confined to a narrow band of ground paralleling a 1-mile stretch of the Firehole River. Additional springs, mostly cool and muddy, extend up the Rabbit Creek drainage to the east. Topographically, the Midway Geyser Basin is a part of the Lower Geyser Basin, but it has always held separate status because it is separated from the Lower Basin by a forest of lodgepole pines. First known as the Halfway Group, then as Egeria Springs, Midway contains only a dozen geysers of note. Possibly dozens of other hot springs are geysers, too, but essentially nothing is known about them. Two such areas are indicated on Map M.

Despite its small size, the Midway Basin is the location of the largest single hot springs in the world. Grand Prismatic Spring ("X" on Map M) is more than 370 feet across. Excelsior Geyser discharges a steady stream of more than 4,000 gallons of water every minute. In fact, almost every spring at Midway is of extraordinary size.

The entire Midway Geyser Basin is readily accessible. The main part is served by a parking lot and boardwalk system. Other geysers can be reached or seen from pullouts along the main road, and the remainder from the vicinity of the Fairy Falls trailhead. One of the best views of the area is obtained by climbing the low bluff across the river and highway from Excelsior. There one is high enough to receive a good view of the pools and their coloration. The hike is well worth the few minutes it takes.

1. **TILL GEYSER** is named for the glacial gravels from which it rises. (Till is the rocky soil that makes up a glacial moraine, the material dumped by a glacier when it melts.) Because of its loca-

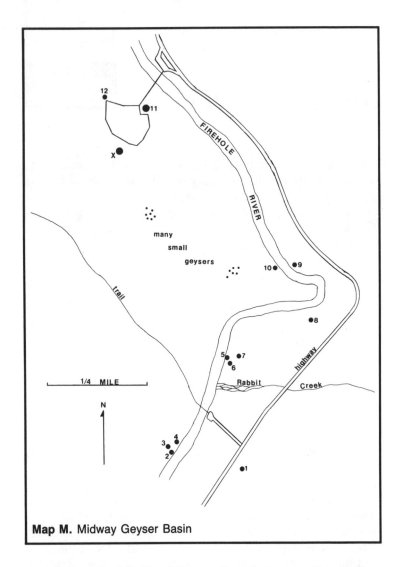

Map M. Midway Geyser Basin

tion against the hillside, Till is easily seen by people travelling south on the highway but almost invisible to those travelling in the opposite direction.

Till erupts from a complex of vents. The two main craters are situated at the top and bottom of the cluster; between them are several smaller apertures that also jet water. The system fills slowly after an eruption, reaching overflow about 30 minutes before the next eruption. The play begins suddenly. The greatest height comes from the upper main vent, where some jets reach 20 feet. At the same time, the lower main vent sprays mostly horizontally to about 10 feet. The smaller vents sputter a few inches to a few feet high. The entire operation lasts about 30 minutes, with only a few brief pauses occurring near the end of the activity. Although invervals are known to range from 5½ to 10 hours, during most seasons Till is very regular at around 9 hours. During 1985 there were at least two sequences of minor, mid-interval eruptions, the first ever observed. These occurred in series, with intervals of 11 minutes and durations of 2½ minutes. Interestingly, there was no delay in the time of the subsequent full eruption.

2. UNNG-MGB-1, along with MGB-2 and MGB-3, is located south of the Fairy Falls trailhead within a small cluster of springs on the west side of the river. Very little is known about this geyser. During most seasons it apparently is nearly dormant, while in others it is seen several times per month. The eruptions, 6 to 8 feet high, may last several hours.

3. UNNG-MGB-2 is located just up the slope from MGB-1. A perpetual spouter, MGB-2 has a 1-foot eruption that issues from a low cone, algae-covered, which makes it less than obvious from a distance.

4. UNNG-MGB-3 is the northernmost of the springs within this small group. It is a true geyser, but the height of the eruptions is less than 1 foot. The play recurs every 1 to 3 minutes and lasts 1 to 2 minutes.

5. RIVER SPOUTER was created by the 1959 earthquake when a crack was formed in the sinter at the base of an old cone. It may be that the old spring had sealed itself in with sinter and that the energy for the present eruptions has always been available, only awaiting release through the new vent. Because the vent is located beneath the water of the Firehole River, River Spouter is evident only when the river is very low. Then the spout, steady during some years and frequently periodic during others, will sometimes reach 10 feet high. During these eruptions the old cone raises a commotion within its vent but seldom splashes any water onto its sides.

6. **PEBBLE SPRING** is a small geyser located near River Spouter. It undergoes continuous eruptions no more than 2 feet high, except that on infrequent occasions much larger activity occurs. These eruptions may reach over 8 feet high and persist for nearly 1 hour. They are typically seen only once or twice per year.

7. **UNNG-MGB-4** is a complex of related geysers and spouters. There is always some degree of eruption going on here. Sometimes it is rather little; most often several vents are active at once. The highest jets reach about 3 feet high, with occasional surges to 6 feet.

8. **CATFISH GEYSER** is different not only from the Catfish in the Upper Geyser Basin, but probably also from the spring originally given the name. That may be the old cone at River Spouter (5). This Catfish is a large intermittent pool, which has shown very little variation in its activity. About every 15 minutes the water rises. Along with the heavy water discharge there is a vigorous boiling. This action throws water 2 to 3 feet into the air. The duration is near 5 minutes.

9. **FLOOD GEYSER** is perhaps the most important geyser in the Midway Basin, frequently active and discharging considerable water. Through much of its recorded history it has been practically ignored; for years, the highway to Old Faithful crossed the river downstream from Flood, leaving it isolated. Now the highway crosses the hillside directly above Flood. In spite of that proximity, no systematic observations of its behavior were made until 1970, and it waited for 1985 to reveal the full extent of its complex behavior.

The vigorous activity of Flood consists of minor, intermediate, and major eruptions. The duration of an eruption is directly related to the length of the interval preceding it. The minor eruptions have a duration of just 10 to 40 seconds following an interval of 1½ to 4 minutes. For the intermediates the durations are 2 to 5 minutes after 15- to 25-minute intervals. Majors last 6 to 8 minutes when the previous interval has been 33 to 45 minutes. Very few eruptions occur with values out of these ranges.

Regardless of variety, all eruptions of Flood look about the same. Water is bulged upwards by expanding bubbles of steam rising into the crater, which burst to produce large globular splashes. The height ranges between 10 and 25 feet. There is a tendency for the bigger splashes to occur during the major eruptions, but this is not an iron-clad rule. All eruptions have a heavy discharge of water, the total during the major play amounting to perhaps 10,000 gallons.

10. WEST FLOOD GEYSER was so named because its eruptions somewhat resemble those of Flood Geyser (9). Although the two geysers are directly across the Firehole River from one another, there seems to be no connection between them. West Flood was reported as active during 1878, but maps and descriptions from that time make it likely that it was Flood that was actually seen. There was no modern activity by West Flood until 1940, and it has usually been active, though highly variable, since then. Eruptions generally recur every 45 to 80 minutes, with little average variation at any given time. The bursts are 10 to 12 feet high and last 1½ to 6 minutes.

11. EXCELSIOR GEYSER is one of the brightest stars of the geyser world – when it is active. The last of its truly stupendous eruptions was in 1890. During the ten years before that it underwent many eruptions during several active episodes. Although most eruptions reached "only" 100 feet, some were fully 300 feet high, and they were as wide as they were high! Considering the size of the geyser, the amount of activity was fantastic. For example, during the eleven days of play from September 27 through October 7, 1881, Excelsior played 63 times, giving an average interval of only a little over 4 hours.

The present Excelsior is quite different, though still impressive. The crater measures more than 200 by 300 feet. The huge, azure pool boils at numerous points, proving an abundant source of heat. The discharge is tremendous, too, amounting to a measured 4,050 gallons per minute. That is more than 5,800,000 gallons of water per day, enough to fill more than 200 railroad tank cars or 300,000 automobile gas tanks. And this flow is constant.

That in itself tells us a lot. Excelsior was a geyser, a periodic hot spring. So, the flow of water might be expected to be peri-

Excelsior Geyser, the only major geyser in the Midway Basin, last erupted during the 1880s, when it played as high as 300 feet.

odic, too, even when no eruptions are occurring. The fact that Excelsior boils from many places other than the main vent indicates that the explosive eruptions of the 1800s tore some of the crater and plumbing system apart. In effect, Excelsior has been leaking, unable to build the high subsurface temperatures and pressures needed for eruptions.

It was, therefore, a very big surprise when Excelsior erupted during September 14–16, 1985. Eruptions were frequent during that 46-hour period. Most were minor in size, with the biggest bursts reaching perhaps 30 feet high. There were also a few major eruptions. Though not nearly of the scale of the activity of the 1800s, some of the play sent jets of muddy gray water to as much as 80 feet. As before, the bursts were at least as wide as they were high. All of the eruptions lasted near 2 minutes, with known intervals ranging from 5 to 66 minutes. During the active episode the water discharge was several times greater than at any other time since 1890.

Whether these eruptions were a preface to renewed activity of a truly major scale or just an aberration, none can tell. Everything about Excelsior's crater is jagged, evidence that its entire history has been recent and explosive. It is probably the nature of Excelsior to experience short periods of immense but damaging eruptions followed by decades of healing. Now, perhaps, it is mended.

12. OPAL POOL is a significant geyser, but its eruptions are rather rare and exceedingly brief. No activity was known until 1947, when Opal played several times as much as 50 feet high. Similar action occurred during 1949 and 1954, but then nothing further was seen until 1979. A few eruptions have been observed during every season since then, except 1982, 1983, and 1990. The modern action is usually less than 30 feet high, but no matter what the size, most eruptions consist only of a single, virtually instantaneous burst of water. At its best, Opal will have several successive bursts a few seconds apart; then the duration may reach as long as 1 minute.

Table 13. Geysers of the Midway Geyser Basin

Name and Number	Interval	Duration	Height (ft)
Catfish Geyser (8)	15 min	5 min	2–3
Excelsior Geyser (11)	rare	4 min–hrs	50–300
Flood Geyser (9)	1½–45 min	10 sec–8 min	10–25
Opal Pool (12)	rare	seconds	10–50
Pebble Spring (6)	steady	steady	1–8
River Spouter (5)	irregular	sec–steady	0–10
Till Geyser (1)	5½–10 hrs	30 min	10–20
UNNG-MGB-1 (2)	irregular	hours	6–8
UNNG-MGB-2 (3)	steady	steady	1
UNNG-MGB-3 (4)	1–3 min	1–2 min	1
UNNG-MGB-4 (7)	near steady	near steady	2–6
West Flood Geyser (10)	45–80 min	1½–6 min	10–12

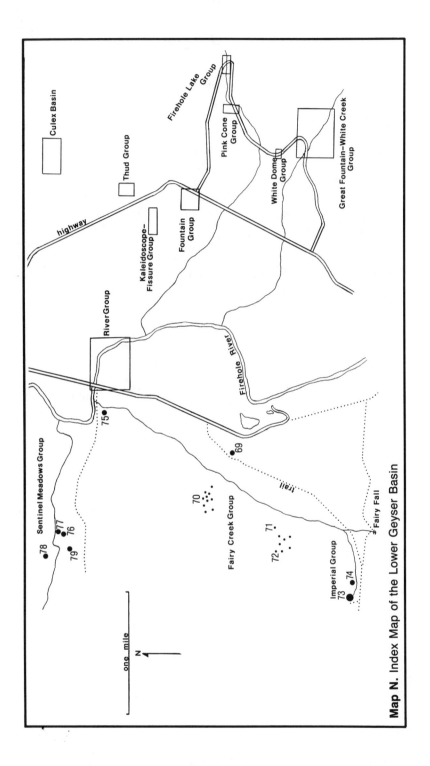

Map N. Index Map of the Lower Geyser Basin

Chapter 6

Lower Geyser Basin

The Lower Geyser Basin (Map N) is the largest in Yellowstone National Park. It covers a 12-square-mile valley within which hot springs are found in over a 5-square-mile area. Within this area are many scattered hot spring groups, most of which include geysers. Several of the spouters are as famous as those of the Upper Basin, and Great Fountain deserves its reputation as one of the most magnificent geysers in the world.

The individual geyser clusters of the Lower Basin are readily accessible. Roads approach them in several areas, and boardwalks allow the visitor to further explore the most important groups. Some of the more remote springs can be reached via primitive but maintained trails. A few groups, however, remain visible only from the highway. The geyser action in all of the areas is vigorous, and seldom are any visited when some geyser is not erupting.

Most of the springs here are of the same clear water type as those of the Upper and Midway basins. But the Lower Basin is notable in that there are some areas of muddy, acidic activity. These are often closely spaced with the geysers, an unusual occurrence. The Fountain Paint Pots, within the Fountain Group of geysers, is the most famous example. They are the single largest cluster of mud pots in Yellowstone.

Great Fountain-White Creek Group

Great Fountain Geyser should probably be assigned to a group consisting of two geysers, including only itself and one other very small spouter. Its activity over the years has varied only slightly and it is certainly a nearly isolated spring. Along nearby White Creek there are many springs including at least nine geysers (Map O, Table 14). Some of the pools of this area are

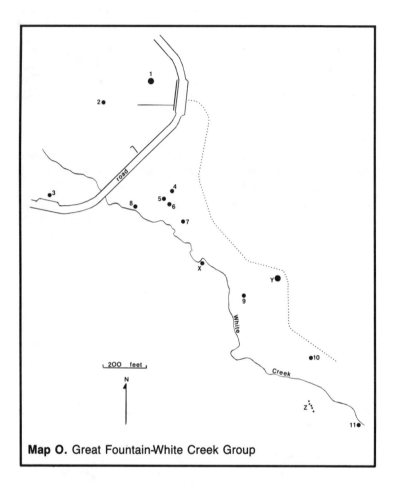

Map O. Great Fountain-White Creek Group

worthy of note in their own right: Verdant Spring ("X" on Map O) is deep emerald green, Octopus Pool ("Y") is crystal clear, and the Five Sisters ("Z") are pretty and support fine algal growths. All in all, this is a group well worth an extended visit.

Great Fountain Geyser is right beside the Firehole Lake Drive (one-way north) and has been provided with a small parking lot. The White Creek area can, to at least some extent, be reached by following the old White Creek-Midway Basin trail, which leaves the road at the parking lot. Much of the pioneering research about hot water life has been conducted in the White Creek area. Please look, but do not touch.

1. GREAT FOUNTAIN GEYSER was the first Yellowstone geyser to be observed by reliable reporters. In 1869 the Cook-Folsom-Peterson party entered their first geyser basin here. They were fortunate in arriving just as Great Fountain began to erupt and were duly impressed. As Cook later wrote, "We could not contain our enthusiasm; with one accord we all took off our hats and yelled with all our might.".For after such a long and dangerous search they had finally found a source of the many rumors. They would be rumors no more.

Great Fountain has always attracted much attention. The large crater is set in the middle of a broad, raised sinter platform. The vent itself is about 16 feet across and filled with clear, boiling water. The setting is impressive even when the geyser is not in eruption.

The eruptions of Great Fountain are regular enough to be predicted. The superheated water surges and boils during the long preplay period. It takes some close looking, but the most significant time for prediction is the time of first overflow from the crater onto the platform. This usually begins about 1 hour before the beginning of an eruption. Meanwhile, the boiling within the crater becomes periodic. Eventually, a heavy surge, several feet high, will precipitate the eruption. The boiling becomes extremely violent, then the geyser bursts into the sky. A great many of the eruptions are little more than 100 feet high, but even these are spectacular since the water column is very wide. Often enough, though, some of the bursts will reach over 150 feet. "Superbursts" are rather rare; coming at the start of play, these are known to reach as much as 230 feet! The activity proceeds with bursts of widely varying heights for several minutes. Then Great Fountain pauses for a few minutes while leading up to a second eruptive period. This process is repeated several times so that the whole eruption lasts 50 to 60 minutes.

During all of the pre-1959 earthquake years, Great Fountain's intervals averaged near 12 hours. The tremors caused some sort of underground changes. Great Fountain continued to be regular, but the intervals were cut to around 8 hours. Even now, after more than 25 years, the average is still only 9½ hours.

Great Fountain Geyser is the largest in the Lower Basin. Eruptions of up to 200 feet in height have been observed.

On rare occasions, Great Fountain enters what is called "wild phase" activity. For many hours to several days it erupts almost continuously. Water is thrown anywhere from 10 to 50 feet high several times per minute. Although not nearly as high as the normal eruptions, this play is very impressive. What causes it is a mystery, as is the cause of somewhat similar periods of excessively long overflow. In an opposite fashion, Great Fountain will sometimes fail to fill normally following an eruption. The water may remain at a low level for as long as three days before normal eruptions resume.

But overall, Great Fountain is an extremely reliable performer. Being predictable, and the only such major geyser in the Lower Basin, it performs for thousands of people every year. Few of them are disappointed by the display.

2. UNNG-GFG-1 made its appearance during 1985. Located downstream and in the middle of Great Fountain's (1) southern runoff channel, this geyser shows some relationship to Great Fountain's activity. While intervals are known to range between 28 and 50 minutes, most are on the short side *unless* Great Fountain has just erupted. Lasting for several minutes, the eruption reaches a height between 1 and 6 feet.

3. FIREHOLE POOL, immediately below the road, before one gets to Great Fountain Geyser (1), is a pretty, rich blue pool that has functioned as a perpetual spouter throughout recorded Park history. One of the very few hot springs of any type to escape earthquake effects, its steady play reaches 6 feet high.

4. UNNG-WCG-1 ("A-O" GEYSER) was so named in allusion to its proximity to the somewhat more officially named A-1 and A-2 geysers. A-0 is erratic in its performances, with the first recorded eruptions apparently taking place during the 1970s. The play generally recurs every 1 to 2 hours, bursting water to between 5 and 10 feet high. Most plays last only a few seconds, but occasional eruptions lasting several minutes and reaching perhaps 15 feet are known.

5. A-1 GEYSER shows clear relationships to A-0 and A-2 geysers and to Botryoidal Spring. If A-1 is active, then A-2 is nearly dormant; if A-2 is active, then A-1 is completely dormant. Of these geysers, A-1 is the closest to the roadway. The crater is an irregular oval, largely filled with rubble, much of which has probably been tossed in by visitors. When A-1 is active, eruptions recur every 30 to 40 minutes and are 6 feet high. More often, A-2 is active.

6. A-2 GEYSER lies about 25 feet east of A-1 (5), and like A-0 (4) and A-1, it is connected with other springs in the area. A-2 plays from a shallow basin containing three large and several smaller vents. The bulk of the eruption comes from just two of these openings. Except in 1970 and 1971, when A-1 was the functional member of this group, A-2 has been the dominant geyser of White Creek. Eruptions may recur as often as every 5 minutes with short durations, but more typical are plays 6 to 8 minutes long separated by intervals of 1 to 2 hours. Either way, the height is about 10 feet.

7. BOTRYOIDAL SPRING erupts from a boiling pool some 100 feet east of A-2 (6) Geyser. The crater is surrounded by thick, massive geyserite shoulders covered with botryoidal (grape-like) globules of sinter beadwork. Botryoidal is essentially a perpetual spouter, the individual eruptions being separated by only a few seconds. On infrequent occasions, Botryoidal has been known to undergo larger eruptions up to 7 feet high.

8. UNNG-WCG-2 ("LOGBRIDGE" GEYSER) is so called because it lies near some cut logs that were placed across White Creek many years ago. Logbridge attracted special attention during 1985, when it began having exceedingly regular eruptions far larger than any seen before. Replacing the long-known nearly perpetual activity are eruptions recurring every 27 minutes. The play, lasting 35 to 55 seconds, is as much as 15 feet high. Some slight erosion in the sinter surrounding Logbridge indicates that such episodes have occurred before, but they cannot have been very extensive. The current activity probably should not be expected to last very long.

9. DIAMOND SPRING was named for the shape of its pool. Always a quiet spring, Diamond erupted powerfully at the time of the 1959 earthquake. No reasonably frequent eruptions were observed until 1973; these were brief and no more than 3 feet

Table 14. Geysers of the Great Fountain-White Creek Group

Name and Number	Interval	Duration	Height (ft)
A-1 Geyser (5)	rare	5–10 min	6
A-2 Geyser (6)	min–2 hrs	sec–8 min	6–10
Botryoidal Spring (7)	seconds	seconds	3–7
Diamond Spring (9)	rare	unrecorded	3
Firehole Pool (3)	steady	steady	2–6
Great Fountain Geyser (1)	7–15 hrs	50–60 min	100–230
Spindle Geyser (11)	1–3 min	1 min	1–10
UNNG-GFG-1 (2)	28–50 min	5–13 min	1–6
UNNG-WCG-1 ("A-0") (4)	1–2 hrs	sec–min	5–15
UNNG-WCG-2 ("Log-bridge") (8)	27 min	½–1 min	8–15
UNNG-WCG-3 ("Tuft") (10)	50–100 min	minutes	2–4
UNNG-WCG-3a ("Eclipse") (10)	infrequent	2 min	8

high. Splashed and washed areas about the crater show that further activity followed the 1983 earthquake, but none of these eruptions were ever witnessed.

10. UNNG-WCG-3 ("TUFT" GEYSER) is a small geyser playing from a number of closely spaced, small openings within a spiny geyserite mound. Nearby is another vent, this one round and about 6 inches in diameter, and beyond that is a small bluish pool. These three features are directly connected. Most often it is Tuft that is active. Its intervals range from 50 to 100 minutes, the entire eruption lasting several minutes. The highest of the fine spray reaches no more than 4 feet. During the eruption, the water level in the pool lowers several inches. On infrequent occasions, such as during 1983–84, the middle vent assumes the geyser function, resulting in near dormancy in Tuft itself. Sometimes called "Eclipse" Geyser because of this role, its play recurs every 35–40 minutes, lasts 2 minutes, and reaches 8 feet high when it is active.

11. SPINDLE GEYSER, though rather remote, is well worth seeing. Few geysers illustrate the "typical" cycle of activity of a fountain-type geyser as well as Spindle does. Eruptions recur every 1 to 3 minutes. Steam bubbles can be seen rising in the crater, expanding as they go, then throwing the water 1 to 3 feet high. Following the eruption the water level drops several inches, far enough to stop all overflow. The pool then begins to rise again almost immediately, flow becoming very heavy just before the next eruption. Thus, the alternating build-up and loss of pressure within the system is readily seen. In 1985, during a more erratic episode, eruptive bursts nearly 10 feet high were seen.

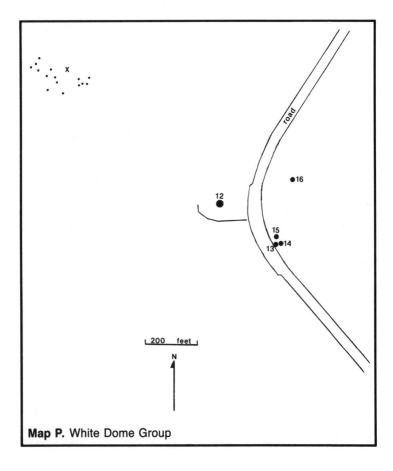

Map P. White Dome Group

White Dome Group

The White Dome Group (Map P, Table 15) is a tiny cluster of hot springs bisected by the Firehole Lake Drive. The area encompassed is scarcely 200 feet square, yet it includes five geysers. Most important of these is White Dome Geyser, one of the oldest hot springs in Yellowstone.

Across the marshy flat area west of White Dome Geyser, another cluster of hot springs can be seen. Virtually nothing is known about the "Tangled Creek" Group except that not fewer than eight springs have been active as geysers. Such action is rare, however, and this group is of limited overall importance. These springs are shown at the "X" on Map P.

12. WHITE DOME GEYSER has been erupting for a long, long time. The massive geyserite cone built up by the spray is over 20 feet high. The cone, in turn, sits atop a 12-foot-high mound of sinter formed by an even older hot spring. Because some structural remains of the older crater can be seen, it is believed by some that it may once have been a geyser of considerable power. White Dome has apparently nearly sealed itself off with deposits of sinter within its vent, for the remaining opening is only 4 inches in diameter. So, while the high cone seems to hold promise of strong eruptions, the resultant display is often disappointing.

White Dome is nonetheless a fascinating geyser, so beautiful and symmetrical that it was selected as a symbol of the Yellowstone Library and Museum Association. The eruption begins after a few moments of splashing preplay. At first the action consists mostly of steam, but water soon makes up the bulk of the discharge. The maximum height of about 30 feet is maintained for most of the 2-minute eruption. White Dome shows a wide variation in its intervals. While most are on the order of 15 to 30 minutes, some are as short as 9 minutes and others as long as 150. There is no way to predict what the next interval will be.

People waiting for Great Fountain Geyser (1) just up the road often see several eruptions by White Dome. Viewed near or far, it is always an impressive geyser.

13. **PEBBLE GEYSER** is the small pool just across the road from the White Dome parking area. This spring was not known to erupt until August 1968, when it underwent several eruptions. Because the spring is located so close to the edge of the road, much gravel gets spilled into the crater. The first several eruptions scattered these pebbles across the road, giving the geyser its name. The 1968 eruptions were brief but over 20 feet high. It continued occasional activity into 1969, when nearby Crack Geyser (14) became active. Since then, any action by Pebble has been infrequent and weak.

14. **CRACK GEYSER** developed along a fissure in the sinter platform. Formed by the earthquake of 1959, this fracture was first the site of a fumarole. By 1960 it was erupting and became known as Crack Geyser. After a few months of activity it went dormant with the rejuvenation of Gemini Geyser (15). Crack remained quiet until 1969, when its renewed activity caused a corresponding dormancy in Gemini and Pebble (13). Since Crack returned to dormancy in 1973 eruptions have been rare.

15. **GEMINI GEYSER** plays from two small cones, each perforated by a tiny vent. During the beginning of an eruption, water begins to well from the cones. Progressively stronger bubbling gradually builds the eruption in size. Within moments the full height of 10 feet is reached. Both water jets are tilted slightly away from the roadway. Gemini is cyclic in its activity, several hours passing between active periods. During the active phases, eruptions recur every 5 to 25 minutes and last around 3 minutes. Gemini is unquestionably connected with Crack (14) and Pebble (13) Geysers; when either of them is active, Gemini is dormant.

16. **UNNG-WDG-1.** About 250 feet north of Gemini is a small pool that began erupting during 1971. During that one season, the geyser was regular, with intervals of 2 to 3 hours. The play lasted 20 minutes and was 5 feet high. Rare eruptions continued through the rest of the 1970s. The water spouted by this geyser was milky looking, an indication that the plumbing system was being damaged by even these little eruptions. The site has been totally inactive during the 1980s.

Table 15. Geysers of the White Dome Group

Name and Number	Interval	Duration	Height (ft)
Crack Geyser (14)	infrequent	1–4 min	10
Gemini Geyser (15)	5–25 min	2–4 min	10
Pebble Geyser (13)	infrequent	seconds	20
UNNG-WDG-1 (16)	rare	20 min	5
White Dome Geyser (12)	9 min–2½ hrs	2 min	30

Pink Cone Group

Pink Cone Geyser, for which this group (Map Q, Table 16) is named, may not be the most important geyser in the cluster, but it is the most powerful. Bead Geyser gained early fame as the most regular geyser in the Park, and so it is today. Of the ten important hot springs in this group, only one – Shelf Spring ("X" on Map Q) – is not a geyser.

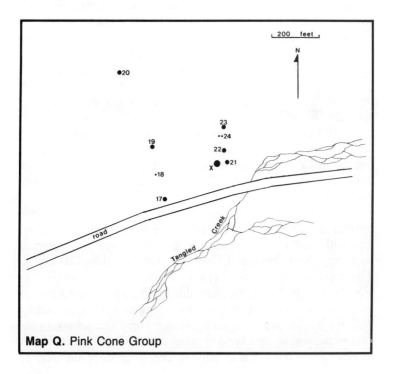

Map Q. Pink Cone Group

Wandering about in the Pink Cone Group is discouraged. There are signs warning you to stay on the roadway, and by positioning yourself properly all of the geysers can be seen from there. The area is perforated by many spring holes with overhanging rims. Shelf Spring is very deep and highly superheated. The thin sinter rim projects far out over the pool, making any close approach very dangerous.

Perhaps no other hot spring group in Yellowstone was more dramatically affected by the 1983 Borah Peak, Idaho, earthquake. While some of the geysers within the group do not seem to have been affected at all, many others increased their activity considerably, nearly doubling their frequencies, and one arose from a long dormancy. This increased action has persisted without evident waning for more than two years and therefore appears to be stable.

17. **PINK CONE GEYSER**, with its 18-inch-high, brownish pink cone, is colored by a trace of manganese oxide; if only a bit more were present the color would be jet black. This same coloration shows up in Pink (19) and Narcissus (20) Geysers. Because of this similarity and the fact that the three lie along a line, they are undoubtedly connected along some sort of subsurface lineation–a long crack or perhaps a fault. The connection cannot be too direct, however, as none of these geysers' performances are affected by the others.

Pink Cone was named by one of the early Hayden Surveys of Yellowstone. They recognized that it must have been a geyser, but no eruptions were seen and, in fact, none were ever recorded until 1937. During this first known activity the intervals were as much as 50 hours long.

The 1959 earthquake markedly increased Pink Cone's performance. For a while, the intervals were less than 50 minutes long with eruptions of the same length. With time, the intervals have very slowly increased; the average is now about 13½ hours. The present activity lasts between 2 and 2½ hours, with occasional steam puffs taking place during the following couple of hours. For most of the duration the jetting of water is constant, with the stream reaching up to 30 feet high. The jet does pulsate some, and as the play continues these pulses become more extreme. Near the end of an eruption they begin to result in brief, total pauses; these then become progressively more dominant and merge into the end of action.

Pink Cone Geyser lies immediately next to the road. When it was built, the route was cut right through the broad mound upon which the geyser sits. Some minor parts of the plumbing system were tapped into along the roadcut, and these sputter a little water when Pink Cone is in eruption. The wonder is that Pink Cone wasn't severely damaged or destroyed. But since it did survive, we now have an excellent cross-section of a geyserite mound, built up layer after tedious layer by uncountable thousands of eruptions.

18. UNNG-PNK-1 plays from a small double vent about midway between Pink Cone (17) and Pink (19) Geysers. The tiny, very brief eruptions of 1985 were hardly worth noting, except that this spring evidently has no previous record of activity. Also, all observed eruptions were far too small to produce runoff, yet the geyser has a considerable runoff channel leading away from it. Sometime, then, this geyser must have had significant activity.

19. PINK GEYSER lies about 200 feet beyond Pink Cone Geyser (17). The rose-colored sinter basin of this spring is 7 feet in diameter; the vent itself is only a few inches across and enters the ground at an angle. Pink is cyclic in its activity. During most years the eruptions do not occur more often than twice per day; during other periods intervals as short as 1 hour have been known. The highly active phases are generally infrequent and brief. For example, for a short while during 1974, Pink played about every 2½ hours, but within weeks it had lapsed back into the less frequent behavior. The 1983 earthquake stimulated Pink into a cycle in which intervals average about 5½ hours. During the play, which lasts from 11 to 17 minutes, the water is jetted about 20 feet high, at an angle in the uphill direction. It's a very pretty eruption, concluded by a briefly loud steam phase as Pink runs out of water.

20. NARCISSUS GEYSER is located farthest from the road, largely hidden behind a band of lodgepole pines. Therefore, it is seldom seen, either close at hand or from a distance. The geyser erupts from a soft pink bowl filled with greenish-tinted water. The setting is lovely.

Narcissus is quite regular in its activity. It is known to have both minor and major eruptions, and the only uncertainty about Narcissus arises because one never knows which type will next occur. Minor eruptions come after an interval of only 2 to 4 hours. Narcissus has not had time to fill its basin before the play starts, resulting in some jets of water over 20 feet high. Minor eruptions last between 5 and 8 minutes. The major eruptions begin after Narcissus has been full and overflowing for more than an hour, the interval being 5½ to 7 hours long. These eruptions last longer than the minors – sometimes as long as 15 minutes – and this duration is the important distinction between the two types of activity. Because of the full crater, some of the eruptive force is lost and Narcissus's major eruptions seldom exceed 15 feet high. After either type of eruption, the crater drains rapidly and completely.

21. BEAD GEYSER has long been known for its extreme regularity. It also used to be known for its fine collection of "geyser eggs," small, loose ¼- to 2-inch spheres of geyserite that slowly form in the splash basins and runoff channels of all geysers. The geyser eggs of Bead are long gone, having been removed by Park visitors almost as soon as their existence was known. They will not be replaced for many human generations.

Bead is one of the most – if not *the* most – regular geysers in Yellowstone. Although the length of the interval does vary some as time passes, eruptions seldom occur more than 30 seconds off the average of any given time. During the past two decades, the average has ranged between 23 and 30 minutes. The duration is equally regular, being just about 2½ minutes with only a few seconds variation.

Bead's eruption begins suddenly after water has slowly risen within its narrow vent. Just when it reaches overflow level, the geyser suddenly surges. Within a few seconds, water jets are reaching 25 feet high. The bursting play is non-stop until it ends as suddenly as it began. The geyser then sucks the remaining water back into the vent.

22. BOX SPRING is a rather small, squarish spring about 50 feet beyond Bead Geyser (21). It had been ignored for many years, and it wasn't until it began erupting following the 1983 earth-

quake that modern observers even realized that it had been named during a similar episode of activity during the 1870s. The eruptions are erratic. In early 1984, some intervals were as short as 7 hours; in time, they have become much longer, and Box will probably return to dormancy soon. The play consists mainly of heavy overflow, punctuated by occasional bursts as much as 5 feet high. The duration is about 5 minutes.

23. LABIAL GEYSER is a complex of several vents, all of which are active at the same time. Labial is an impressively loud and pretty geyser, so it is fortunate that it is one whose action was greatly increased by the 1983 earthquake. During the quiet interval water rises and falls every few minutes. Best observed in a small related vent a few feet from Labial itself, the high water results in boiling, sloshing, and a loud commotion within Labial. As an indication of how near Labial is to eruption, the related vent will begin overflowing about an hour before the play. Each overflow period will be heavier than the one before. During one of these periods Labial's own surging will become heavy, and the eruption is triggered. The play lasts less than 2 minutes, but the strongly angled water jet reaches as much as 25 feet high. A second vent bursts to 6 feet. Following the main eruption, Labial continues occasional bursting; it never falls completely silent. For most of its known history, eruptions have occurred about twice per day with a great deal of irregularity. Since the 1983 earthquake, Labial has been much more frequent and regular, playing every 4½ to 7½ hours and with most intervals very near 5½ hours long.

Table 16. Geysers of the Pink Cone Group

Name and Number	Interval	Duration	Height (ft)
Bead Geyser (21)	23–30 min	2½ min	25
Box Spring (22)	infrequent	1–5 min	2–5
Labial Geyser (23)	4½–15 hrs	2 min	15–25
Labial's East Satellite (24)	frequent	sec–min	1–6
Labial's West Satellite (24)	irregular	seconds	3–10
Narcissus Geyser (20)	2–7 hrs	5–15 min	15–20
Pink Geyser (19)	1–12 hrs	11–17 min	15–20
Pink Cone Geyser (17)	13½ hrs	2–2½ hrs	30
UNNG-PNK-1 (18)	1–2 min	seconds	1

24. LABIAL'S SATELLITE GEYSERS, East and West, vary their action directly in correspondence to Labial Geyser's (23) period. The Satellites are very active shortly before Labial plays and essentially inactive for a couple of hours after Labial. At their best, eruptions may recur as often as every 2 minutes in the East Satellite, and these may last several minutes. Discharge is considerable as the play reaches up to 6 feet high. The West Satellite plays much less frequently, but it is the larger of the two geysers, sometimes reaching 10 feet high.

Firehole Lake Group

The Firehole Lake Group (Map R, Table 17) is an area of very high water output. The total discharge is about 3,500 gallons per minute, which flows from the area via Tangled Creek. Most of the hot springs are large, quiet pools. The biggest is Firehole Lake. Supplied with water through several vents, its temperature is about 160°F (70°C). Hot Lake covers a much larger area, but it is not a hot spring as such, only a collecting basin along the runoff; its temperature is about 100°F (38°C). The Firehole Lake Group contains four geysers, one of which—Steady—is of considerable interest.

The springs around Firehole Lake have formed some unique deposits. Many of them are dark in color. Their craters are coated with a heavy, powdery deposit of black manganese oxide minerals. That is not unusual in itself, but nowhere is so much being deposited as here. Also, this is the only geyser group in Yellowstone where travertine, a form of the mineral calcite, is deposited along with siliceous sinter. Young Hopeful Geyser deposits calcite within its vents, Steady Geyser forms travertine geyser eggs, and Firehole Lake is bordered in places by low travertine terraces. There is no mystery as to how this travertine forms; the water here contains somewhat more carbon dioxide than usual, and that allows the water to also transport more calcium. The two combine to form the travertine, calcium carbonate. The bigger question is why is there more CO_2? There is no pat answer.

On the north side of Firehole Lake a short trail can be seen looping across the hillside. This is the Three Senses Nature

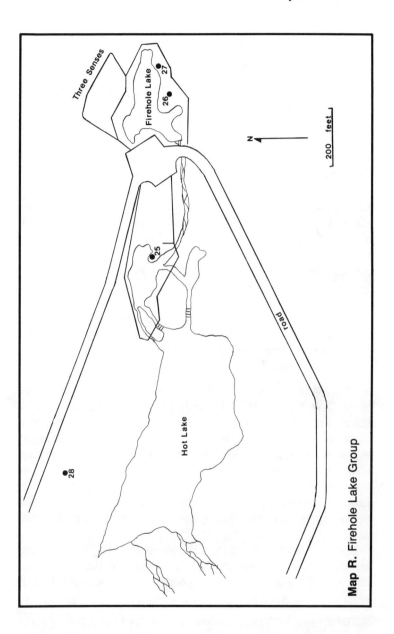

Map R. Firehole Lake Group

Trail. The exhibits here emphasize sound, smell, and touch. Though designed especially for the deaf and blind, they encourage everybody to experience the area without vision. Try it!

25. STEADY GEYSER, also called Black Warrior Geyser, has been the largest perpetual spouter in Yellowstone and the world, but during the past several years it has declined to a very much smaller size. It has erupted continuously since discovery. Steady has two vents, which curiously alternate between eruptive and dormant periods. The shifts of energy between these closely spaced openings are very slow, sometimes taking several years to complete. The top vent spouts straight up, in good times reaching 30 feet high. The other vent plays at an angle, and may be 10 feet high. The lower vent has been active for a number of years, with only a bit of action being seen in the upper vent, and the play is currently less than 5 feet high.

Steady Geyser, being part of the Firehole Lake Group, is forming some unusual deposits. The cone is tinted dark gray by the inclusion of small amounts of manganese oxides in the sinter. In the splash basins and runoff channels are some ¼-inch "geyser eggs" of rounded, pearly travertine (calcium carbonate) nodules; elsewhere, geyser eggs are composed of silica.

26. YOUNG HOPEFUL GEYSER was named by the Hayden Survey of 1872. It spouted from 11 vents for about 100 years, until a steam explosion opened two larger craters. Most of the force of the eruption now comes from these two vents. The eruption is a surging, splashing sort of play with some spray reaching 6 feet high. It used to be that Young Hopeful alternated active and dormant phases, each part of its period lasting from a few hours to several days. Since the explosions, however, quiet periods have been rare. Young Hopeful is essentially a perpetual spouter.

Like most other springs in the Firehole Lake Group, Young Hopeful has exceptional amounts of travertine in the sinter about its vents. The more obvious deposits were destroyed by the steam explosions that enlarged the craters.

27. GRAY BULGER GEYSER was known as a perpetual spouter for all of its known history until 1975. The play was a series of small splashes, never more than 3 feet high. Without warning, Gray Bulger began having far larger eruptions during the summer of 1975, and these persisted into 1977. Recurring every few seconds and lasting a few seconds (so that, overall, it was playing about half the time), the geyser jetted water as much as 25 and 30 feet high. A second vent, which had hardly been noticed before, began playing almost horizontally, squirting water as much as 20 feet outward. After a short dormancy, Gray Bulger resumed activity. The present eruptions are only slightly weaker than those of the 1970s.

28. UNNG-FLG-1 was active during the first few years after the 1959 earthquake, then not again until a short time following the 1983 earthquake. The play was never frequent, and its duration was not recorded. Some bursts reached as high as 10 feet, however, making this quite an impressive geyser.

Table 17. Geysers of the Firehole Lake Group

Name and Number	Interval	Duration	Height (ft)
Gray Bulger Geyser (27)	seconds	seconds	2–25
Steady Geyser (25)	steady	steady	1–30
UNNG-FLG-1 (28)	rare	unrecorded	10
Young Hopeful Geyser (26)	steady	steady	6

Fountain Group

The Fountain Group (Map S, Table 18) is the largest collection of geysers in the Lower Basin. Many of these spouters are large, and most of them are connected, forming the Fountain Complex. The activity of this complex is intense, perhaps more so than in any other similar area of Yellowstone, but exchange of function also causes a high degree of irregularity among the geysers.

Located here, also, are the Fountain Paint Pots ("X" on Map S). These are the largest easily accessible mud pots in the Park. Since the 1959 earthquake increased their activity, the basin in which they lie has been considerably enlarged. At one time the expansion threatened to engulf walkways and roadways, and

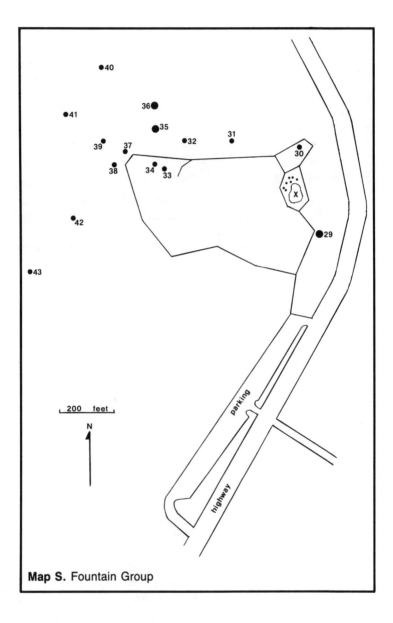

Map S. Fountain Group

remnants of the old construction can be seen overhanging the mud at several points beneath the modern boardwalk.

The Fountain Group is traversed by a boardwalk with access from a large parking lot. Leaflets are available for self-guided tours of the ½-mile loop trail, and they point out many fascinating aspects of the area. During the peak of the summer season, there is often a Park ranger-naturalist stationed here to answer questions or guide you about the area.

29. SILEX SPRING fills a deep sinter-lined crater below the boardwalk. The overflow runs across a wide area and supports a profuse growth of multicolored hot water algae. The name "Silex" might have been derived from either of two sources: it is the Latin word for silica, but some people feel that the activity of the spring resembles that of the silex-type coffee percolator. Whatever the case, Silex is a geyser.

Silex has always been observed to undergo occasional boiling periods with consequent heavier overflow. That is enough to qualify Silex as a geyser, but it was never known to actually throw water into the air until following the 1959 earthquake. First the water level dropped several feet, then for several days it surged steadily, throwing water 10 feet into the air. The steady activity died down as the crater slowly refilled, and it ceased when overflow was reached.

No further eruptive action was seen until 1973. Silex then began having small eruptions rather often. The increased activity continued into 1979. The most powerful eruptions ever seen from Silex took place at the very end of this active period. After one eruption, it took between 2 and 4 hours for the crater to refill. Almost without warning, the pool would begin to surge and boil. Silex required several minutes to reach full force, which at its peak could send some bursts as high as 20 feet. Silex has been dormant since 1979, but it remains one of the prettier pools in Yellowstone.

30. RED SPOUTER is a direct product of the 1959 earthquake. This was a flat, grassy area until two new mud pots formed following the shocks. After a while these became steam vents. Now, during the seasons of high water table, these vents act as perpetual spouters, throwing muddy, red water as much as

8 feet high. At low water, Red Spouter reverts to being a steam vent. Thus, Red Spouter is really nothing more than an occasionally drowned fumarole, and to call it a geyser is stretching the definition.

31. UNNG-FTN-1 is very informally known as "Volcanic Tablelands" Geyser since its vent lies down the slope directly below a sign with those words. This geyser plays from an old rift. Until action began during 1985 the crack was filled with soil and grew grasses and wildflowers. The eruption, a rather unimpressive commotion throwing water 1 to 2 feet high, recurs every 10 to 15 minutes and lasts about 2 minutes.

THE FOUNTAIN COMPLEX. All but the last two of the remaining geysers of the Fountain Group belong to the Fountain Complex, geysers of complex subterranean relationships. The activity of everything within the complex is dependent on the current behavior of the other geysers. Three of them — Morning, Fountain, and Clepsydra — are large and must be included in any list of the most important geysers of Yellowstone.

On the hill above the Fountain Complex, a short boardwalk spur serves as an overlook. From there nearly every spring in the complex can be seen in action.

Twig, Morning, Fountain, Jet, FTN-2, Spasm, Sub, and Clepsydra Geysers are unquestionably connected with each other; Jelly, New Bellefontaine, and others are probably related, too. There is often a well-established pattern of behavior in all of these springs. These patterns vary over the years, but the 1985 performances will serve as an example. After Fountain Geyser had erupted, it took several hours for it to refill. During all of this time practically the only active geysers in the complex were Twig and Clepsydra. FTN-2, Jet, and Jelly had occasional plays. Once Fountain began its next eruption, things became much more exciting. Jet began playing very frequently, usually just after FTN-2 had started.Clepsydra lost the water supply to one of its vents, which then loudly ejected steam under great pressure. Spasm burst distinctly higher than otherwise, and even distant Sub could be seen, which is not the usual case. This action would continue for some minutes after Fountain ended, then Clepsydra would stop and Twig would sometimes undergo a brief steamy sort of play. Slowly, the group returned to the normal, weaker activity typical of Fountain's quiet interval.

The above description should be taken only as a guide to the kinds of relationships that exist here. The Fountain Complex is an extremely dynamic set of geysers. Their activity can change dramatically over short periods of time.

32. TWIG GEYSER lies near the foot of the stairway leading down from the overlook. To the right of the boardwalk, the shallow crater is about 4 feet in diameter; near it are two smaller vents. The only time when Twig shows clearly that it is a part of the Fountain Complex comes at the end of eruptions by Fountain Geyser (35). Then it sometimes (definitely not always) begins to enter a steam phase sort of play, in which steamy spray is played several feet high. Otherwise, its eruption is a bursting action up to 10 feet high. Overall, Twig seems to be in eruption about half the time.

33. JET GEYSER is most directly related to Fountain Geyser (35) and the nearby unnamed geyser (34). The elongated cone appears to have developed along an old fracture in the sinter. This break also extends through Spasm (37), Clepsydra (39), and New Bellefontaine (41) Geysers and in total is several hundred feet long. Jet, though it has been known to have dormant periods, is usually active. It is at its most frequent and powerful when Fountain is playing, infrequent and weak at other times, and inactive when Morning (36) is active. Water is jetted from at least six different vents. The highest stream comes from a central one and may reach 20 feet. The other vents play much lower, and the opening on the far right (west) plays mostly steam during weaker action. Typical eruptions are brief, most lasting much less than 1 minute. Intervals are also short, varying from 1 to 20 minutes.

34. UNNG-FTN-2 is known to some as "Super Frying Pan" Geyser. Not only is that a very long-winded name, but it is also an unfortunate one in that a frying pan is a type of acid hot spring vastly different from a geyser. In any case, this geyser is a rather recent development, first showing signs of its existence during 1966 but not breaking out in distinct form until 1975. The main vent lies near enough to the boardwalk to occasionally spray it with a bit of water; this vent produces most of the runoff. Two other spots in the gravel, both about 20 feet from the main vent, also sputter a little during the eruptions. Eruptions, clearly controlled to some extent by the activity of Fountain (35) and Jet (33) Geysers, generally recur every 2 hours, lasting 8 to 29 minutes.

35. FOUNTAIN GEYSER has long been considered the major geyser of the Fountain Group. Only Morning Geyser (36) can play higher, but it is seldom active. The pool of Fountain is the nearer of the two beyond the name sign. Broad and deep, it is a rich azure-blue color. The high sinter shoulders about the crater suggest that Fountain has been active for a *very* long time.

The pool is calm throughout the long quiet period. About an hour before an eruption a few small bubbles can be seen rising from the vent, but these are so slight that they go unnoticed unless one knows exactly where to look. The eruption begins without further warning with a sudden rise in the water level. Huge bursts propel water from the crater, sometimes appearing as gigantic blue bubbles that explode to throw water in all directions. The play is often as wide as it is high. Most bursts are 10 to 20 feet high, but bursts reaching 40 to 50 feet are common. During some seasons, "superbursts" reaching over 80 feet are seen during nearly every eruption. The eruptions may last anywhere from 35 to 60 minutes, but the usual duration is just about 50 minutes. An interesting pattern shows up in Fountain's intervals. Most of the time they average about 11 hours and are regular enough that Fountain certainly could be predicted. Now and then, however, without warning or evident transition, Fountain doubles its frequency, maintaining 5½-hour intervals for a few days before lapsing back to the normal. Yet whichever interval the geyser is having, the eruptions maintain the same duration and force. (Though uncommon, Fountain will sometimes maintain 4- to 6-hour intervals over an extended period; the duration then tends to be just about half as long as those otherwise seen.)

36. MORNING GEYSER is one of the most powerful geysers in Yellowstone, and its eruptions are often more spectacular than anything seen in the Park since the days of Excelsior Geyser (see #11 of the Midway Geyser Basin). Tremendously explosive bursts reach over 150 feet high and may be more than 60 feet wide. Unfortunately, Morning is almost never active.

The first recorded eruptions of Morning were in 1899. At first it was called New Fountain Geyser. Some of the eruptive bursts were estimated to have been at least 200 feet high. The geyser continued to have occasional active periods until sometime in the 1920s. From then on it was dormant until 1944, when there was one eruption recorded; there were two more in 1946. Finally, during 1947 it began to display the power and frequency it had shown in 1899. Eruptions were irregular but occurred about once every 3 or 4 days. Curiously, of the 36 eruptions recorded during that summer, all but one began during the morning hours, hence the new name, "Morning."

Morning continued to have active periods until the time of the 1959 earthquake. That jolt apparently caused a shift in the energy flow of the Fountain Complex. Clepsydra Geyser (39) became more and more active and the activity of Morning became weaker. By early September, Morning was dormant. It did not erupt again until 1974, when there were several 100-foot eruptions with durations of about 40 minutes. Additional active episodes, these approaching the power of old, occurred during 1978, 1981, 1982, and 1983.

Morning, as a major member of the Fountain Complex, is severely affected by any other activity in the complex. So it is that it is seldom active. Simply too much water and heat are lost from the system through the other geysers. Its eruptions truly are special sights to behold.

37. SPASM GEYSER was named for its ragged, jerky pattern of play. Because of its connections with other geysers in the Fountain Complex, Spasm is very irregular in its performances. The nearly constant action of Clepsydra Geyser (39) during recent years has rendered Spasm nearly dormant. The typical current play is no more than a boiling and surging, which domes the water about 1 foot high without really jetting into the air. At times, Spasm has been an impressive geyser, with intervals as short as 5 minutes and heights to 30 feet. In 1963, however, an explosion occurred during an eruption. The old crater was considerably altered and enlarged, and it may be that the system was changed enough that none of the large eruptions of old will ever occur again.

38. JELLY GEYSER erupts from a crater measuring 16 by 30 feet, one of the largest in the Fountain Group. A small eruptive satellite vent within the runoff channel from Spasm Geyser (37) also takes part in the eruption. Jelly's intervals are usually very regular at any given time, but over the years it has also shown a great deal of variation. Before the 1959 earthquake it erupted every 10 minutes. Now interval lengths are known to range from 10 minutes to well over an hour. The play, less than 1 minute long, ranges from 3 to 12 feet high. Long dormant periods are known, too, when the crater becomes lined with thick, jelly-like masses of brown algae.

39. CLEPSYDRA GEYSER was named after a mythical Greek waterclock. For years it erupted for a few seconds at intervals of almost exactly 3 minutes. All this changed at the time of the 1959 earthquake. Clepsydra entered what is called "wild phase" activity. Without any known pause, Clepsydra erupted from the time of the earthquake into 1963. At that time, Fountain (35) reactivated from a dormancy. Clepsydra would stop playing only for a short time following an eruption by Fountain. When Fountain returned to dormancy in 1964, Clepsydra immediately resumed its steady eruptions. This activity has characterized Clepsydra and Fountain ever since. If Fountain is dormant, Clepsydra rarely stops playing; when Fountain is active, Clepsydra will normally quit about 10 minutes after Fountain quits. This pause lasts about 30 minutes.

Clepsydra plays from several vents. The two largest open to a cone of geyserite stained a distinct yellow color. One of the vents jets to about 45 feet while the other, at a slight angle, reaches about 25 feet. A number of other openings splash a few feet high. This forceful wild phase is showing no sign of slowing down more than twenty-six years after the earthquake. It certainly must now be considered the normal behavior of Clepsydra, and of the Fountain Complex.

40. SUB GEYSER plays within a deep crater far out across the sinter flat to the northwest of Fountain Geyser (35). Most of its activity has been confined to levels deep within the crater, hence the name. Since the 1983 earthquake, Sub has frequently played powerfully enough to be seen from the boardwalk. These eruptions reach as much as 10 feet above the ground and, therefore, probably 25 feet above the pool level.

41. NEW BELLEFONTAINE GEYSER is located beyond Clepsydra Geyser (39), at the far end of the rift. A very active geyser, it repeats its fountain-like play with never more than a few seconds between eruptions, which in turn usually last less than 1 minute. The height is as much as 20 feet.

Down the hill, beyond New Bellefontaine and out of sight of the boardwalk, is another rift in the geyserite. Along it are at least four geysers, none named, one of which plays as much as 12 feet high.

42. OLD BELLEFONTAINE GEYSER, not a member of the Fountain Complex, does not fit its name, which is French for "beautiful fountain." Old Bellefontaine is irregularly and generally infrequently active. The eruptions are less than 6 feet high, being no more than occasional bursts rising above a small, unnotable pool.

Table 18. Geysers of the Fountain Group

Name and Number	Interval	Duration	Height (ft)
Clepsydra Geyser (39)	near steady	near steady	20–45
Fountain Geyser (35)	4–12 hrs	35–60 min	50–80
Jelly Geyser (38)	10–90 min	seconds	3–12
Jet Geyser (33)	1–20 min	seconds	10–20
Morning Geyser (36)	seldom	18–60 min	100–200
New Bellefontaine Geyser (41)	seconds	sec–min	10–20
Old Bellefontaine Geyser (42)	irregular	minutes	2–6
Red Spouter (30)	steady	steady	3–8
Silex Spring (29)	rare	minutes	10–20
Spasm Geyser (37)	irregular	5–20 min	1–3
Sub Geyser (40)	frequent	seconds	10
Twig Geyser (32)	frequent	5 min–hrs	5–10
UNNG-FTN-1 (31)	10–15 min	1–2 min	1–2
UNNG-FTN-2 (34)	1–3 hrs	8–29 min	3–8
UNNG-FTN-3 (43)	days	hours	20

43. UNNG-FTN-3 erupts from a vent far beyond Old Bellefontaine. Though it was noted during a mapping project in 1968, almost nothing is known about this geyser. It is seen in eruption a few times each season. Evidently, the intervals are days long while eruptions may be hours long. The play is fully 20 feet high.

Kaleidoscope and Fissure Groups

The Kaleidoscope and Fissure Groups (Map T, Table 19) are two barely separated assortments of hot springs. In total, the two groups probably include more than thirty geysers. Most of these are small, however, and cannot be seen from a distance. They aren't described here since at a distance is the only way to experience these groups. No trails lead into the area, and the closest public approach is either the highway or the Fountain Group, both several hundred yards away. Therefore, only those geysers large enough to be seen at a distance are described here.

At the far eastern end of the Fissure Group is a large, bright blue pool. Gentian Pool ("X" on Map T) is 88 feet long and among the largest pools in the Park.

44. KALEIDOSCOPE GEYSER is the largest in the two groups, but it unfortunately undergoes rather frequent dormant periods. When active, the eruptions recur every 1 to 25 minutes. Lasting 15 to 20 seconds, they play over 40 feet high. Because of exchange of function with Drain Geyser (45), Kaleidoscope has been dormant since the early 1981 season.

To the south and southwest of Kaleidoscope are several springs of recent origin, and some may have formed as a result of the 1959 earthquake. Three of these are known to have been active as geysers during the 1970s. The eruptions of one reached more than 15 feet high.

45. DRAIN GEYSER is so named because most of the runoff from an erupting Kaleidoscope runs into its crater. However, when Kaleidoscope is dormant, then Drain is active as an impressive geyser. Eruptions recur every 5 to 35 minutes, usually nearer the longer interval. Shortly before the play the growth and collapse of steam bubbles at depth cause a pulsating of the water surface in the large pool. Progressively larger waves wash shore-

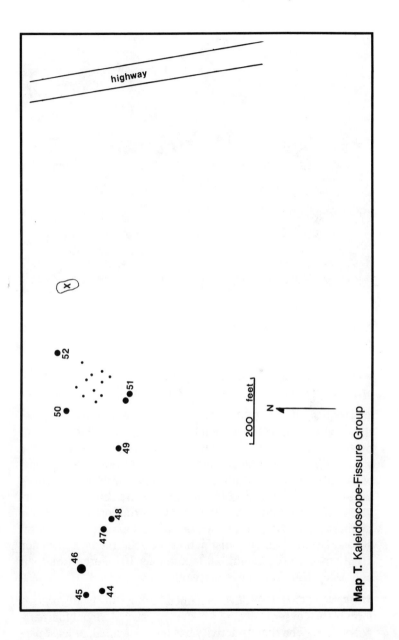

Map T. Kaleidoscope-Fissure Group

Kaleidoscope Drain Geyser is one of the several large pools that produce occasional spectacular eruptions within the Kaleidoscope and Fissure Groups.

ward, culminating in the bursting eruption. The play is a series of distinctly separate bursts reaching from 6 to 25 feet high.

46. DEEP BLUE GEYSER is the largest spring in the area other than non-erupting Gentian Pool. The main crater measures 30 by 40 feet and is surrounded by an extensive area of shallower water. The water is deep enough to produce a rich sapphire color. Deep Blue has both major and minor eruptions. Majors take place about once in 24 hours, minors in a series with intervals of about 20 minutes. Each kind of eruption lasts about 5 minutes, consisting of a series of bursts separated by several seconds each. The only distinction between major and minor eruptions is in the height, 30 feet versus 10. More often than not, Deep Blue Geyser is dormant.

47. HONEYCOMB GEYSER, so named because of the decorative form of the geyserite about its crater, has been dormant for many years. It may be that its activity has been assumed, at least partially, by nearby Honey's Vent Geyser (48). When active, Honeycomb plays every few hours for about 10 minutes, some bursts reaching 30 feet high.

48. HONEY'S VENT GEYSER formed as a result of a steam explosion sometime during the early 1960s. Almost certainly a delayed response of the 1959 earthquake, Honey's Vent was a periodic geyser with both major and minor eruptions during its first decade of life. Since then it has acted as a perpetual spouter playing several feet high. Every few minutes a surge in action produces jets as much as 12 feet high.

49. ANGLE GEYSER plays from one of about a dozen vents within a single large crater. Actually, just which of these is Angle itself is uncertain. Angle played frequently to about 20 feet high, with the water column distinctly angled from the vertical. A geyser playing within the complex now is of about the same size but essentially vertical (and so has been called "Vertical" Geyser). This geyser is cyclic in its performances. A series of minor eruptions, lasting about 5 minutes and recurring every 12 to 20 minutes, is ended by a major eruption lasting more than 35 minutes. A recovery period of 1 to 2 hours is then needed before the geyser resumes the minor play.

50. FERRIC GEYSER, surrounded by sinter heavily stained with iron oxides, is the only geyser of the Fissure Group to have formed a distinct cone. For a while following the 1959 earthquake, it played every hour as much as 25 feet high. The activity has since regressed into more or less perpetual spouting just a foot high; an occasional surge may send some spray up to 8 feet.

51. SPRINKLER GEYSER lies within a richly iron oxide-stained crater of red-brown color. Evidently a cyclic geyser, it has periods of relatively frequent eruptions separated by dormant periods of several hours. The play consists of sharp jets of water 8 to 15 feet high.

More impressive, perhaps, is "West Sprinkler" Geyser. Rising from the same crater complex as Sprinkler, it erupts with a very high degree of regularity after intervals of 1 to 2 minutes, bursting water to about 12 feet. After an eruption the water level drops about 18 inches within the crater; it doesn't begin to rise again until a bare instant before the next eruption.

52. EARTHQUAKE GEYSER merits a place in this book because of its size. Its entire history as a significant geyser spans a few weeks following the 1959 tremors. From a point along an old rift, Earthquake Geyser began to erupt to as much as 100 feet high. A tremendous volume of water was discharged, but the eruptions ended when a steam vent developed nearby. Earthquake now plays steadily about 2 feet high.

Table 19. Geysers of the Kaleidoscope and Fissure Groups

Name and Number	Interval	Duration	Height (ft)
Angle Geyser (49)	rare?	4 min	20
Deep Blue Geyser (46)	20 min	5 min	10–30
Drain Geyser (45)	5–35 min	seconds	6–25
Earthquake Geyser (52)	steady	steady	2
Ferric Geyser (50)	steady	steady	1–8
Honeycomb Geyser (47)	rare	10 min	30
Honey's Vent Geyser (48)	steady	steady	4–12
Kaleidoscope Geyser (44)	1–25 min	seconds	45
Sprinkler Geyser (51)	15–40 min	1–2 min	8–15
UNNG-KFG-1 ("Vertical") (49)	12–20 min	5–35 min	12–20
West Sprinkler Geyser (51)	1–2 min	10–20 sec	12

Thud Group

Once known as the Hotel Group because of the site of the old Fountain Hotel on the hill right next to Thud Geyser, this group (Map U, Table 20) reverted to its original name when the hotel was razed during 1927. Although the springs of this group are generally of minor size, character, and activity, they have received much attention because of the former presence of the hotel. Also, nearly all have been active as geysers.

Many visitors and employees of the hotel used these springs as trash receptacles. Especially damaged was Thud Geyser, the closest member of the group to the building. In 1948 an attempt was made to clean it. The amount of material removed was astonishing. For the sake of interest (and wonderment), here is the complete list of recovered trash: 3 one-gallon crocks, a frying pan, a duster, 7 soda pop bottles, 4 quart whiskey bottles, several beer bottles, a cog wheel, bones, 1 penny, 2 Colorado tax tokens, a 40-gallon drum, 2 wooden kegs, a bath towel, a bath mat, 1 rubber boot, a raincoat, some screen wire, 2 bricks, 1 horseshoe, 16 handkerchiefs, a copper plate, a pitchfork, 1 ladle, a large piece of canvas, a stew kettle, a gunny sack, 17 tin cans, 1 napkin, 1 pie tin, 1 window sash, 2 drawer handles, 1 cooking fork, 2 cake molds, 1 broom, 1 porcelain plate, 1 china plate, a surveyor's stake, 2 wagon braces, a blue dishpan, 2 knives, 1 fork, 1 spoon, a cigarette pack, a 1913 guidebook to Yellowstone, 2 marbles, 1 film box, 4 .22 caliber shells, 1 .45 caliber shell, 1 light bulb, 1 apron, a large piece of pipe, a mix-

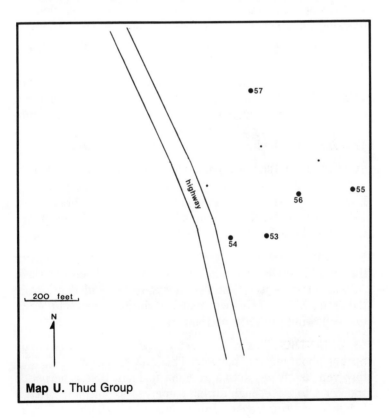

Map U. Thud Group

ing bowl, a set of men's outer clothing, 1 butter tub, 1 kerosene lamp, 1 large copper lid, an oak evener, a single tree, several barrel staves, 2 ear tags for cattle belonging to a Rexburg, Idaho, rancher, several pieces of window glass, an oven rack, a cotton coat, miscellaneous pieces of iron, copper, and aluminum wire, paper, 1 Mason jar, 1 Vaseline bottle, *and* 1 seltzer bottle. Enough? Let's hope so, for all this was taken from a crater just 15 by 18 feet!

Please throw your trash in the real trash cans. After the abuse experienced by Thud Geyser, it's a wonder that the spring was able to survive at all.

The Thud Group contains no trails. It is possible to view the springs from pullouts along the roadway or from the site of the old hotel. As is the case with the Kaleidoscope and Fissure Groups, the intent is to keep this area inaccessible and, therefore, untouched.

53. THUD GEYSER, despite the treatment it received over the years, continues to have occasional active periods. The last such was during the early 1970s. When it is active, the collapse of steam bubbles within the plumbing system at depth causes a pounding, or thudding, of the ground. The eruptions last 4 minutes and recur every 3 to 4 hours, some bursts ranging between 12 and 15 feet high.

54. FUNGOID SPRING was named for the thick, brownish-orange jelly-like mat of algae that once grew along its runoff channel. Fungoid has been known as a geyser during just three years: 1929, 1948, and 1972. During an active period the eruptions recur hourly and are 12 feet high.

55. GOURD SPRING undergoes such infrequent geyser activity that no full details about its activity have ever been recorded. As with Thud Geyser, Gourd's crater was filled with debris from the hotel. Much of this was expelled during a powerful eruption following the 1959 earthquake.

56. UNNG-THD-1 lies a few feet below non-eruptive Stirrup Spring, about midway between Thud (53) and Gourd (55). The tiny vent is always active in some fashion. It is a perpetual spouter 1 to 2 feet high during some years, but more often it behaves as a true geyser. Intervals are typically about 5 minutes and durations 1½ minutes. Water jets up to 7 feet high have been observed.

57. KIDNEY SPRING, the northernmost spring in the Thud Group, is the only regularly active geyser in the group. The crater is roughly kidney-shaped, some 34 feet long and 6 feet wide. Kidney is a very regular geyser. Intervals average about 25 minutes, and any variation of more than 2 minutes from the average is uncommon. Each eruption lasts 3 to 4 minutes, during which the play is mostly less than 4 feet high; an occasional burst will jet to 10 feet. Kidney was apparently inactive during the detailed geological surveys of the 1870s, but it has been continuously functional for more than 50 years now.

Table 20. Geysers of the Thud Group

Name and Number	Interval	Duration	Height (ft)
Fungoid Spring (54)	rare	5 min	12
Gourd Spring (55)	rare	1 min?	2–20
Kidney Spring (57)	25 min	3–4 min	4–10
Thud Geyser (53)	rare	4 min	10–15
UNNG-THD-1 (56)	5 min	1½ min	2–7

Culex Basin Area

The Culex Basin (see Map N) is an isolated group of hot springs located well to the northeast of the rest of the Lower Geyser Basin. It includes two distinct groups of hot springs, each of which contains some geysers.

To reach the area one must hike about 1½ miles up the Mary Mountain trail. In doing so, a number of hot springs are encountered along the way, but it isn't until a grove of trees is reached and passed that the valley again opens out into these springs. The area is unmistakable because towering above the roadway (which is open only to Park Service vehicles and doubles as the hiking trail) is the face of a large rock quarry. Long abandoned, it now has some trees beginning to grow among the boulders.

The first group of springs encountered is the Morning Mist Group. It includes the only truly significant geyser of the area, Morning Mist Geyser itself. Besides it, there are two or three other geysers of very small size and generally infrequent performance.

Up the hill, around and to the right of the quarry, is Culex Basin proper. Among its several dozen springs are at least four geysers. Again, none is of any particular significance, and because of the remote location essentially nothing is known about any of them.

58. MORNING MIST GEYSER is the only truly important geyser in the general Culex Basin area. It lies directly between the creek and the quarry, about 75 feet to the south of the trail/road into the area. The eruption of Morning Mist isn't particularly large, the highest bursts reaching no more than 6 feet, but in terms of water discharge it is important. A single eruption lasts about 12 hours and pours about 126,000 gallons of water down the channel. That is almost exactly the amount discharged by Old Faithful in any 24-hour period. Once one eruption ends, the water level of Morning Mist drops about 12 feet within the crater. Refilling takes place at about 1 foot per hour. Once overflow is reached, anywhere from 12 to 36 hours of slight discharge will occur before another eruption begins. Thus, the intervals range from 24 to 48 hours and are quite easy to judge on the basis of water level and overflow. Given the long intervals, you will most likely have to enjoy the greenish pool without seeing its eruption.

59. PORCUPINE HILL GEYSER is one of the first springs encountered as you begin to hike in to Morning Mist. Perhaps 300 yards from the parking area at the trailhead, the geyser is to the north of the trail at the summit of a broad sinter mound. Whether Porcupine Hill Geyser has ever had a strictly natural series of eruptions is unknown. The only recorded activity was during 1969 and 1970, shortly after a research drill hole was completed nearby. The play was as much as 30 feet high but was very brief,

Table 21. Geysers of the Culex Basin Area

Name and Number	Interval	Duration	Height (ft)
Morning Mist Geyser (58)	24–48 hrs	12 hrs	3–6
Porcupine Hill Geyser (59)	rare	seconds	25–30

usually lasting much less than 1 minute. Some intervals were known to be more than a week in length.

River Group

Of all the hot spring groups in the Lower Basin, only the River Group (Map V, Table 22) lies along the banks of the Firehole River. Thus, the setting of these springs is much like that of the Upper Geyser Basin. The geysers of this area are relatively small compared with those of other areas, and there are some rather wide spaces between the individual hot springs.

Much of the River Group is within an oval valley known as Pocket Basin. It formed during a large hydrothermal explosion shortly after the end of the last glaciation of the Ice Age, about 10,000 years ago. The ridge that forms the rim around the basin is composed of the angular debris that was blasted out to form the valley. In power, the energy released during this explosion about equalled that of the bombs dropped on Japan at the end of World War II. Associated with this geological situation, over the ridge to the east, are the Pocket Basin mud pots. They are the largest collection of mud pots in Yellowstone. Rangers lead hikes into the area two or three times per week during the summer season. Reservations are required as this is a very popular and interesting trip.

There are no established trails in the River Group, but it is traversed on both sides of the river by paths worn into the ground by thousands of fishermen and geyser gazers. You can drive to the parking lot at Ojo Caliente Spring on Fountain Flats Drive; from there simply go to the appropriate side of the river and begin walking. As you go, remember the hazards of the geyser basins and stay well clear of all hot springs.

Ojo Caliente Spring (at "V" on Map V) is a part of the River Group but is well separated downstream from the rest of the group. It is a superheated spring and smells strongly of hydrogen sulfide gas. Ojo Caliente had a brief eruptive episode during 1968, at the same time that a geothermal research drill hole was being sunk nearby; eruptions ended as soon as the drilling was stopped and the well was capped. The group contains several other large springs: on Map V, Grotto is at "W," Azure at "X," Cavern at "Y," and Bath at "Z."

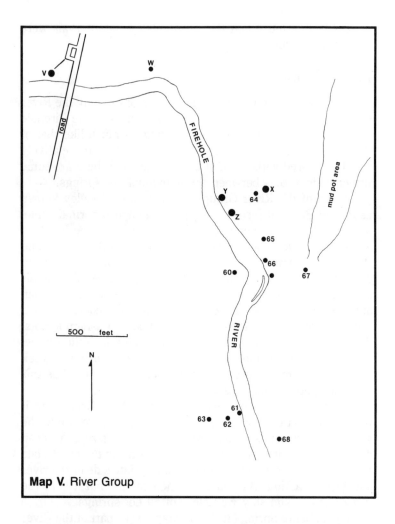

Map V. River Group

The geysers of the River Group will be discussed in turn, first those on the west side of the Firehole River, then those on the east side.

60. MOUND GEYSER is the most important named geyser in the River Group. Its crater measures about 25 by 10 feet and lies at the summit of a large sinter mound that was initially formed by a much older hot spring. Mound is quite regular in its activity; intervals range from 11 to 35 minutes but usually average just about 22 minutes. The eruptions last 5 minutes and take the form of a series of heavy surges ranging from 6 to 12 feet high. Mound itself discharges almost no water, but a number of spring holes just down the slope to the north gush a heavy flow just before and during the play. This flow amounts to at least 150 gallons per minute.

61. **UNNG-RVG-1** is a large pool near the level of the Firehole River about 700 feet north of Mound Geyser. At times of high water the river covers this spring and renders it dormant. Water levels low enough to allow eruptions occur only during the driest of seasons. Then, after intervals generally only a few seconds long, the pool displays brief eruptions up to 5 feet high.

62. **UNNG-RVG-2** had its first known activity during late 1985. The eruptions proved to be very regular at any given time but widely variable when a span of days was considered. The known range in interval was from 20 to 50 minutes. Eruptions begin when the water level in the crater abruptly begins to rise. First a small, subsidiary vent causes jetting 2 or 3 feet high; then the main vent bursts up to as much as 7 feet. Several minutes of minor boiling and splashing follow the 2-minute play.

63. **UNNG-RVG-3** is located in a grassy meadow area about 150 feet from RVG-2. Its only known activity occurred during 1973, when it played frequently as much as 15 feet high. Within this general area are a dozen or more additional hot springs, most of which show signs of having had geyser activity in the past. Now, however, eruptions such as those of RVG-2 and RVG-3 are unusual, and the springs are normally of relatively low temperatures.

64. **UNNG-RVG-4** is found on the east side of the Firehole River, near Azure Spring. There is no record of this geyser erupting prior to the mid-1970s, which is not surprising since this is one of the most dynamic areas of the geyser basin, and change is to be expected. For example, big Azure Spring, with a crater measuring 31 by 56 feet, is not mentioned by the geological surveys of the 1870s; there seems to be little question that it formed sometime since then. RVG-4 is highly variable in its activity, with periods of dormancy or quiet intermittency much more common than episodes of geyser action. Intervals range

from seconds to a few minutes, with all of the brief eruptions reaching 2 to 5 feet high.

65. DIADEM SPRING is one of the largest and prettiest pools in the River Group. Although never really a geyser by strict definition, Diadem is sometimes a very impressive intermittent spring. When active the water level slowly rises; just as overflow is reached a surge sends water cascading over all sides of the crater. Although the height of the eruption is zero, the flood amounts to more than 2,500 gallons per minute. Just a few feet from the spring, the stream drops over a waterfall and almost directly into the river. The steaming cascade is remarkable. Runoff channels suggest that Diadem has seen a lot of activity in its history, but it has been dormant since the early 1970s.

66. CONE SPRING sits in the top of a 4½-foot-high cone perched on the steep bank of the Firehole River. A short distance farther upstream is Horn Spring, with an almost identical cone. Both of these springs bubble and spout slightly. It is doubtful that they have ever had large eruptions, as the slender cones would best be formed by seeping flow running down their sides. Both, however, do erupt to a slight extent. Steady bubbling splashes water a few inches high. During the early 1970s Cone Spring was sometimes seen to throw a little spray as high as 3 feet, but that seems to have been exceptional behavior.

67. POCKET BASIN GEYSER, as often as not known simply as "Pocket" Geyser, lies near the natural drainage exit of the Pocket Basin mud pot area. It is evidently a young geyser, as it is not mentioned in any report, including some as recent as the early 1970s. Its deep alcove and runoff channel argue that this is a reactivated spring. Pocket Basin Geyser is clearly cyclic in its activity. Times are known in which it has not erupted for several days at a stretch, while at other times intervals are regular and as short as 23 minutes. When it is active the water periodically rises and falls within the vent. Each rise brings the level a bit higher than before. Sometimes requiring several overflow periods and other times none, eruptions begin at the time of highest water. The play is a series of strong bursts, some jets reaching over 15 feet high. The entire play lasts about 45 seconds, whatever the interval.

68. FORTRESS GEYSER, also known as Conch Spring, looks as if it should be a powerful geyser. The superheated pool lies within a massive geyserite cone rising more than 4 feet above its surroundings. The boiling is periodic. Quiet intervals are extremely brief, typically only 2 to 4 seconds in length. The play is violent boiling with occasional bursting to about 5 feet above the rim of the cone. Rare bursts may reach 10 feet high. Wide and deep runoff channels lead away from Fortress, indicating that it did undergo major eruptions some time in the past. The only such play in recent history occurred the night of the 1959 earthquake. Although it wasn't seen, it is estimated from the area washed by the water to have been at least 40 feet high.

Up the hill to the east of Fortress Geyser is an extensive area of hot springs. Several of these have histories of brief geyser existence, but evidently none have sustained such action beyond a few days. Occasional eruptions as much as 20 feet high have been seen in this area. Much more typical, and almost always present, are a few spouters 1 to 2 feet high.

Table 22. Geysers of the River Group

Name and Number	Interval	Duration	Height (ft)
Diadem Spring (65)	rare	2–3 min	boil
Fortress Geyser (68)	2–4 sec	seconds	5–10
Horn Spring (66)	steady	steady	inches
Mound Geyser (60)	11–35 min	3–8 min	6–12
Pocket Basin Geyser (67)	min–days	45 sec	15
UNNG-RVG-1 (61)	seconds	seconds	5
UNNG-RVG-2 (62)	25–50 min	2 min	2–7
UNNG-RVG-3 (63)	seldom	5–10 min	15
UNNG-RVG-4 (64)	sec–min	seconds	2–5

Imperial and Fairy Creek Groups

Along the broad valley of Fairy Creek, much of which is meadow land, are several small groups of scattered hot springs. There are few geysers of significance among these groups; those of note are approximately shown on Map N and listed in Table 23. Access to the area is via a trail that leaves the dirt portion of Fountain Flats Drive about 0.4 mile from the end of the pavement; this trail is not well marked. Access to the Imperial Group can also be gained via the Fairy Falls trail, which begins in the

Midway Geyser Basin. Fairy Falls is one of the nicer waterfalls in Yellowstone, with a delicate 200-foot sheer drop. The two trails merge into one about halfway between the Falls and Imperial Geyser; the round-trip hike to Imperial, via either trail, is about 6 miles.

69. UNNG-FCG-1 is a superheated pool just a few feet east of the trail, about ½ mile from the road. It is perhaps more of an intermittent spring than a true geyser. As the water drops within the crater at the end of an eruption the boiling decreases to near quiet. At high water the boiling causes a doming of the water, with some jets reaching 3 to 4 feet high. Eruptions last more than an hour, with intervals of much shorter length.

70. UNNG-FCG-2. Only one spring, called Locomotive, has been named along Fairy Creek, and just which one it is is uncertain. The groups have not been mapped in detail, and they are totally undeveloped. Accordingly, there is virtually nothing to serve as a guide to the area. However, what may be called the "Lower Fairy Creek Springs" are those located most directly to the west of FCG-1, lying beyond the creek a few hundred yards across the meadow. This group contains several dozen springs, including a few beautiful, deep pools, and at least seven geysers. The largest of these geysers has been seen to erupt as much as 10 feet high, such eruptions lasting only a few seconds. Eruptions are frequent on some occasions but more often are very infrequent. None of the other geysers here plays more than 2 or 3 feet high.

71. UNNG-FCG-3. When looking up-valley from the Lower Fairy Creek Springs, one sees a second group to the right (west) of an isolated stand of trees. These might be called the "Upper Fairy Creek Springs." The closest spring to those trees is a large, rarely active geyser. Eruptions observed during the early 1970s were as much as 30 feet high with a duration of 5 minutes. Since that time, however, this spring has dramatically changed its appearance: at some time a stream explosion enlarged the crater. What was a vent only about 4 feet across is now a pool closer to 10 feet in diameter, surrounded by tilted, broken blocks of geyserite. It is likely that the geyser has thoroughly changed its structure and activity and, in fact, that it probably is no longer a geyser at all.

72. UNNG-FCG-4 is located up a small valley to the west of the Upper Fairy Creek Springs. A perpetual spouter, it sprays water 6 feet high while giving rise to an impressively large runoff stream.

73. IMPERIAL GEYSER was born in 1927. If there was a hot spring at the site before then, it had never been recorded. Imperial probably had some eruptions during 1927, but none were directly observed until the following July. Drs. Allen and Day of the Carnegie Institute conducted extensive observations on the development and behavior of Imperial for their classic work, *The Hot Springs of the Yellowstone National Park.* They were instantly impressed by the geyser, and its fame rapidly spread outside the Park. It received its name as the result of a newspaper contest.

Erupting from near one side of a crater nearly 100 feet across, Imperial would continuously shoot bursts 30 feet wide to as high as 80 feet. An eruption would last about 2 hours, during which time over 360,000 gallons of water were expelled. The quiet intervals of 12 to 20 hours were periodically interrupted by brief splashing to 25 feet. Even during the quiet phase the discharge averaged 700 gallons per minute. In every way, Imperial was one of Yellowstone's most significant geysers. But after 15 months of activity, Imperial fell dormant in September of 1929. Because of many apparent steam leaks in the floor of the crater, Allen and Day surmised that Imperial had ruined its plumbing system, never to erupt again.

The dormancy lasted 37 years. Throughout that time the high water discharge continued and there were periodic episodes of small splashing. Major activity did not again take place until sometime in August 1966. Possibly a delayed effect of the 1959 earthquake, the first new activity was never more than 40 feet high, but it was non-stop. Through the succeeding years, Imperial gained in strength. In 1973 measurements proved some bursts to be more than 70 feet high. Although seemingly steady, the activity was, in fact, intermittent, with average intervals of 20 seconds and durations of 40 seconds.

From the time of its 1966 rejuvenation through 1984 Imperial showed no signs of slowing down. It came as a complete surprise, then, to find it barely active in 1985. Though still nearly constant in its play, the height was never more than 6 feet. At times the eruption declined to gentle boiling. What the future holds for Imperial, of course only Time knows.

74. SPRAY GEYSER has been known since the earliest days of the Park, one reason why an earlier existence for Imperial Geyser (73) is unlikely. When the first huge steam clouds of Imperial were seen at a distance it was thought that the source was Spray. It sits back in the woods, up a small tributary a few yards from the runoff from Imperial and perhaps ¼ mile from that geyser.

Spray is one of the few geysers whose intervals are consistently shorter than the durations. Although the length of these times can vary greatly, the relationship between the two is always the same. In 1929 the quiet intervals lasted from 2 to 31 minutes, the eruptions from 12 to 38. During the 1950s the intervals were around 2 minutes and the durations 5. Most recently, Spray's eruptions have lasted 3 to 5 minutes, separated by intervals of less than 1 minute. The eruption includes two main jets of water. One is nearly vertical and reaches 25 to 30 feet; the smaller, angled column is about 12 feet high. Several other openings play water between 2 and 6 feet. The entire cone and vicinity is thickly covered with some of the lushest algal growth anywhere.

Table 23. Geysers of the Imperial and Fairy Creek Groups

Name and Number	Interval	Duration	Height (ft)
Imperial Geyser (73)	seconds	seconds	1–70
Spray Geyser (74)	1 min	3–5 min	25–30
UNNG-FCG-1 (69)	minutes	1–2 hrs	4
UNNG-FCG-2 (70)	unrecorded	seconds	10
UNNG-FCG-3 (71)	rare	5 min	30
UNNG-FCG-4 (72)	steady	steady	6

Sentinel Meadows Group

The hot springs of the Sentinel Meadows Group (Map N, Table 24) have not, except in this book, been described in over 50 years. They lie scattered about a broad valley, forming several clusters. Three of the springs have formed large geyserite mounds. Known as Flat Cone, Sentinel Cone, and Mound

Spring, each is capped by a deep, boiling pool. The spring on the highest and steepest of these mounds has been reported to erupt, but absolutely no details are known. A fourth major spring is Queen's Laundry. The origin of that name is uncertain, but the pool is also known as Red Terrace Spring because of the wide overflow terraces that are coated with orange-red algae. Nearby is a wooden structure, the remains of a bath house dating to the first decade of Park history.

The Sentinel Meadows Group contains at least four geysers. Little is known about any of them since this is a rather remote area. From the road it is 1.7 miles to the Queen's Laundry. The trail begins directly across the Firehole River from Ojo Caliente in the River Group.

75. BOULDER SPRING is immediately at the base of a low, boulder-strewn hill about 300 yards southwest of Ojo Caliente. Not a part of the Sentinel Meadows Group, it is included here since access to it is from that trail. Boulder Spring is a perpetual spouter, playing from two main vents within a pool. The height of the eruption constantly varies in a pulsating motion while it also waxes and wanes in overall force. The height ranges from less than 1 foot to more than 6 feet.

Around the hill to the northwest of Boulder Spring, between the hill and the Sentinel Meadows trail, is an area of old hot spring craters and sinter platforms. The activity here was very vigorous at one time, but it is now so dead that only a slight seepage of steam can be seen on cold days. Near here, however, showing that all is not done in, a mud pot at the base of the hill opened a 10-foot-wide crater full of boiling mud during 1985.

76. UNNG-SMG-1 is located on the northern flank of the wide, low mound of Mound Spring, the first of the large superheated pools encountered when entering the area. The geyser plays from a beaded vent stained orange by iron oxide minerals. The interval of this geyser is unknown. Eruptions last no more than 20 seconds. The play is a series of distinct squirts of water, reaching up to 20 feet at first but rapidly dying down to just 3 feet at the end of the eruption. For several minutes following the eruption the water remaining in the vent boils violently before abruptly draining. Evidently, several hours are required for the system to refill, and even then eruptions take place only after long periods of overflow. It seems like the interval might well be 12 hours or longer. That, the brevity of play, and the infrequency of observation make it remarkable that any eruptions have been seen at all.

77. UNNG-SMG-2 lies about 50 feet towards the stream from SMG-1. Playing from a vent about 6 inches in diameter, its interval and duration are both about 10 seconds long. The height is 2 feet.

78. ROSETTE GEYSER was named after the shape of its crater, at a time in the 1870s when only a single, 30-foot eruption was seen. No further mention was made of Rosette until 1928. At that time it erupted every 2 minutes, its play of 10 feet lasting just a few seconds. In more recent years it has been weak and irregular. Intervals are apparently several hours long, culminating in eruptions only 2 to 4 feet high and lasting no more than 20 seconds.

79. IRON POT is the name of a geyser occupying a deep sinter basin partially surrounded by trees. It is about 200 yards south of Sentinel Cone. Little is known about the eruptions by Iron Pot. It was named in the 1870s, but no further note about its activity was made until the 1980s; it may have been dormant throughout that century. Eruptions probably recur every several hours. Every few minutes during the interval the water level rises a few inches, accompanied by minor bubbling. It is only at the time of eruption that the level rises significantly above a point about 10 feet below the rim. The play is several minutes of bursting and sloshing, water reaching the rim but never forming any runoff. Some fine droplets may extend as much as 15 feet above the pool.

Table 24. Geysers of the Sentinel Meadows Group

Name and Number	Interval	Duration	Height (ft)
Boulder Spring (75)	steady	steady	1–6
Iron Pot (79)	hours	minutes	15
Rosette Geyser (78)	hours	20 sec	2
UNNG-SMG-1 (76)	hours	20 sec	3–20
UNNG-SMG-2 (77)	10 sec	10 sec	2

Chapter 7

Norris Geyser Basin

The Norris Geyser Basin is, in several ways, very different from any other basin in Yellowstone. Only the geysers themselves look the same. The casual visitor immediately notices that the scene is stark. The Porcelain Basin is a barren depression almost totally devoid of plant life. It is drab gray with none of the pastel shades of other areas. Stream channels are only sporadically lined with green algae, and the few other visible colors are caused by thin surficial mineral deposits.

Norris's unique appearance is due to the presence of acidic water, which is not common in the other geyser basins. Large amounts of sulfur are being brought to the surface. In the springs it is oxidized to form sulfuric acid. The siliceous sinter deposited in the acid water is spiny and does not form the thick masses so common in the alkaline areas such as the Upper Geyser Basin.

Norris is also the hottest geyser basin in Yellowstone and certainly one of the hottest in the world. The water tempera- tures are higher and the geyser activity more vigorous than else- where. One research drill hole here reached a temperature of more than 459°F (237°C) at a depth of only 1,087 feet below the surface.

One curious aspect of the activity at Norris occurs during the summer season of each year. Popularly known as the "dis- turbance," its exact cause is uncertain. There is evidence that at Norris the hot springs are served by two separate geother- mal systems, one deep and the other shallower. Also, because of the lack of extensive geyserite deposits, which might other- wise seal the upper part of the system from inflowing ground water, there is some recycling of hot spring water back into the shallow portions of the geothermal system. Whatever the cause, the result is that quite suddenly, often within a few hours, a great many of the Norris springs and geysers become muddy. Pools that are normally quiet spring to life as powerful geysers; existing geysers become much more frequent in their activity. Usually, the disturbance occurs just once per year, most commonly during August or September. In 1984, however, a series of many more localized disturbances was distributed between May and October. The results, in any case, can be very spectacular. In any situation where an individual spring is especially affected by the disturbances, the fact is noted in the following descriptions.

The only public facility at Norris is a small museum. It contains excellent displays about the different kinds of hot springs and the life of the geyser basins. At the peak of the season, naturalists conduct several guided walks each day. There are no other services.

Porcelain Basin

The Porcelain Basin (Map W, Table 25) comprises the northern half of the Norris Geyser Basin. It was named for one of the few masses of alkaline sinter found at Norris. Porcelain is a relatively small area, but geyser and other hot spring activity is highly concentrated. A single glance from the museum might easily take in a dozen or more erupting geysers.

Porcelain Basin is also an extremely changeable area. The larger, long-lived geysers of the area, those that have names, are never quite the same from one year to the next. Most of the geysers are small and very short-lived. During their brief existence they act as perpetual spouters. Because of the internal deposition of minerals (mostly clay), they soon seal themselves in. The hot water that they gave off soon finds exit through new geysers. These spouters, possibly numbering 50 or more at any given time, obviously cannot be included in the descriptions here. Look for them in the central part of Porcelain Basin, especially on the wide flat beyond Pinwheel Geyser.

The Porcelain Basin trail doubles as a self-guiding nature trail. Signs along the way explain the thermal features, algae, and related matters. The entire trail system covers about 1 mile.

1. **HARDING GEYSER** had its first known eruption in 1923, the year President Harding visited Yellowstone. Harding Geyser

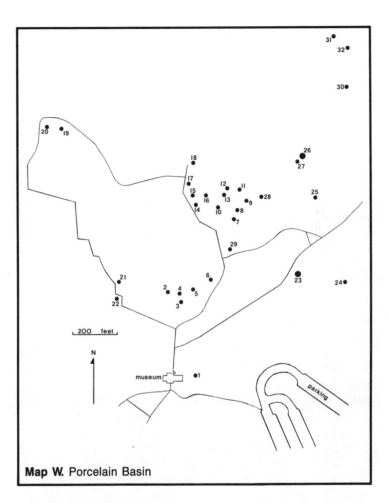

Map W. Porcelain Basin

rarely erupts. Records pertaining to its activity are scarce, and it has probably erupted during only a few seasons since its initial activity. The best seasons on record are 1975 and 1982, with several eruptions each. The play lasts about 5 minutes, and the 50-foot water jet is concluded with a short steam phase.

2. DARK CAVERN GEYSER is a faithful and frequent performer. It issues from a cave-like opening in a pile of dark gray geyserite. The water jet would be higher and more pronounced if it didn't strike a projecting piece of sinter. Deflected as it is, the maximum height is still as much as 20 feet. Dark Cavern is known to have both minor and major eruptions, the distinction between them being mostly a matter of duration. Both kinds included, several eruptions occur every hour.

3. VALENTINE GEYSER had its first known eruption on St. Valentine's Day in 1902. Located in a wide, deep alcove below the trail, its 6-foot-high cone is the largest at Norris. Valentine's activity is highly variable. In some years it erupts almost daily, while in others many weeks will pass during the interval. The eruption is spectacular but strangely quiet. Only the sound of falling water can be heard. Near the beginning of play the jet may reach as much as 75 feet. The water rapidly gives way to steam, and the remainder of the 90-minute eruption is an impressive cloud of steam and fine spray shooting to 40 feet. Valentine has now been dormant since 1978.

4. GUARDIAN GEYSER rarely performs. It lies at the narrow exit of the alcove containing Valentine Geyser (3) and spouts from a small pile of iron-stained rocks. When active, Guardian often acts as a precursor to Valentine, preceding that eruption by a few moments. The play, 20 to 25 feet high, lasts only a few seconds. Starting with Valentine's dormancy in 1978, Guardian has behaved differently. Independent eruptions, although very rare, are sometimes observed to last as long as 4 minutes and reach up to 30 feet. Guardian has also recently undergone a number of noisy steam-phase eruptions.

Just a few feet from Guardian Geyser is another geyser, first seen during 1984. Its activity corresponded with the onset of the steam eruptions in Guardian. Eruptions recurred every 9 to 26 minutes, lasted up to 19 minutes, and very much resembled the action of a squirt gun. The height was about 6 feet.

5. LEDGE GEYSER is, aside from Steamboat (36), the largest geyser at Norris, but it is highly irregular in its activity and is dormant during most seasons. Its best year on record was 1974, when its predictable eruptions occurred every 14 hours with extreme regularity. It continued such action until the earthquake of June 30, 1975, and only a few comparatively weak eruptions have occurred since then.

When active, there is an extraordinary amount of preplay from Ledge. It plays from five vents that are aligned so that the activity resembles the human hand. Three of the central vents jet water a few feet high; they are known as the "finger vents," and their activity is almost constant before an eruption. At the point nearest the trail is a deep cavity with a small vent at the bottom. This "little finger" slowly fills with water during the preplay; when Ledge is very frequent and regular, the water level in this "pressure pool" can be used to predict the time of eruption. The main vent is difficult to see from the trail. It lies to the far right, in the area where the bench containing the finger vents drops off to lower ground. This opening, the "thumb," penetrates the hillside at an angle. During the preplay, water occasionally splashes out of this vent. When Ledge is ready to play, one of these splashes becomes a steady surge then suddenly bursts into a tremendous eruption. It is surely one of the most impressive anywhere, reaching the full force in a matter of seconds. The water shot from the thumb reaches a height of 125 feet but, because it is jetted at a 40-degree angle, it may land as far as 220 feet from the vent. Meanwhile, the fingers are playing slender columns of water to 30 feet and more, and the pressure pool may burst to more than 60 feet. The booming and roaring spectacle cannot be matched anywhere.

The major activity of Ledge lasts about 20 minutes, throughout all of which the maximum height is maintained by the main vent. Thereafter the eruption slowly subsides. After about 2 hours it is finished, although Ledge never falls completely silent.

Ledge last erupted in 1979. Whatever affected it might well be what caused the dormancy in Valentine beginning in 1978. Though there are still some noisy steam vents in the area, the overall activity in this part of the Porcelain Basin is much less than it was during the early 1970s.

6. BASIN GEYSER used to erupt from the center of its pool, and its play was frequent but small. Then some new vents developed at the left end of the crater, and most of the eruption issued from them, reaching 6 feet high. Then during the late 1970s the crater drained, and dormancy has allowed wildflowers to grow deep within the vent.

7. UNNG-NPR-1 ("GEEZER" GEYSER) erupts from an unimpressive little hole among some jagged rocks. It is active essentialy only at the time of a disturbance, and then not always. Always irregular, the play can last as long as 15 minutes and reach up to 15 feet high.

8. ARSENIC GEYSER erupts from a symmetrical vent lined with pearly gray sinter. Sometimes it is nearly inactive and the eruptions are hardly more than a bubbling in the crater. At other times it is more active, and the play can be seen several times per day. The eruptions last as long as 20 minutes, and the height is as much as 20 feet. During the disturbance events, Arsenic is very much more active. Eruptions lasting as long as 3 hours reach fully 35 feet.

9. LAVA POOL COMPLEX is a group of vents at the base of the hillside beyond Arsenic Geyser (8). There is nearly always at least some eruptive activity among the seven vents, but its nature changes rapidly. At times, especially during the disturbances, all of the Lava Pool vents are active. These eruptions have durations upwards of several hours and may reach 10 feet high.

10. AFRICA GEYSER developed in a previously inactive crater during 1971. The eruptions were 45 feet high and very regular, with almost clockwork-like intervals of 90 minutes. As time progressed the intervals shortened and the force weakened. By 1973 Africa had become a perpetual spouter perhaps 20 feet high. Change continued. By the later 1970s the water gave out, and only a steady steam phase activity occurred. Slowly, Africa declined into dormancy, and now it is only another hole in the ground.

11. PINTO GEYSER spends most of its time as a calm blue pool. At the time of the summer disturbances, however, it becomes a geyser of considerable power. Muddy water is thrown to 40 feet in eruptions that can last as long as 30 minutes. Its irregular intervals range from 5 minutes to several hours.

12. FAN GEYSER is located a few feet beyond Fireball Geyser (13). The pearly, orangish vent is almost impossible to see from the boardwalk. Fan is a very irregular geyser. It may erupt as often as 2 or 3 times per day, but it is often dormant for long periods. Eruptions 10 minutes long jet water to about 10 feet high. During the disturbance episodes Fan develops a nearly constant bubbling and splashing, which is punctuated by frequent eruptions 15 to 25 feet high.

13. FIREBALL GEYSER shoots out of several small vents among a low pile of red, iron-stained rocks about 100 feet beyond Little Whirligig Geyser (14). Each of the openings jets water at a different angle and height. The largest is vertical and 12 feet high. Eruptions by Fireball are frequent and last about 5 minutes. During the disturbances, durations as long as 1 hour can be separated by intervals as short as 5 minutes. During 1984, when a series of minor disturbances was recorded, Fireball was in eruption about half the time.

There has been discussion as to which geyser, #12 or #13, is Fan and which is Fireball. The play of #13 is distinctly fan-shaped while that of #12 certainly is not. Nonetheless, the original descriptions of the vents indicate that the names as given here are correct. Undoubtedly, the names were inadvertently switched sometime in the past so that we now have a non-fan-shaped geyser named Fan and a fan-shaped geyser named Fireball!

14. LITTLE WHIRLIGIG GEYSER erupts from a crater colored bright orange-yellow by iron oxide minerals. It is one of the more colorful points in the Porcelain Basin. Sometime prior to the 1930s Little Whirligig seldom erupted, if it even existed. References to it are few. In that decade, nearby Whirligig Geyser (15) declined in activity until it seldom played. By then, Little Whirligig was playing almost steadily. It wasn't until 1973 that Little Whirligig began taking occasional rests, pausing for about 20 minutes just 2 or 3 times per day. During 1974, Whirligig began erupting regularly for the first time in many years, and by June 1975 Little Whirligig was again completely dormant. With rare exceptions, so it has remained. When active, the eruption of Little Whirligig is jetted at an angle directly toward the boardwalk; its maximum height is 20 feet.

15. WHIRLIGIG GEYSER, also known as Big Whirligig, was so named because the water swirls about the crater during an eruption. After many years of dormancy, Whirligig rejuvenated in the summer of 1974. Eruptions were frequent and regular, lasting between 3 and 4 minutes. During the 1980s they have declined in frequency, so that the intervals are more irregular and near 12 hours in length. The play begins with a sudden and rapid filling of the crater. The largest portion of the activity comes from the central vent, where the water is thrown to 15 feet by a series of closely-spaced bursts. The most interesting play is from the "rooster-tail vent" on the far side of the crater. It shoots water in a series of puffs, looking much like the bird's tail plumes and sounding like an old steam engine. During an eruption of Whirligig, the water running beneath the boardwalk at this point will be about 180°F (82°C).

16. CONSTANT GEYSER has never seen anything approaching constant activity, but at one time it was of constant regularity. That has certainly changed, and on most modern occasions the action has been erratic and infrequent. Constant is clearly related to the two Whirligigs; it is most active when Whirligig (15) is active, and nearly dormant when Little Whirligig (14) is active. When active, the intervals may range from a few minutes to many hours. The one sign to look for is a pulsation of the surface of the shallow pool, which is located just beyond Whirligig. Look closely! After only a few seconds of such warning, the entire 30-foot play lasts only 5 to 10 seconds.

17. SPLUTTER POT, once known as the "Washing Machine," plays from a small crater in the midst of the runoff from Pinwheel Geyser (18). The rim of the crater often forms an island in the middle of the stream. Splutter Pot currently plays every 4 to 6 minutes for 1 to 2 minutes, reaching a height of about 6 feet. Its history has also seen many long dormancies.

18. PINWHEEL GEYSER was once one of the stars at Norris. Its eruptions were frequent and over 20 feet high. Several years ago the ground on the far (upstream) side of the crater settled a few inches, allowing the runoff from other springs to enter the pool. This cool water was able to lower the temperature of Pinwheel enough to stop all eruptive activity. During the late summer disturbance of 1974 the runoff decreased markedly. Within a day Pinwheel began having minor eruptions. Whenever

observed, it seemed about to explode with the power of old. But that never happened; the runoff was soon back to normal and all activity again ceased. It may be that through the years enough gravel and silt has washed into the vent to effectively seal Pinwheel off. If so, it may never again erupt as it did in the past.

19. BEAR DEN GEYSER comes as a complete surprise to those who manage to see an eruption. It is situated at the base of a cliff where it issues from a narrow defile among some rhyolite boulders. The site attracts little notice as it is partially hidden by some trees below the trail and because there is no pool to emit steam. The eruptions, though, are very impressive. Water is squirted by a series of distinct pulses to heights as much as 70 feet. The jets are at an angle so that the water falls well downhill from the vent. An eruption may consist of anywhere from just one to as many as thirty-five bursts. The intervals range from 3 to 7 hours.

Bear Den apparently came into existence in the late 1950s after the crater of nearby Ebony Geyser (20) was choked by debris thrown by visitors. Unquestionably, Bear Den developed as a new outlet for Ebony's blocked energy.

20. EBONY GEYSER erupts from a yawning crater lined with dark gray sinter. Until the mid-1950s, Ebony was one of the largest and most faithful geysers at Norris, but the constant throwing of debris by Park visitors spelled its demise. Even though the vent now appears to be clear of rubble, eruptions are rare. The energy has largely shifted a few feet east to Bear Den Geyser (19). Major eruptions, 75 feet high, have not been seen in many years; smaller eruptions, in which some bursts may reach 10 feet, are almost equally rare.

Ebony and Bear Den give us a lesson. Geysers are very fragile features. Just a few rocks thrown into a crater can plug a geyser, causing it to stop erupting. In the case of Ebony a new, large geyser came into existence as a replacement as the energy shifted elsewhere. But in most cases of this sort the energy is distributed among a number of existing springs. There is no new geyser. Please do not throw anything into any geyser, and help keep others from doing so, too. The geysers of Yellowstone are much too rare to be lost through such carelessness.

21. GLACIAL MELT GEYSER was so named because of an opalescent appearance to its water. This is caused by a high content of suspended, colloidal silica particles. The result is similar in color to the meltwater from glaciers. This geyser is most active during the summer disturbances, when individual splashes several seconds apart reach 5 feet high. At other times, Glacial Melt is usually a quiet pool.

22. UNNG-NPR-2 ("TEAL BLUE BUBBLER") is a small, sometimes-spouter that plays from a small pool perched on the hillside. The boardwalk stairway passes immediately next to it. Although it is not active during most seasons, eruptions as much as 6 feet high have been seen.

23. CONGRESS POOL began life in 1893 as a geyser. Within weeks it had become a large and regular performer. Much to everybody's disappointment, though, it soon stopped erupting and became a quiet pool. From that time into the 1970s there was little activity from Congress. In 1974 it began some "almost eruptive" behavior. Constantly roiling, it would periodically throw muddy water as high as 20 feet. As this activity continued, the water level dropped lower and lower until it was down fully 5 feet. After about two weeks, Congress began to decline in force, the crater refilled, and the pool was soon back to normal. This activity began earlier than, but otherwise coincided with, that year's disturbance. Since then, Congress has continued to exhibit disturbance-related behavior, but never to the degree shown in 1974.

24. CARNEGIE DRILL HOLE. Across the flat, barren area to the back left of Congress Pool is what looks like a small rock pile. Water spurts from a little pool at the base of the mound. What you cannot see from the trail is that the entire area, rocks and all, pulsates up and down by as much as several inches every second or so. Actually, the rock pile is cemented together, marking the site of a drill hole sunk for research purposes. The work was done in 1929 by Dr. C. N. Fenner of the Carnegie Institute of Washington. This project was one of the earliest attempts at drilling in a thermal basin; certainly it had never been done in an area as active as Norris. The purpose of the drill hole was to gather data about the alteration of the rocks in a geothermal system and to learn something about the subsurface temperatures. The results were surprising. First, all notable rock alteration was confined to within a few feet of the surface. Second, the hole had to be abandoned at a depth of only 265 feet – the steam pressure was so great that it threatened to blow up the drill rig. At that shallow depth the temperature was 401°F (205°C)! After abandonment the hole was filled with cement, but the hot water soon found a way around the plug. The pool that developed is now a perpetual spouter.

25. FEISTY GEYSER was once one of the finer geysers of the Porcelain Basin area, but if it still exists it cannot be distinguished from the many other geysers and spouters in its vicinity. Feisty's site is immediately below the Porcelain Springs, which flow alkaline water and are depositing geyserite at the fastest rate ever measured in Yellowstone. New formations sometimes grow nearly 1 foot per year (compared with a more typical 1 inch per century). As a result, existing springs change rapidly. Feisty was always somewhat irregular but usually played several times per hour. Lasting several minutes each time, the play was as much as 25 feet high. No such geyser exists in the area now, but at least a dozen vents are known to play to about 10 feet. One of them may be Feisty.

26. BLUE GEYSER, also known as Big Blue Geyser, lies far out on the barren flats beyond Feisty Geyser (25). The large pool is active most of the time, sending up periodic large domes of water as high as 15 feet. Eruptive periods may be as short as 15 minutes, but most last several hours. By the way, Blue is pale gray most of the time, especially during disturbances.

27. IRIS SPRING occupies a small crater immediately in front of Blue Geyser (26). It is a perpetual spouter. Most of the splashes are quite small, but a few reaching perhaps 15 feet are occasionally seen.

28. THE PRIMROSE SPRINGS extend along a shallow "valley" extending toward the main flats of Porcelain Basin. Within this group are about a dozen perpetual spouters. Primrose Spring itself plays about 3 feet high.

29. SUNDAY GEYSER is so called because it first erupted on a Sunday. It is dormant nearly all the time. The last active episode was during 1981–82, when it was a frequent performer. Eruptions 30 feet high recurred every 15 to 20 minutes, each lasting more than 5 minutes. When not active, the site is occupied by a shallow, bluish pool which often becomes muddy gray at the time of a disturbance.

30. RAGGED SPOUTER is one of several recent developments in the far northeastern portion of Porcelain Basin. Its vent appears to be simply a wide spot along an old fissure. When first seen, during 1981, it was described as having "Echinus-like" bursts approaching 50 feet high (see Echinus Geyser, #38). It rapidly died down, and although still active on irregular intervals, the greatest height is now only about 10 feet.

31. GRACEFUL GEYSER became active at about the same time as Ragged Spouter (30), in late 1981 or early 1982. At first the eruptions played from a small cone. Being very old and badly weathered, the cone did not last long. Now Graceful erupts from a large, jagged crater, some of the spray reaching about 20 feet high.

32. UNNG-NPR-3 ("COLLAPSE CAVE" GEYSER) is another little-known, recently reactivated geyser in the far corner of the Porcelain Basin. It erupts within a large, cavernous opening, from which part of the roof collapsed many years ago. The eruptions, though lasting no more than 10 seconds, play up to 20 feet high. They generally recur about every 5 minutes.

Note: Numerous other geysers are known to have been active within Porcelain Basin during the past few years. Most have played only for a year or two, however, and whether they will make future appearances is, of course, not known. For the record, some of the informal names involved are: Moxie Geyser, Poquito Geyser, Ramjet Springs, Crackling Lake Geyser, Porcelain Springs Geyser, Norris Geyser, Green Apple Cider Spring, Junebug Geyser, Blowout Geyser, and Christmas Geyser. This is only a sampling, and for each of these there are several smaller, less significant geysers that have been observed from time to time. As stated in the introduction to Norris, this is an extremely changeable area.

Table 25. Geysers of the Porcelain Basin

Name and Number	Interval*	Duration	Height (ft)
Africa Geyser (10)	dormant	steady	20–45
Arsenic Geyser (8)**	irregular	5–20 min	10–35
Basin Geyser (6)	dormant	steady	6
Bear Den Geyser (19)	3–7 hrs	sec–min	10–70
Blue Geyser (26)**	frequent	min–hrs	15
Carnegie Drill Hole (24)	steady	steady	1–4
Congress Pool (23)	disturbance	minutes	4–20
Constant Geyser (16)	irregular	seconds	10–30
Dark Cavern Geyser (2)	minutes	sec–min	20
Ebony Geyser (20)	rare	3–5 min	10–75
Fan Geyser (12)**	irregular	10 min	10–25
Feisty Geyser (25)	irregular	2–20 min	10–25
Fireball Geyser (13)**	frequent	5 min	12
Glacial Melt Geyser (21)	disturbance	steady	5
Guardian Geyser (4)	seldom	minutes	3–30
Graceful Geyser (31)	irregular	minutes	20
Harding Geyser (1)	rare	5 min	50
Iris Spring (27)	steady	steady	5–15
Lava Pool Complex (9)**	frequent	min–hrs	1–10
Ledge Geyser (5)	rare	2 hrs	125
Little Whirligig Geyser (14)	irregular	min–hrs	15–20
Pinto Geyser (11)	disturbance	2–30 min	20–40
Pinwheel Geyser (18)**	rare	5 min	20
Primrose Spring (28)	steady	steady	3
Ragged Spouter (30)	irregular	minutes	10–50
Splutter Pot (17)	4–6 min	1–2 min	6
Sunday Geyser (29)**	rare	5 min	30
UNNG-NPR-1 ("Geezer") (7)	disturbance	15 min	15
UNNG-NPR-2 ("Teal Blue") (22)	infrequent	steady	1–6
UNNG-NPR-3 ("Collapse Cave") (32)	minutes	10 sec	20
Valentine Geyser (3)	rare	90 min	40–75
Whirligig Geyser (15)	min–hrs	3–4 min	15

*Under Interval, "disturbance" indicates geysers that are active essentially only at the time of a disturbance.

**Indicates geysers that show more frequent and/or more powerful activity at the time of a disturbance.

Back Basin

Hot spring activity in the Back Basin (Map X, Table 26), that is, the southern half of the Norris Geyser Basin, is much less concentrated than in the Porcelain Basin. Pines separate small groups of hot springs from one another, often even isolating individual springs. Because of this, the Back Basin is a better area in which to stroll on a hot summer day. Here not only will you see abundant geyser activity, but you may also see some wildlife – elk, moose, sandhill cranes, and even bear have been seen in the area. Before you leave the museum area be sure to check on the status of Echinus Geyser, the only large, predictable geyser at Norris.

The loop trail around the Back Basin is about 0.9 mile long. For those who do not wish to walk the entire distance, a cutoff just about halves the round-trip distance.

33. STEAMVALVE SPRING was known during the early days of the Park, but a dormancy of many decades left it all but forgotten. During the late 1970s, though, Steamvalve suddenly reappeared as a geyser. Its activity is quite constant, and predictable. About 1½ hours before an eruption, bubbles begin to rise through the water in the crater, which is slowly filling. The eruption begins abruptly before overflow is reached. Bursts are thrown as high as 12 feet, the biggest bursts usually coming near the end of the 15-minute eruption.

34. BATHTUB SPRING is usually an acidic spring splashing from a massive geyserite crater. The geyserite was formed at times when Bathtub was alkaline rather than acidic. Bathtub has been known to switch back and forth several times. It *may* also be identical to a geyser of the 1800s known as the "Schlammkessel." In more recent years, Bathtub Spring has acted as a perpetual spouter, most play reaching 3 feet high.

35. EMERALD SPRING spends most of its time as a beautiful yellow-green pool. The color arises from the combination of the blue of the water and the yellow of sulfur lining the crater walls. The color is intense and very different from that produced by yellow algae. No spring was better named.

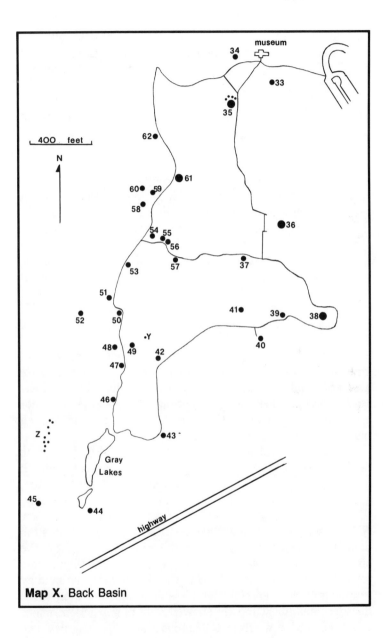

Map X. Back Basin

Most of the time, Emerald Spring calmly bubbles over the vent. The bubbling is not boiling – the temperature of 195°F (90°C) is several degrees below the boiling point – but rather due to mixtures of steam and carbon dioxide. At the time of the disturbances Emerald Spring abruptly becomes turbid gray-brown, and then it does sometimes act as a geyser. Such eruptions are usually about 6 feet high. During 1931 it had an extraordinary episode of activity, when it played at least 87% of the time with bursts reaching 60 to 75 feet!

Just to the right of Emerald Spring are several ephemeral springs and spouters. First active in the 1930s, they were not seen again until some brief action during 1971. Then in 1974 they became active again. Within about 30 minutes, over a dozen spouters made their appearance. Their development was the first sign of the onset of a disturbance, one that proved to be basin-wide in effect and one of the most intense ever. Some of these spouters played 10 feet high. Most had disappeared within a few weeks, but two or three continued their activity into 1975. Very shallow depressions in the gravel now mark their sites.

36. STEAMBOAT GEYSER is the largest geyser in the world – when it is active. Most of the time the only eruptions seen are a series of minor splashes every few minutes. Actually, the boardwalk is farther from the vent than it looks, and the minor eruptions are as much as 40 feet high. But for Steamboat such bursts are almost insignificant.

Steamboat has an interesting history. According to some descriptions there was no spring of any kind here before 1878; more likely, it did exist but was largely inactive. In any case, 1878 is the year of Steamboat's first known series of major eruptions. The new geyser was variously known as New Geyser, New Fissure Geyser, and Steamboat Geyser; Steamboat is the name that stuck. The destruction the eruptions brought to the surrounding forest was unmistakable: trees were killed, huge rocks thrown about, and plants covered with sand and mud by eruptions well over 100 feet high. Through the next three decades Steamboat mostly showed only minor action; major eruptions are known from 1891, 1894, and 1902, and may well have occurred during other years as well. The next year in which there was a series of major eruptions was 1911. The height was said to be over 250 feet. Steamboat again fell quiet, with only minor activity for fifty years. Then, starting in 1961 and continuing into 1969, Steamboat had its best active period yet. All told, there were ninety major eruptions during those eight years, twenty-nine of them in 1964 alone.

It is difficult, if not impossible, to adequately describe a major eruption of Steamboat. It begins with a normal-looking minor sort of play, except that the action persists and continues to build in height. It may exceed 100 feet. More often than not, this "superburst" will fail to trigger a full eruption. But there simply is no describing the scene when the superburst proves to be the major play. The height simply continues to grow, almost beyond belief. A number of eruptions have been measured at about 380 feet high, more than 3 times the size of Old Faithful, and none are less than 250 feet. The water phase of the eruption lasts anywhere from 5 to 20 minutes, during which well over a million gallons of water are discharged. Then comes the steam phase. The roar is tremendous and may last several hours. Some say that one eruption, on a cold, crisp and windless winter day, was heard in Madison Junction, 14 miles away! At times it is literally impossible for people to yell at one another and be heard—as if anybody had anything sensible to say.

After its major eruption on March 20, 1969, Steamboat failed to play again until nine years had passed. There is no chance that any eruptions were missed, as any eruption of Steamboat leaves abundant signs. So it was hoped that the eruption of March 28, 1978 presaged a new series of activity. And so it did, although eruptions were sparse until 1982. There were twenty-three eruptions that year, the third best year on record; twelve more occurred during 1983. It is a great disappointment that this cycle appears to have ended, as only five eruptions happened in 1984 and none during 1985.

Aside from the joy of seeing eruptions by Steamboat, the geyser's activity has revealed something about the water circulation of the Norris geothermal system. A geyser as large as Steamboat obviously must be served by a very abundant supply of water. It seems likely that Steamboat's deeper plumbing taps rather directly into a second, hotter and deeper, geothermal system than do many of the other hot springs at Norris. At the times of the Norris disturbances, however, there is a mixing of the two waters. Recently, the onset of a disturbance has always first appeared in Steamboat, sometimes as long as two days before it becomes evident elsewhere. Quite often this has happened when Steamboat appeared to be approaching another major eruption. The disturbance ends any such possibility until its effects have passed. Known as the "zap," its effect is also seen in Echinus Geyser (38), Emerald Spring (35), and Steamvalve Spring (33), indicating that these geysers may be associated along some sort of fracture system.

So, for both geyser gazing and geothermal research, Steamboat is a very important geyser. It is not likely that you will get to see it have a major eruption. Then again, somebody will be there when it happens next, and just maybe it will be you.

37. CISTERN SPRING is the only spring known to be directly affected by an eruption of Steamboat Geyser (36). Every major eruption there causes Cistern to drain by as much as 12 feet; Steamboat's superbursts have also been observed to have an effect. Cistern has been known to erupt on two occasions, both shortly after major eruptions by Steamboat; these were in 1978 and 1982. The height of play was about 20 feet.

Cistern Spring is building a sinter terrace about its crater at a very rapid rate. The deposit is growing upward at the rate of about 1½ inches per year. The trail has had to be moved, and several additional trees are entombed each year.

38. ECHINUS GEYSER is a favorite of nearly everybody. Very regular and predictable, it is also large and beautiful. Overall, it is the "best" geyser at Norris. Nowhere can you get so close to a large geyser as you can at Echinus.

The name "Echinus" comes from the Greek word for spiny. The same root gave the sea urchins and starfish their collective name of "echinoderms." The name was applied to the geyser because an early visitor thought some of the stones about the crater resembled sea urchins. And indeed they do. They are rhyolite pebbles that have been coated with the typically spiny sinter of acid water. This is one of the better examples of such geyserite. The prominent reddish and yellow-brown colors are

Echinus Geyser, with bursts up to 125 feet high, is the largest predictable geyser in the Norris Basin.

due to iron oxide minerals that are deposited along with the sinter. This is also one of the rare cases where arsenic compounds are being deposited by the hot water—the sinter at Echinus is about 5% arsenic pentoxide. But don't worry about the water if you happen to be sprayed. The arsenic content is far too low to be harmful.

Echinus's activity begins with its large crater slowly filling with water. The water level is easy to gauge by watching some specific point within the basin. As the filling progresses and the eruption time nears, the filling becomes faster. In some years the crater must completely fill and overflow before the eruption starts; in others, the play begins while the level is still several feet below the rim. Either way, the boiling over the vent becomes a surging, and the eruption is on within seconds. Echinus is a typical fountain-type geyser, throwing its water in a series of closely-spaced bursts. Each burst is different from every other, some small, others nearly 125 feet tall, some straight up, and others so sharply angled that they can soak people on the benches with warm water (not hot after its flight through the air). How long has it been since you took a geyser shower? It's a unique experience—and a harmless one.

After the eruption, the water remaining in the crater slowly recedes. In some years it drops no more than 4 feet, and in others the crater empties entirely. Then it begins the slow, steady refilling toward the next eruption. The average interval is quite different every year, but it generally ranges between 20 and 80 minutes. The durations also vary, from just a few minutes to as long as 70 minutes. Echinus is at its most variable at the times of basin-wide disturbances. Then it may undergo what has been termed a "gran-mal eruption," during which the water turns from nearly clear to very muddy during the play, which will always be of considerable power and very long duration. Like the "zap" at Steamboat, the "gran-mal" is often one of the first signs of the onset of a disturbance. The one thing you can count on, though, is that regardless of the specifics of its action, Echinus will be active and will provide one of the best eruptions to be seen in Yellowstone. Echinus is one geyser you should not miss.

39. CRATER SPRING has also been called Collapse Crater Spring, for reasons that should be clear to an observer. At sometime in the rather distant past the entire undercut rim of the crater collapsed inward. The rubble still lies there. During most of Crater Spring's known history, a steady eruption jetted above the boulders. During a disturbance in May 1983, Crater Spring began playing as a true geyser. Eruptions, lasting as long as 10 minutes and recurring as often as every 30 minutes, jetted water as high as 20 feet. The main jet was angled to the north, reaching over the trail so that a new route had to be constructed. By mid-summer of 1983, Crater Spring had regressed to a pool, but then it was nearly full and slightly overflowing. Since then, eruptive activity has been weak and unusual.

40. ARCH STEAM VENT undergoes rare major eruptions. This is positively known from splashed areas, runoff channels, and killed vegetation, but apparently no reporter has ever seen one of the plays. The greatest number known for any single year was four, in 1974. The signs indicate that the eruption is jetted at about a 45-degree angle down the slope, reaching perhaps 40 feet high. The deep runoff channels just below the vent indicate that Arch has probably had considerable eruptive activity in the past.

41. TANTALUS GEYSER has had important eruptive activity only during 1969, and in fact is probably no different from any of the great many other ephemeral geysers and spouters so common to Norris—except for its size. During its few days of activity, Tantalus played as high as 35 feet. It is now a quiet pool, which becomes muddier and may splash weakly during disturbances.

42. MUD POOL is, contrary to its name, clear most of the time. If it is eruptive, however, it will be muddy. Most eruptive periods are associated with disturbances, when some bursts have reached 30 feet high. Somewhat more typical is a steady surging 1 to 2 feet high. During 1984, Mud Pool performed as a small but regular geyser, with durations of 12 to 20 minutes separated by intervals of 40 to 60 minutes. The height was 1½ feet.

43. PUFF-N-STUFF GEYSER is right next to the trail. The dissected cone constantly rumbles and gurgles, sending a fine spray of water a few feet high. Puff-N-Stuff looks and acts as if it could do more at any time, but it never has.

44. BIG ALCOVE SPRING is not accessible to the general public, lying in an area not served by a trail, but it merits description since it can be one of the larger geysers at Norris. It plays from a crack in the rhyolite bedrock exposed within a deep, alcove-like crater. The pulsating jet has been known to reach over 25 feet high, though most eruptions are less than 10 feet. Both intervals and durations are only a few seconds long.

45. MEDUSA SPRING is another geyser not accessible by trail; though awkward, it can be observed from the main highway from a point about ¾ mile south of Norris Junction. Medusa is a pretty, greenish pool about 10 feet across. It is unusual in that its acidic water is forming a geyserite more typical of alkaline water. Medusa is a geyser, irregular in its performances, but reaching as much as 12 feet high.

46. BLUE MUD SPRING is a constantly active spouter immediately below the trail. More often than not it does not send water above ground level, but sometimes the play will briefly send fine, muddy spray as high as 10 feet.

In the flat area below Blue Mud Spring is a group of springs known as the "Muddy Sneaker Complex." These features began to make their appearance during 1971, with a small mud pot right in the middle of the old trail. Since then the individual springs have come and gone frequently, and a few temporary geysers have been observed. To the north a few feet from Blue Mud Spring, occupying the bottom of a shallow draw, another group of springs known as the "Tangled Root Complex" also made its first appearance during the 1970s and, again, some brief geyser activity has been observed. In both of these groups the springs often have a beautiful opalescent blue color. This is caused by an extremely high silica content in the water.

47. UNNG-NBK-1 ("SON OF GREEN DRAGON" SPRING). The unofficial name for this small perpetual spouter seems to be catching on, although the spring bears little resemblance to the much larger, cavernous, muddy Green Dragon Spring a few hundred feet away. Actually, this spring involves three different spouting vents. The biggest bursts are about 2 feet high.

48. ORBICULAR GEYSER plays from a shallow, round (orbicular) crater. Most of the time this is a quiet, insignificant spring, sometimes even filled with *cold* water. When active, though, it can be very noticeable. Orbicular tends to be most active at the time of a disturbance, when it plays as much as 90% of the time; intervals may be a few seconds long while durations sometimes exceed 10 minutes. The maximum height is 6 feet. In some seasons Orbicular is active without disturbance-related behavior; then the geyser plays much less frequently and reaches no more than 3 feet high.

49. DABBLE GEYSER is active almost exclusively at the time of summer disturbances. Then its activity is highly variable. Eruptions consist of a splashing reaching about 8 feet high. During a disturbance, the intervals may range from 30 minutes to several hours in length, while the play lasts about 4 minutes.

50. DOUBLE BULGER is only half alive now. The larger crater is a muddy perpetual spouter, throwing water 2 or 3 feet high. The smaller, more symmetrical vent used to perform in the same manner, but it has been choked by rocks and gravel for many years.

51. PEARL GEYSER is one of the few hot springs at Norris to resemble those of the other geyser basins. Its massive sinter crater is occupied by a shallow pool of crystal clear water. Occasional bubbles rise from the vent. During most years, that is the eruption – totally erratic and with splashes no more than 2 feet high. During 1984, Pearl proved to have a cyclic pattern of more truly eruptive episodes. During an active phase the intervals ranged from seconds to minutes in length, and some bursts reached 8 feet high.

52. PORKCHOP GEYSER plays from a crater that is, indeed, shaped like a porkchop. The vent is a hole 2 inches in diameter lying at the far western (narrow) part of the crater. Eruptions are erratic at Porkchop. In some seasons it is a very regular geyser, with intervals on the order of 3 hours and durations of 75 minutes. These "normal" eruptions sound like an old steam engine, several chugs per second sending bursts of water 15 to 20 feet high. During some other seasons, evidently not directly associated with other disturbance activity, Porkchop develops a steady eruption. Lasting for as long as several weeks, the nonstop steamy spray reaches over 30 feet high.

53. VIXEN GEYSER plays from a reddish vent right beside the trail. It always pleases those who spend a few minutes waiting for it. Vixen has two types of activity. Minor eruptions are generally the rule. They last only a few seconds but recur every few minutes. The maximum height is 10 feet. Major eruptions, which hadn't been observed for more than a decade until 1984, are relatively rare. Lasting anywhere from only 30 seconds to as much as an hour, this play is at least 35 feet high. It is only a major eruption that discharges enough water to form a runoff away from the vent. The shallow channel leading toward Tantalus Creek is quite small, an indication that Vixen has never had many major eruptions.

Tantalus Creek, by the way, is almost entirely hot water runoff from the springs and geysers. It was named for the Greek god Tantalus, one of the sons of Hades, the god of the Underworld.

54. RUBBLE GEYSER first erupted in 1972. Before then there was no evidence of any spring ever having existed at the site, but its coming was foretold by the small lodgepole pine trees of the area. In 1970 they began dying as the ground warmed up and exceeded their temperature tolerance. Judging by the ragged vent, Rubble was formed by a small steam explosion. At first, Rubble played frequently and regularly, but the activity rapidly decreased. By the time it was four years old, Rubble was nearly dormant, and so it remains. A few eruptions are seen each year, and their nature hasn't changed. Lasting about 6 minutes, the splashing play begins after 1 to 2 minutes of overflow. The bursts reach as much as 10 feet high, but the force rapidly declines near the end of the duration.

55. CORPORAL GEYSER hardly merits attention, whether active or inactive. The eruption consists of nothing more than an intermittent overflow, at which time there may be a few 1-foot-high splashes. Intervals range from 20 minutes during active years to many hours during less active episodes. The duration is about 3 minutes.

56. UNNG-NBK-2 ("DOG'S LEG" SPRING) is located about 6 feet to the east of Corporal Geyser. When active as a geyser, it far overshadows Corporal. During some seasons, it has been seen to erupt as much as 3 feet high and to do so for durations of several hours. More often, its level drops when Corporal erupts and refills when Corporal stops playing. There is considerable complexity here, though, as no disturbance has been known to affect Corporal while many have been seen to increase the activity of Dog's Leg Spring.

57. VETERAN GEYSER is a spell-binder. People will sit here for long periods, waiting for an eruption that always seems about to happen. Often they are not disappointed, but some must wait quite a while. The intervals are always irregular – 15 minutes on some days, more than 3 hours on others. The main vent of Veteran is a large hole on the far side of the deep crater. Between the main vent and the crater is a hole connecting the two. A third vent is on the near side of the basin, right next to the trail. When it is time for an eruption the already turbulent water in the main vent becomes violent. Water is shot through the small opening into the crater. Once that pool is high enough to cover the opening the eruption begins in earnest. Water is jetted from the main vent at an angle, reaching as much as 25 feet high and 40 feet out. Meanwhile, water also escapes from the third vent, shooting across the trail at a very low angle. The eruption ends very abruptly after anywhere from 10 seconds to 2½ minutes have passed.

A few feet to the east of Veteran's pool is another crater with the same overall appearance. This is known as "Veteran's Auxiliary Vent." It was only realized during 1984 that this spring will fill only shortly before Veteran begins a new cycle of eruptions. Since those cycles last at least 14 hours and more typically several days, the Auxiliary is not seen often.

58. PALPITATOR SPRING is a geyser, first observed to be so during 1974. Prior to then it had always been a quiet pool with the water surface bouncing (palpitating) over the vent. Since the first observed eruptions, the duration has gradually increased while the interval has decreased. Currently, Palpitator takes about 7 hours between eruptions, which last around 3 hours. The play is about 3 feet high.

59. FEARLESS GEYSER doesn't seem to erupt any more. It used to be reported to play several times per day, though to only 3 feet high. Perhaps there has been some change in the plumbing system, for Fearless is certainly hot enough to be a geyser. The pool is superheated, with a temperature several degrees above boiling, yet the only activity is a steady boiling.

60. UNNG-NBK-3 is a set of perpetual spouters that made their appearance during the late 1970s. Spouting muddy brown water, some of the play has reached 6 feet high. At least six separate vents have been active here, the action constantly shifting around.

61. MONARCH GEYSER, as the name implies, is a major geyser. But its days are probably past, for the pool at the site is very different from that present when the geyser was active. Monarch's play was as much as 200 feet high. Lasting around 10 minutes, the eruption would throw out so much water that the old road through Norris had to be closed every time the geyser was active. The last few eruptions threw out muddy water, indicating that the plumbing system was being damaged at depth. It is interesting to conjecture that the death of Monarch was in some way related to the 1911 rebirth of Steamboat (36). The two geysers are actually rather near one another, and the changes in activity took place within weeks of each other. Of course, since then Steamboat had a dormancy lasting 50 years, and no activity occurred in Monarch. Perhaps there's no relationship at all.

62. MINUTE GEYSER received its name because of the very regular but brief nature of its eruptions many years ago. It has so thoroughly been changed since then that it has also appeared in literature as mĭn-ūt′, meaning something very small. The early eruptions of Minute were sometimes as much as 100 feet high. Then somebody threw a boulder into the main vent. The geyser was unable to dislodge it, so the activity shifted to a second nearby vent. Now the eruptions are almost constant, any true pauses lasting no more than a few minutes. The maximum height is 4 feet, a far cry from what it was before.

Note: As is the case with the Porcelain Basin, a great many other geysers have been observed in the Back Basin area. Most of these have been very temporary in their existence; the vast majority have also been of small size. Therefore, very few of these geysers have ever been named, even informally.

Among the geysers of the Back Basin, perhaps two are worth special mention. Pebble Geyser (at "Y" on Map X) was a large, well-known geyser in the first fifty years of Park history. It stopped playing during the 1920s, and nobody is now certain as to just which vent it played from. In the southwestern portion of the Back Basin are the Hydrophane Springs (at "Z"). This is a very active area, where three or four small geysers have been active within the last few years. Some of the play has reached 10 feet high, but it is ephemeral.

Also to be noted is the area called the One-Hundred Springs Plain. This is the northwestern portion of the Norris Geyser Basin. Not accessible by any trail and, because of the great number of hot spring vents, a dangerous area to explore, it is the site of a few small geysers.

Table 26. Geysers of the Back Basin

Name and Number	Interval*	Duration	Height (ft)
Arch Steam Vent (40)	rare	unrecorded	30–40
Bathtub Spring (34)	steady	steady	3
Big Alcove Spring (44)	1–5 sec	2–10 sec	6–25
Blue Mud Spring (46)	steady	steady	1–10
Cistern Spring (37)	rare	minutes	10–20
Corporal Geyser (55)	20 min–rare	2–4 min	1
Crater Spring (39)**	rare	minutes	10–20
Dabble Geyser (49)**	disturbance	2–9 min	8
Double Bulger (50)	steady	steady	2–3
Echinus Geyser (38)**	20–80 min	3–70 min	60–125
Emerald Spring (35)**	rare	hours	2–75
Fearless Geyser (59)	steady	steady	boil
Medusa Spring (45)**	irregular	1–15 min	2–12
Minute Geyser (62)	steady	steady	4
Monarch Geyser (61)	dead?	5–10 min	100–200
Mud Pool (42)**	40–60 min	12–20 min	1–30
Orbicular Geyser (48)**	sec–min	sec–10 min	3–6
Palpitator Spring (58)	4–9 hrs	2–5 hrs	3
Pearl Geyser (51)	sec–min	seconds	1–8
Porkchop Geyser (52)	irregular	45–90 min	15–30
Puff-N-Stuff Geyser (43)	steady	steady	1–3
Rubble Geyser (54)	rare	6 min	5–10

Table 26. Continued

Name and Number	Interval*	Duration	Height (ft)
Steamboat Geyser (36):			
minor	frequent	seconds	20–100
major	rare	hours	250–386
Steamvalve Spring (33)**	4–5 hrs	12–15 min	8–12
Tantalus Geyser (41)**	rare	minutes	2–35
UNNG-NBK-1 (47)	steady	steady	2
UNNG-NBK-2 ("Dog's Leg") (56)**	infrequent	min–hrs	1–3
UNNG-NBK-3 (60)	steady	steady	1–6
Veteran Geyser (29)	15 min–3 hrs	10 sec–2½ min	25–40
Vixen Geyser (53)	sec–min	sec–1 hr	10–35

*Under Interval, "disturbance" indicates geysers active essentially only at the time of a disturbance.

**Indicates geysers that show more frequent and/or more powerful activity at the time of a disturbance.

Chapter 8

West Thumb Geyser Basin

The West Thumb Geyser Basin (Map Y, Table 27) is one of the smallest such areas in Yellowstone, just about matching the Lone Star Geyser Basin (Chapter 10) in size. The major portion of its thermal activity occurs within an area less than 1,000 feet long. The basin skirts the shore of the West Thumb of Lake Yellowstone and extends inland only a few hundred feet from the water.

Compared to the other areas of clear, alkaline water, the activity at West Thumb is limited and generally weak. Only about half a dozen geysers have ever been observed within the basin proper. The three geysers currently of greatest import are to the north, near one another within a very narrow tract of thermal ground squeezed between the lake and the highway. Even farther to the north is the Potts Hot Spring Basin, in which there are several small geysers.

West Thumb is, perhaps, better known for its hot pools. Some of these are among the largest in Yellowstone. The beautiful colors of Abyss and Black Pools ("X" and "Y" on Map Y) would be notable anywhere in the Park. Here, too, are the Thumb Paint Pots ("Z"). Well-known in the early days of the Park because of their variety of pastel colors, these mud pots are far less active than they used to be. Within the limited depression are a few low gray mud cones and not much else.

For reasons that are anything but clear, the main portion of the West Thumb Geyser Basin underwent a sudden and drastic decline in water levels during the 1970s. Activity abruptly declined so that, in fact, there is very little actual geyser action there.

The West Thumb Geyser Basin is serviced by a boardwalk system. Also in the immediate area are a store and a photo shop, although these facilities are slated to be removed shortly. The

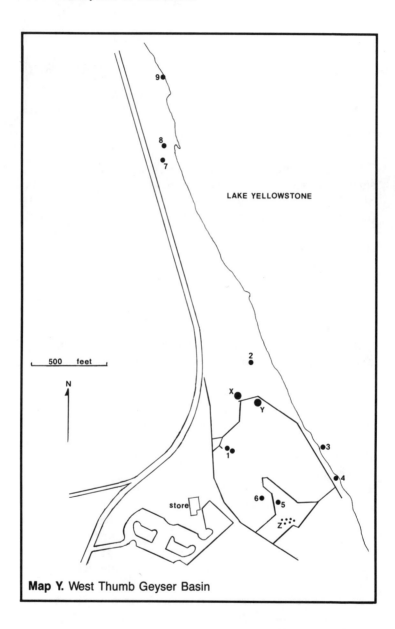

Map Y. West Thumb Geyser Basin

LAKE YELLOWSTONE

500 feet

N

store

areas to the north, outside of the basin itself, are not accessible but are sometimes visited during ranger-led walking tours.

1. **TWIN GEYSER** is the largest and most spectacular geyser at West Thumb. During most of its history, however, it has been dormant. When in such a state the water constantly boils in the crater nearest the boardwalk overlook. The farther of the two basins is active only just before and during a major eruption. The first recorded activity in Twin was during 1933, when a single eruption 30 feet high was reported. The next activity came during 1949. In that year there were infrequent eruptions, but the play reached over 100 feet high. Then Twin was dormant again until 1971, when it began its best active episode.

The renewed activity was typically about 60 feet high, but a number of eruptions exceeded 100 feet and a few were estimated at fully 120 feet. The geyser became known as "Maggie and Jiggs" after the cartoon characters. First one crater would erupt, and as its water jet reached 50 feet the other would begin spouting. The two columns converged far above the ground and, just as Maggie often ended the great plans of Jiggs, the second column would take over the eruption, reaching the maximum height as the other rapidly died to only a few feet high.

During 1971 the eruptions recurred every 4 to 8 hours. For a few weeks they were regular enough to be predicted. The activity lasted from 3 to 4 minutes. Since then Twin has largely been dormant.

2. **KING GEYSER** erupts from a pool at the far northern end of the main basin. Deep and clear, it is a very pretty spring, but not much of a geyser. Eruptions have always been rare, with none recorded during most seasons. When King does erupt the play reaches 6 feet high and lasts around 10 minutes.

3. **FISHING CONE** is one of the most famous hot springs in Yellowstone. As the story goes, it was possible to stand on the cone while fishing in the lake; then the catch could be cooked in the boiling hot spring without having to be removed from the hook. Sometimes this could actually be done, but Fishing Cone is usually too cool to cook in. The cone itself is completely surrounded by lake water except at times of extremely low water

Twin Geyser, though seldom active, is the most important geyser in the small West Thumb Basin. (Photo courtesy of R. B. Dent, with permission.)

levels. During the 1920s and 1930s, eruptions were common at Fishing Cone, the play reaching 3 feet high. None have been seen for many years.

4. LAKESHORE GEYSER has a cone much like that of Fishing Cone. It sits within the lake, too, but unlike Fishing Cone its vent is usually covered by water. It can erupt only when the vent is high and dry. Even then Lakeshore is nearly always dormant. When in an active phase it erupts every 30 to 60 minutes. The play usually lasts about 10 minutes, reaching 25 feet high.

5. LEDGE SPRING is one of those in the middle portion of West Thumb that has suffered a water level drop. Accordingly, it is nearly inactive. On rare occasions, Ledge Spring does erupt. The play is a massive bursting, only 3 feet high but involving a large volume of water, accompanied by heavy discharge.

6. THUMB GEYSER is now totally inactive, as it has been covered by the cool runoff from other springs. When active, though, it can be an impressive geyser. It has always been erratic in its performance, even when at its best, but Thumb has been seen to play more than 10 feet high in eruptions lasting several minutes.

7. OCCASIONAL GEYSER is the first of those outside the main West Thumb Geyser Basin proper, being near the lakeshore about ½ mile to the north. In spite of its name, Occasional is a frequently and regularly active geyser. During most years the eruptions recur every 30 minutes or so. Lasting 4 to 5 minutes, its height is about 10 feet. The crater of Occasional sits atop a high sinter platform, and the runoff goes only a few feet before plunging directly over a fall into the lake waters.

8. LONE PINE GEYSER is now the largest active geyser in the West Thumb area. It received its name in 1974, the year of its first recorded activity. The crater lies near a small peninsula of sinter that extends into the lake; this land projection is decorated by a single, small pine tree. The first activity consisted of eruptions recurring every 20 minutes or so. The duration was 5 minutes and the height was 25 feet. As time progressed the eruptions came less frequently, but they also grew in strength. Since the early 1980s there has been little further change in the action. Intervals are longer than a day—usually about 29 hours and highly regular. The play still lasts 5 minutes but may reach more than 75 feet high. A few minutes following the major eruption will be a minor play lasting a few seconds and reaching perhaps 40 feet high. Following that comes another, and so on. At times there will be as many as five such follow-up minor eruptions before Lone Pine falls silent and begins to refill. Slight overflow occurs for several hours before an eruption.

9. OVERHANGING GEYSER is so named because erosion caused by waves on Lake Yellowstone has undercut the crater so that it is actually perched out *over* the water. It must be a miracle that the erosion did not tap into the plumbing system. The activity of Overhanging is quite variable from one year to the next, but rather regular at any given time. Intervals range from 2 to several hours. The eruption usually lasts about 3 minutes, bursting water 6 feet high.

THE POTTS HOT SPRINGS BASIN is an area of several hundred individual hot springs visible below the highway roughly 1 mile north of Thumb Junction. Whether this is really the thermal area written about by Daniel T. Potts in 1827 is uncertain. It is only within the 1980s that an understanding of the true nature of activity here has been gained. The overall activity seems to be cyclic, with all geysers being affected in similar ways. At times as many as fifteen geysers are active, some of the eruptions reaching more than 10 feet high. On other occasions it is difficult to find more than two or three geysers a foot tall. Some additional springs show evidence of being the sources of even more powerful eruptions, but none of those has ever been recorded. It seems amazing that so little should be known about such a visible area, and Potts is probably of greater importance than the developed, main portion of West Thumb. Its fifteen geysers are, in fact, more than all those ever observed in the rest of West Thumb, or in the Gibbon and Lone Star Geyser Basins.

Table 27. Geysers of the West Thumb Geyser Basin

Name and Number	Interval	Duration	Height (ft)
Fishing Cone (3)	rare	hours	3
King Geyser (2)	rare	10 min	6
Lakeshore Geyser (4)	rare	10 min	25
Ledge Spring (5)	infrequent	1 min	2–3
Lone Pine Geyser (8)	24–36 hrs	5 min	20–75
Occasional Geyser (7)	25–40 min	4–5 min	10–25
Overhanging Geyser (9)	2–12 hrs	2–5 min	6
Thumb Geyser (6)	irregular	minutes	1–10
Twin Geyser (1)	rare	3–4 min	60–120

Chapter 9

Gibbon Geyser Basin

Between the Norris Geyser Basin and Madison Junction are many scattered groups of hot springs. The greatest number of these are in and about the grassy fields of Gibbon Meadows, about 5 miles south of Norris Junction. This is the Gibbon Geyser Basin (Map Z, Table 28). For various reasons, these hot springs contain elements of interest even though geysers are few.

The Gibbon Geyser Basin includes all of the hot spring clusters that lie around the perimeter of Gibbon Meadows. True geysers are confined to three of the five important groups. A fourth area has probably included some in the past and may again in the future; meanwhile, it does contain some spouting springs (not true geysers). The last group will never hold any geysers, but it is described here because it lies immediately next to the road where relatively cool springs are forming some unique deposits.

The main highway runs through the middle of the Gibbon Basin. Trails proceed to the hot spring areas, although some of them are old and no longer maintained.

Artists Paint Pots Group

The Artists Paint Pots are probably the best-known features of the Gibbon Geyser Basin. The trail to them is well marked, heading east from the highway at the south end of Gibbon Meadows. The path is very well maintained and incorporates some boardwalks where it passes among the hot springs. The round trip to the area is about 1 mile.

The group was named for the numerous bright colors that characterize the springs. Most predominant are oranges and reds created by iron oxide minerals. Clay minerals form pastel pinks and blue-grays, while hot water algae add other oranges plus

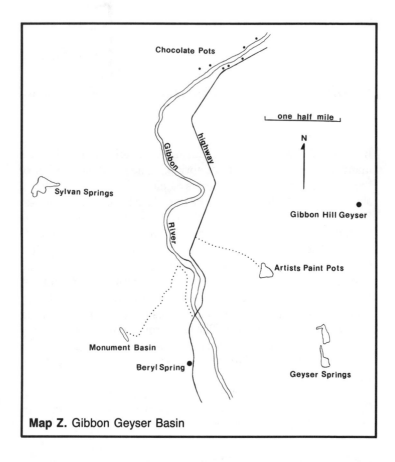

Map Z. Gibbon Geyser Basin

browns and greens. Add to these the usual blues of the pools and the greens of the forest and the overall effect is striking. The scene is one of the most colorful in Yellowstone.

The Artists Paint Pots themselves are located up the hillside, somewhat separated from the other hot springs. Although restricted to just two basins, they tend to be very active. At times the gray mud is tossed as much as 20 feet high. Despite their proximity to one another, the two sets of mud pots are always of different thicknesses.

The clear water springs, including two geysers, are located at the base of Paint Pot Hill. Several other springs in the area appear to be geysers but aren't. Their spouting is due to both steam and carbon dioxide, but the water temperatures are below boiling.

1. UNNG-GIB-1. Playing from a shallow basin at the far east end of the Artists Paint Pots Group is a perpetual spouter. Since its activity was first described in 1926 its spouting has never been known to cease. The maximum height is about 6 feet. The water discharge of this one spring amounts to at least 150 gallons per minute, about half that of the entire group. The small alcove surrounding the spring is highly colored by iron oxides and, in fact, the water contains a far greater than normal concentration of iron in solution. A sample, allowed to cool and sit quietly, will develop a precipitate of reddish iron oxide within a few minutes; the only other Yellowstone spring water known to do this comes from the Chocolate Pots, elsewhere in the Gibbon Basin.

2. UNNG-GIB-2 is located about 25 feet to the right (west) of GIB-1. A true geyser, its activity is difficult to see from the trail, so look closely – but stay on the trail. The vent of the geyser is nothing more than a crack in a large rhyolite boulder. A small pool at the base of the rock constantly pulsates and splashes a few inches high. The activity is irregular, but every few minutes a brief squirting rises from the crack, reaching as much as 4 feet high.

Geyser Creek and Gibbon Hill Groups

The Artists Paint Pots trail ends at that group, and signs there admonish the visitor to go no farther. Doing so can therefore be a bit tricky. What appears to be a good trail beyond the signs rapidly deteriorates to nothing. The path used to continue through the forest – traces of it in the form of cut logs still show in places – extending ½ mile around the hill to the Geyser Creek Group. The walk now involves some bushwacking but is well worth the effort.

The Geyser Creek Group is the site of the most vigorous geyser activity in the Gibbon Basin. This is an extremely dangerous area. Perhaps no place in Yellowstone contains more

This "monument" is typical of the geyserite cones in the Monument Geyser Basin, one of the several hot spring groups in the Gibbon Basin.

fragile crust areas, and the temperatures are very high. Any exploration of the area should be confined to the hillsides. The Geyser Creek area is naturally divided into two sections. First is an open valley in which most of the larger springs are found. Farther upstream, and separated from the lower area by a forested ridge, is a smaller area that includes several pools and at least two geysers.

The Gibbon Hill Group is an entirely separate area and the home of Gibbon Hill Geyser, the only geyser within the group. Finding Gibbon Hill Geyser can be very difficult. There never has been a trail to it, and the best guide is the steam cloud that is visible on cool days when the geyser is active. It is located about ½ mile northeast of the Geyser Creek area.

If you decide to visit either of these areas you definitely should notify somebody, preferably the rangers in the Norris area and family members, and then check in after your trip. Again, this is a very dangerous area, and your safety is in your own hands.

3. UNNG-GIB-3 ("ANTHILL" GEYSER) is among the first hot springs encountered when entering the lower portion of the Geyser Creek Group. It erupts from a complex of vents next to Geyser Creek, dominated by a small symmetrical geyserite cone that looks something like an anthill. This is a geyser of considerable regularity. Although the intervals can vary from just 1½ to 5 minutes, so do the durations vary in like fashion; the net result is that the period of the geyser (that is, the interval plus the duration) is of little variation, generally ranging from 11 to 13 minutes. The play is a noisy mixture of steam and spray jetted from the cone, sometimes reaching 4 feet high, while an associated pool splashes to about 1 foot.

4. UNNG-GIB-4 was first seen during 1985. Near the only deep blue pool in the lower portion of the area, it was seen to erupt muddy water to about 4 feet. Eruptions lasted only a few seconds.

5. OBLIQUE GEYSER has also been known as Avalanche, Rockpile, Talus, Marvelous, Geyser Greek, and Spray Geyser. Any of the names is applicable, providing good descriptions of the setting and activity. Oblique spouts from not less than seventeen separate vents and the play from each has its own character. The vents open among a pile of boulders that have been covered by a spiny, pale brown sinter.

Oblique is a frequent and highly regular performer, a geyser that would do justice to any geyser basin. Its activity has been remarkably constant over the years. During 1928 the 25-foot eruptions recurred every 6 minutes. In 1974 the average was 7 minutes, 48 seconds with no more than 45 seconds of variation. By 1985 the intervals were about 10 minutes long. Any change in interval is balanced by a change in duration, so that under all known conditions, Oblique has erupted about 25% of the time. The current duration is just about 3 minutes.

The eruption begins with a sudden gush of steam from the two main vents. This is rapidly followed by steam comingled with water and, before many seconds have passed, Oblique is in full eruption. The main jets shoot water at slight angles to 25 or 30 feet high. A third important vent erupts out away from the others at a low angle with the water falling fully 30 feet from the opening. Most of the other vents play only 2 to 5 feet high, but much steam is discharged. Finally, several vents emit only steam under pressure. The display is very impressive, roaring and spraying water in all directions. The end of the eruption is abrupt. The water suddenly gives out and Oblique falls quiet with 2 or 3 dying gasps of steam. Occasional gurgling interrupts the quiet interval.

6. **BIG BOWL GEYSER** is about 150 feet north of Oblique Geyser (5), on the slopes of the eastern side of the valley. Activity in the deep basin is nearly constant. Highly superheated, the water boils continuously, but this is punctuated by truly periodic eruptions. The interval is only around 15 seconds and durations are perhaps 5 seconds. Most of the play is less than 10 feet high, but occasional heavy surges send spray to as much as 30 feet.

7. **UNNG-GIB-5 ("TINY" GEYSER)** is near the center of the dense cluster of springs in the upper portion of the Geyser Creek Group. The geyser is extremely small, but Tiny is a true geyser. The vent is marked by a shallow depression in the geyserite platform and is surrounded by beaded yellowish sinter. Water rises within this hole then sputters a small amount of spray to

a few inches. After about 5 seconds of play, the vent drains. Eruptions recur every 2 to 3 minutes. Because of the many other hot springs in the immediate vicinity, any close approach to Tiny Geyser is hazardous.

8. UNNG-GIB-6 ("BAT" POOL) is a deep blue, superheated spring within the upper area. The boiling is steady but normally rather gentle. On occasion it increases in vigor and bursting action can then throw water to about 3 feet high.

At the base of the hillside next to this spring is a rhyolite boulder that was fractured by its fall from the mountain above. Within this crack is a colony of bats. Take a close look. They'll scurry about, twitter, and glare back at you with beady eyes. Obviously, the crack is not a place for fingers.

9. GIBBON HILL GEYSER plays from a broad, shallow pool. The vent, near the front side, measures 8 inches by 4 inches. When periodic in its action, the crater slowly fills between eruptions. Shortly after the first seeping overflow the filling rate greatly increases, causing a disturbance of the water over the vent. Within several minutes this has built into the full eruption. The 25-foot-high bursts are continuous for the entire 20- to 30-minute duration. The eruption ends without warning and the basin drains. Just as in a kitchen sink, the water forms a whirlpool over the vent as it is sucked below ground. Refilling begins before the crater has completely emptied. At times like these the regular intervals average about 5 hours long. At other times Gibbon Hill Geyser acts like a perpetual spouter. It has not been known to quit during the 1980s. Unfortunately, this play is much weaker, with few bursts more than 6 feet high.

Monument Geyser Basin Group

High on the hill above the south side of Gibbon Meadows, 600 feet above the valley floor, sits the Monument Geyser Basin. It is a long, narrow area of little activity. According to some it extends eastward far enough to include Beryl Spring. Beryl is a crystal clear superheated pool right beside the highway, 1 mile south of the Artists Paint Pots trailhead.

Monument was named for the weird sinter cones that are

scattered along the southwestern margin of the basin. Built up
by geysers with spraying eruptions, they are totally unlike the
cones of other areas. Only one – Thermos Bottle – is still active.
No other spring in the group contains alkaline water. Were it
not for these strange formations, the Monument Basin would
never have attracted much attention.

A 1-mile trail leads to the basin. It begins next to the highway bridge across the Gibbon River, between Beryl Spring and
the Artists Paint Pots trail. The entire 600-foot climb is accom-
plished within the second half-mile. It is a rigorous hike but well
worth the effort. Monument is a unique area, and the view from
the mountain top is terrific.

10. **THERMOS BOTTLE GEYSER**, or Monument Geyser, spouts
from one of the largest cones in the Monument Geyser Basin.
Unlike the others, it has not quite sealed itself off by the internal
accretion of sinter. As it is 10 feet tall, that time is not far off.
During the 1930s Thermos Bottle played most of the time with
fine spray being jetted to 15 feet. Now very little water is ejected,
and it never reaches more than 3 feet high. Otherwise, Thermos
Bottle hisses under slight pressure.

Sylvan Springs Group

Sylvan Springs is the most visible hot spring group in the Gibbon
Geyser Basin. It is the large, barren, steaming area at the far
western end of the meadow. The hot springs are almost entirely
acidic, relatively cool, and often muddy. The only important
springs of the group have undergone frequent drastic changes.
Evening Primrose Spring was once regarded as one of the more
beautiful pools in the Park, and it was probably the one reason
why a maintained trail used to lead here. In shape and color it
was comparable to Morning Glory Pool in the Upper Geyser
Basin. Sometime (just when does not seem to have been recorded) the water changed from alkaline to acidic. The surface
became covered with a thick froth of pure elemental sulfur. Then
during 1972 Evening Primrose was invaded by *sulfolobus,* an
archaeobacteria that directly metabolizes sulfur. Today's pool has
become one of Yellowstone's ugliest. Another important Sylvan

spring is Dante's Inferno. Although it is not a geyser as such, the shocks of the 1959 earthquake caused it to erupt violently to more than 100 feet high. The activity still has not completely died down, as the milky pool churns and boils vigorously while rapidly depositing an extensive geyserite terrace. A number of other springs at Sylvan appear to be perpetual spouters. Their temperatures, however, are below boiling and these are not true geysers.

To reach Sylvan Springs, begin by following the Monument Geyser Basin trail. Where it begins the steep climb up the mountainside, you strike out across Gibbon Meadows. An alternate route begins from the Gibbon River picnic area at the north end of the meadows. Either route tends to be very wet, even late in the summer.

Chocolate Pots

Next to the highway in the small canyon between Gibbon Meadows and Elk Park are the Chocolate Pots. The highest temperature in these small springs is only around 130°F (54°C), but the deposits being formed are unique. Rich red-brown, they are more than 50% iron oxide minerals, 5% aluminum oxide, and 2% manganese oxide; their silica content is only 17%. A sample of the clear water allowed to sit for a few minutes will become cloudy brown as the iron oxide spontaneously precipitates from the water.

Table 28. Geysers of the Gibbon Geyser Basin

Name and Number	Interval	Duration	Height (ft)
Artists Paint Pots Group			
UNNG-GIB-1 (1)	steady	steady	5–6
UNNG-GIB-2 (2)	minutes	seconds	4
Geyser Creek Group			
Big Bowl Geyser (6)	10–15 sec	2–5 sec	10–30
Oblique Geyser (5)	6–11 min	2–3 min	25–30
UNNG-GIB-3 ("Anthill")			
(3)	1½–5 min	7–8 min	4
UNNG-GIB-4 (4)	unrecorded	seconds	4
UNNG-GIB-5 ("Tiny") (7)	2–3 min	seconds	inches

Table 28. Continued

Name and Number	Interval	Duration	Height (ft)
UNNG-GIB-6 ("Bat" Pool) (8)	irregular	seconds	3
Gibbon Hill Group Gibbon Hill Geyser (9)	steady–hrs	steady–20 min	6–25
Monument Geyser Basin Group Thermos Bottle Geyser (10)	steady	steady	3

Chapter 10

Lone Star Geyser Basin

In the early days of Yellowstone National Park most of the attention paid to geysers was in the basins along the Firehole River. The Lone Star Geyser Basin (Map AA, Table 29) is one of these, lying about 5 miles upstream from Old Faithful. The present Upper Geyser Basin was originally known as the Great Geyser Basin; today's Lone Star Basin was the original Upper Basin.

The basin was named for Lone Star Geyser, which was named not after the state, but because of its isolated position. Until 1973 it was believed to be the only geyser in its basin. One of the more obvious benefits of having a larger cadre of geyser gazers has been the increase in knowledge about the Lone Star area. Enough is now known about nine geysers for them to be described in this book.

The Lone Star Geyser Basin naturally divides itself into five parts, only one of which is not known to include any geysers. These groups are located on Map AA, with their informal names. Continuing along the Shoshone Lake trail beyond the Campsite Group takes the hiker into another meadow. There, between the trail and the hillside to the east are several hot pools.

The Lone Star Basin is reached via a wide trail beginning from the main highway near the Kepler Cascades of the Firehole River. An old road, it is mostly paved and recommended as a bike trail. It is about 2½ miles from the highway to Lone Star Geyser; from the geyser it is another mile to the Campsite Group farther along the trail.

Lone Star Group

The Lone Star Group is a compact cluster of hot springs, most of which are acidic, small, and of no importance. Separated slightly from the hillside, though, are three springs of alkaline

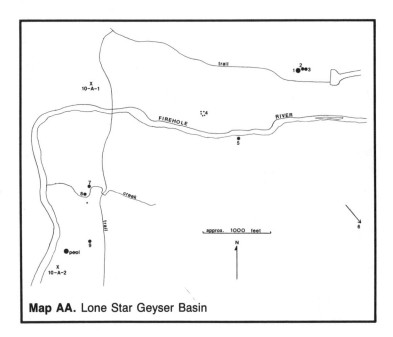

Map AA. Lone Star Geyser Basin

water, each of which is a geyser. The star attraction is, of course, Lone Star Geyser itself. To help the visitor better anticipate when Lone Star might erupt, the National Park Service maintains a logbook. It is hoped that visitors who see Lone Star erupt will write the time into the book. That way later visitors know when it last played and the Park Service is able to garner the data needed for a better understanding of the area.

1. **LONE STAR GEYSER** gained early fame because of its very large geyserite cone. Over 9 feet tall and very steep-sided, it is one of the three biggest cones in Yellowstone (along with Castle Geyser [Upper Basin #48] and White Dome Geyser [Lower Basin #12]). Lone Star erupts from one main and several minor vents at the summit of the cone.

The cone was built to its present height by the frequent splashing of the geyser during its quiet phase. This activity may start within an hour of an eruption. With gradually increasing force, the preplay leads into a minor eruption. Usually Lone Star has just one minor preceding the major eruption; on relatively rare occasions there may be a second and even a third minor,

Lone Star Geyser is the only important geyser in the Lone Star Basin, the smallest geyser basin in Yellowstone, yet its cone is one of the Park's largest.

each followed by a few minutes of quiet. The usual single minor play lasts about 5 minutes and reaches as high as 45 feet. After a rest of 25 to 35 minutes, renewed splashing builds into the full, major eruption. It too jets water to 45 feet, but the eruption lasts fully 30 minutes. In the waning stages the water gives out and the final part of the play is a powerful steam phase. Lone Star is a very regular geyser. The interval between major eruptions is always very close to 3 hours exactly. No dormant period has ever been recorded.

2. UNNG-LST-1 ("BLACK HOLE" GEYSER) is just a few feet from the base of Lone Star's cone. Its vent is a symmetrical funnel penetrating the geyserite of a broad mound that predates the modern activity of the area. The geyser was never observed to erupt prior to 1973. Early that year it played every few minutes for 3 to 4 minutes and reached 15 feet high. By the end of that summer it had grown more erratic, with activity that seemed to be related to the build-up of pressure within Lone Star. These eruptions lasted more than 15 minutes and were 25 feet high. Since 1973, Black Hole has been very erratic. It will spend long hours gently bubbling and overflowing, looking like it should erupt at any moment, only to abruptly drain. Eruptions are usually unheralded.

3. UNNG-LST-2 is located within a geyserite mound directly on the opposite side of LST-1 (2) from Lone Star (1). The mound is perforated by numerous small holes. Eruptions are rather infrequent and consist of nothing more than minor sputtering out of the holes. For that reason, the geyser is variously known as "Perforated Cone" and "Sputtering Mound" Geyser.

"Channel" Group

Along both banks of the Firehole River, roughly ¼ mile upstream from Lone Star Geyser, are numerous hot springs. The majority are on the south side of the river. With few exceptions, all are small and of little importance, but some small geysers are included.

4. UNNG-LST-3 is an assortment of small springs surrounded by meadow on the north side of the river. These are clearly related to one another as they are all active at the same time. Several of the vents are tiny but very symmetrical geyserite cones. The largest spring is only about 3 feet in diameter. On infrequent occasions, these springs are known to erupt, with some of the play reaching 2 or 3 feet high.

5. UNNG-LST-4 is across the river and slightly downstream from LST-3 (4). A small pool only a few inches above the stream level constantly surges and bubbles. Its eruptive activity may be cyclic, as it is often seen to play with short intervals but sometimes also goes for long periods without activity. The eruptions, when they do occur, last only a few seconds, sending splashes 1 foot high.

"Bassett" Group

The origin of this group name seems to be unknown, but it has been used in reports dating since the mid-1970s. Well separated from the rest of the Lone Star Basin springs, the group is easiest to first locate from Lone Star Geyser, where the steam of the one geyser can be seen, and then hike in that direction. Access is either via fording the Firehole River at Lone Star, or by crossing on the footbridge about ½ mile upstream and backtracking. The geyser is the first hot spring encountered in this group. Just beyond it, over a low ridge, are several additional small springs, and at the summit of the steep slope above them is a fine mudpot.

6. BURIED GEYSER is probably a more significant geyser than is Lone Star Geyser. Although not as high, its eruptions are frequent, powerful, and with great water discharge. Buried was so named because its crater was once partially covered by a sinter ledge; that is now virtually gone, removed by the bursting activity of the past decade. Buried Geyser has both minor and major eruptions. Long intervals are caused by long durations, which are the major eruptions. About ⅔ of the eruptions are minors. Their duration is about 3½ minutes, followed by intervals of 7 to 9 minutes. Minor eruptions may have some bursts as much as 15 feet high, but there is little runoff from the area. Major eruptions have durations of 4 to 5 minutes involving bursts 15 to 25 feet high. It is a violent spectacle. The interval following a major eruption ranges from 13 to 15 minutes and always results in a minor eruption. There is no clear relationship between the two types of eruption, except that consecutive majors have never been observed.

"Campsite" Group

About 1 mile from Lone Star Geyser via the Shoshone Lake trail is the Campsite Group, located immediately north of backcountry campsite 10-A-2. This is an extensive group of hot springs. Most are small and many are muddy, but the area also includes one large blue pool and at least three geysers.

7. UNNG-LST-5 plays from a shallow crater lined with spiny, yellowish geyserite; it is just downstream along a small creek crossed by a low bridge. Eruptions by this geyser are not more than 1 foot high and their duration has not been recorded; the intervals are several hours long.

8. UNNG-LST-6 is nearly identical to LST-5 (7) and only a few feet farther down the small stream. As with LST-5, the intervals of several hours lead to eruptions about 1 foot high; again, the duration has not been recorded but it may also be hours long. Just across the creek from this geyser is a muddy pool with an intriguing red-orange color.

9. UNNG-LST-7 is, by size at least, the most important geyser in the Campsite Group. Its eruptions are infrequent. The plays that have been observed all lasted about 10 minutes and reached 3 feet high.

Table 29. Geysers of the Lone Star Geyser Basin

Name and Number	Interval	Duration	Height (ft)
Buried Geyser (6)	7–15 min	3–5 min	8–25
Lone Star Geyser (1)	2½–3½ hrs	5–30 min	45
UNNG-LST-1 ("Black Hole") (2)	erratic	3–15 min	3–25
UNNG-LST-2 (3)	unrecorded	minutes	inches
UNNG-LST-3 (4)	irregular	sec–min	2–3
UNNG-LST-4 (5)	minutes	seconds	1
UNNG-LST-5 (7)	hours	unrecorded	1
UNNG-LST-6 (8)	hours	hours?	1
UNNG-LST-7 (9)	infrequent	10 min	3

Chapter 11

Shoshone Geyser Basin

The Shoshone Geyser Basin (Map BB) is one of the most important thermal areas in the world, even though it measures only 1,600 by 800 feet. The basin probably includes seventy geysers. Many of them are infrequent performers, however, and since the Shoshone Basin is a remote area, essentially nothing is known about them. Accordingly, only thirty-five of the geysers are being described here. Much of the spouting at Shoshone is of considerable size, and one geyser – Union – is of truly major proportions.

The Shoshone Geyser Basin resembles in general the Upper Basin. The hot springs form compact, closely-spaced groups along the course of Shoshone Creek. But Shoshone has its own special attributes, too. The deposits are often brightly colored by iron oxide minerals, and small amounts of arsenic sulfides spot the ground in a few places. Both of these features are rarely found in the other major alkaline basins.

The first written description that can be ascribed to a particular geyser was written by trapper Osborne Russell in 1839. Calling it "Hour Spring" because of its regular activity, he was probably describing Minute Man Geyser; though it must have changed the character of its action in the years since then, Minute Man still plays with a high degree of regularity. During the 1870s the Shoshone Basin was no more remote than any other area of Yellowstone, and it was extensively studied by the early scientific surveys. Most of the recognized names were given to the springs during the 1870s. From that time on no detailed studies or maps were made of the area until the late 1960s and since. The Heart Lake Geyser Basin (Chapter 12) is the only other geyser basin in Yellowstone that has been as ignored over the years. It is likely that geyser activity is even more extensive than that recognized here.

The Shoshone Basin is most easily reached by way of the

same trail that passes Lone Star Geyser (see Chapter 10). The total distance from the highway at Kepler Cascades is about 8½ miles, one way. The entire route is well maintained and generally easy. The basin can also be reached via other, longer trails that lead in from the east, and by canoe over Shoshone Lake.

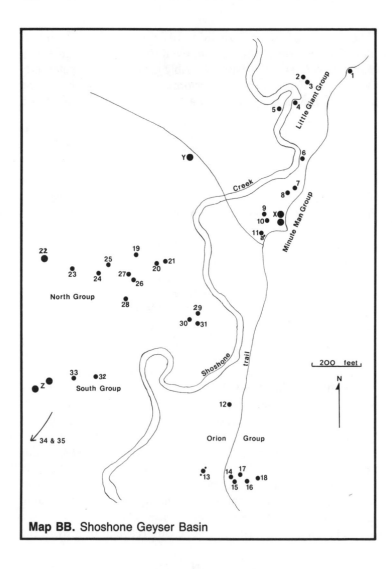

Map BB. Shoshone Geyser Basin

Shoshone is virtually untouched. It is easy to imagine yourself as the first person ever to see these geysers. When in the area please do everything you can to avoid damaging any of the springs and geysers or their deposits. And, as always, remember the dangers of the thermal basins; a thermal burn would be a severe injury in a place as remote as this.

Little Giant-Minute Man Group

The Little Giant-Minute Man Group (Table 30) includes the most intense geyser activity at Shoshone. Little Giant Geyser is the second largest geyser in the basin, though it rarely plays now. Minute Man Geyser is overall the most reliable and most frequent performer, and it also must be considered a major spouter. These and the numerous other springs and geysers of the group are scattered along a 600-foot stretch of ground, all lying very close to Shoshone Creek.

1. **TRAILSIDE GEYSER** is the northernmost at Shoshone, immediately left of the trail as you enter the basin. The trail here is a bridge-like affair made of cut logs. Only constructed during the late 1970s, it wasn't necessary before; geyser activity by Trailside is a recent development, never noted before the 1970s. The geyserite of the shallow crater is lightly stained by iron oxides. During the quiet intervals, which range from 10 to 16 minutes in length, the crater is about half full of water. Eruptions begin with a sudden filling of the crater. Water is splashed from 1 to 5 feet high. The duration is very regular at 30 to 40 seconds.

At the base of the slope just behind Trailside is another geyser, first seen to play in 1981. Its eruption is little more than intermittent superheated boiling, recurring every several minutes.

2. **LITTLE GIANT GEYSER** plays from a heavily iron-stained vent in the middle of a round sinter platform. In the early days of Yellowstone it was a significant geyser, with spouts as much as 50 feet high. Nothing of that sort has been observed during this century. The little bit that Little Giant does now is directly associated with eruptions by Double Geyser (3), just a few feet

away. When Double is erupting, Little Giant splashes erratically, the biggest bursts reaching about 4 feet above the rim.

3. DOUBLE GEYSER jets two columns of water into the air; although there is actually only one vent, above it is a piece of geyserite containing two holes, which split the stream. It has also been known as "The Pirates" because of the certainty that it is the cause of Little Giant Geyser's (2) weak activity. Double Geyser is a very regular performer. For years now its intervals, which range from 52 to 76 minutes, have averaged almost exactly 1 hour. The play begins with a progressively more vigorous welling of water out of the vents. It takes several minutes to build to the full height. Of the twin jets, the vertical one is the highest, reaching about 10 feet; the other shoots at an angle and is 6 feet high. The duration is 10 to 15 minutes.

4. MEANDER GEYSER erupts from a small cone at the foot of a large meander in Shoshone Creek. When first noticed in the 1970s, it behaved as a perpetual spouter just 2 feet high. Since then it has acted as a true geyser. Some of the irregular eruptions, which last 12 to 30 minutes, reach 4 feet high. Intervals are typically hours in length.

Of nearly as much interest as Meander itself are two independent vents nearby. One is a small steam vent in Meander's geyserite shoulder; when Meander is active this vent is periodically drowned, and it then sputters its own fan about 1 foot high with great commotion. The second vent is at the stream's edge so that a periodic withdrawal of water causes a loud gurgling.

5. LOCOMOTIVE GEYSER was originally described in 1947 when its water jet was periodically cut off by a puff of steam. The resulting sound resembled that of a steam locomotive. The action shown by Locomotive has changed considerably since then, but there is still a pulsating action to the eruptions. These occur very irregularly. Over the years, intervals have been known to range from as little as 4 hours to more than 24 hours. Lasting as long as 2 hours, the slender water jet squirts to as much as 15 feet high. Every few seconds there is a brief pause to the play, but the eruption never stops completely until the entire active period has ended; then it quits abruptly, with absolutely no warning. The vent and surrounding sinter platform at

Locomotive Geyser is typical of the small but vigorously active geysers in the Shoshone Basin.

Locomotive are colored a very dark gray, possibly due to the presence of manganese oxide minerals.

6. BLACK SULPHUR SPRING erupts from a vent within the steep sinter embankment above Shoshone Creek, so that the water falls directly into the stream. Black Sulphur is a perpetual spouter, the water being jetted about 6 feet outward at a 45-degree angle. The vent is black, probably due to manganese oxides incorporated into the geyserite.

7. SOAP KETTLE is a superheated spring within a massive sinter cone near the trail that in some years exhibits geyser activity. Soap Kettle tends to be highly regular when active, with intervals in the range of 9 to 21 minutes. During the 1980s it had occasional powerful eruptions. Accompanying bursts up to 8 feet high was enough runoff to cause substantial erosion in the surroundings, including the trail. These major eruptions might be the cause of the near dormancy in nearby Little Bulger Geyser (8); whenever Little Bulger has been frequent and regular, Soap Kettle has been weak or dormant.

8. LITTLE BULGER GEYSER met its partial demise in the early 1980s. At about the time that Soap Kettle began having frequent and strong eruptions, a subsidiary vent at the edge of Little Bulger's crater began weak eruptions of its own. No eruptions by Little Bulger were seen for a few years. Starting in 1986, although the parasitic vent was still active, Little Bulger often played just when an eruption in Soap Kettle began to decline. Though still irregular, by 1989 Little Bulger had improved so that its bursts of 8 to 10 feet about matched those seen before 1980, when the regular action recurred every 10 to 13 minutes.

Immediately south of the rock outcrop next to Little Bulger is Rosette Spring (at "X" on Map BB). Famous during the early days of Yellowstone because of its delicate sea-green color, it has only recently been recognized as being an intermittent spring and, possibly, a small geyser.

9. GOURD SPRING is the first of the three members of the Minute Man Complex. Its squat sinter cone is occupied by a crudely gourd-shaped crater; the massive geyserite is also punctured by numerous minor vents. Like nearby Shield Geyser (10),

Gourd is cyclic in its action. The intervals between active phases range from a few minutes to several hours, the length being dependent on the previous duration. When active, the play is almost continuous splashing 2 to 3 feet high.

10. SHIELD GEYSER erupts from a somewhat squarish cone a few feet from Gourd Spring (9). It is also cyclic, but there is no absolute relationship between Shield's and Gourd's active periods. Shield will erupt only when its crater is full of water. Usually, that means that Gourd is also full and playing, but not always. Also, on those occasions when Gourd goes several hours between active phases, Shield will often undergo independent, albeit short, active periods of its own. Usually, however, the springs do fill, erupt, and drain together. Shield's splashing play reaches 10 feet high.

11. MINUTE MAN GEYSER is probably the feature called "Hour Spring" by Osborne Russell way back in 1839. It erupts from a prominent cone 5 feet high and 12 feet long. Most of this sinter is exquisitely beaded, unlike any other formation that can be seen at close hand elsewhere in Yellowstone. Minute Man, like the other geysers in the complex, is cyclic, but these cycles bear no relationship to those of Gourd (9) and Shield (10).

During active periods Minute Man jets water every 1 to 3 minutes, roughly, with the longer intervals exclusively near the end of an active episode. The play lasts just a few seconds. The heights range from near 40 feet at the beginning of an active period to as little as 10 feet. Overall, the active episodes are usually considerably longer than the quiet ones, and the length of the entire cyclic period involves several hours.

11a. MINUTE MAN'S POOL. During the 1870s the pool between Minute Man's cone and the hill was reported to "sometimes spout." Such activity was not seen again until 1974. These eruptions, 2 to 4 feet high, would occur several times during each of Minute Man's active periods. Then, beginning in 1975 and increasing in frequency and power through 1977, the pool began exhibiting unprecedented major action. The eruptions were so strong and persistent that they became the major part of Minute Man's activity; indeed, at times Minute Man itself was practically dormant. During an active period the bursts would recur as often as every 6 minutes. They were brief, usually lasting less than 20 seconds, but throughout the play jets of water were propelled as high as 50 feet; certainly every eruption included bursts of 35 feet, and some were reported to have exceeded 75 feet. The explosions were loud enough to be heard throughout Shoshone Basin. These eruptions took out a section of the trail through the basin, washed away some of the hillside, and considerably widened Minute Man's runoff channel. All this makes it likely that such eruptions have been rare in the past. Unfortunately, this activity came to an end during 1978, and the pool seldom even bubbles now.

Table 30. Geysers of the Little Giant-Minute Man Group

Name and Number	Interval	Duration	Height (ft)
Black Sulphur Spring (6)	steady	steady	6
Double Geyser (3)	52–76 min	10–15 min	10
Gourd Spring (9)	min–hrs	15–70 min	2–4
Little Bulger Geyser (8)	8–10 min	3–5 min	1–3
Little Giant Geyser (2)	52–76 min	seconds	3–4
Locomotive Geyser (5)	4–24 hrs	45–120 min	6–15
Meander Geyser (4)	hours	12 min	1–3
Minute Man Geyser (11)	40 sec–3 min	2–8 sec	10–40
Minute Man's Pool (11a)	rare	10–30 sec	35–75
Shield Geyser (10)	min–hrs	15–70 min	2–10
Soap Kettle (7)	9–21 min	1–3½ min	4–6
Trailside Geyser (1)	10–16 min	30–40 sec	1–5

Orion Group

The Orion Group (Table 31) contains seven geysers of note and numerous other hot springs. Union Geyser is the largest of all the geysers at Shoshone, although it has unfortunately been dormant for most of its known history. The Orion Group is an area subject to drastic changes in activity. For reasons that are entirely unclear, the group underwent a severe decline in water levels during the late 1970s, and since then there has been little activity in the area. The Orion Group is reached via the old trail leading south from Minute Man Geyser.

12. TAURUS SPRING is a small but very deep pool located just where the basin begins to open out into the Orion Group. Superheated, Taurus boils constantly and vigorously, and this is usually the only activity observed. On rare occasions Taurus does have regular, bursting eruptions when water is sprayed as much as 4 feet high. These are most often seen when Union Geyser (13) is in actual eruption and may indicate a connection between the two.

13. UNION GEYSER is a spouter of the first rank. Unfortunately, it alternates between periods of extreme activity and others of very little. The latter are by far the more common, and Union may go many years without erupting at all. The last active phase was during the mid-1970s.

Union erupts from three distinct geyserite cones. About 4 feet tall, the center cone is the largest and shoots the highest water jet. When Union is active, during the quiet period all three cones are nearly full of water. On occasion an increase in the superheated boiling will splash some water out of the cones. An eruption begins with a series of heavy surges. Once triggered, the water column rapidly climbs to its maximum height. The jet from the central cone will be over 100 feet high, and its play will last with diminishing power for about 12 minutes. The northern, second largest cone begins spouting shortly after the largest. It plays its own water jet to over 60 feet. Longest lasting of the three cones, it persists for over 20 minutes. The southern, smallest cone shoots a double stream of water to about 30 feet, but only briefly. As each jet gives out a steam phase takes over, and when the third spout dies the entire eruption briefly becomes violent. The roar can be heard throughout the Shoshone Basin. The entire eruption, including the steam phase, lasts over an hour.

Union's active periods are separated by about 5 days of inactivity. Once an active phase begins, there will usually be three, but sometimes four or only two, eruptions in the next few hours. The second normally follows the first by about 3 hours; the next interval is about 7 hours. All of the eruptions are of equal force, but each in succession is of shorter total duration.

When Union is inactive for long periods the water level remains well below overflow. It is always superheated, so the inactive periods are apparently due to an exchange of function that draws water volume away from Union. Where it goes is unknown; many other springs in the area are similarly affected at the same time as Union, and a correspondingly significant increase in activity is nowhere to be seen. These dormant periods have been known to last for several decades. Sad to say, Union's activity of the 1970s is apt to have been the last for a long time to come.

14. UNNG-SHO-1 ("SEA GREEN" POOL) was observed as an active geyser only during 1976, at a time when Union was in active eruption. The eruptions lasted only a few seconds but recurred as often as every 2 or 3 minutes. The height was about 10 feet. It is interesting to note that this was the first recorded active period for this geyser and that since 1976 it has never been known to fill as it had before. What had been a beautifully beaded geyserite crater is now severely weathered.

15. WHITE HOT SPRING has a cavernous vent that opens out into a broad shallow pool. Records of its geyser activity date to some of the earliest years of Yellowstone, but apparently at no time was it ever a frequent and regular performer. During the last active episode of Union Geyser (13), White Hot erupted quite often for long durations. The water burst out of the vent, reaching about 2 feet high. Like UNNG-SHO-1 (14), White Hot has remained at a very low level since the late 1970s.

16. UNNG-SHO-2 ("FIFTY" GEYSER) was located just a few feet east of the crater of White Hot Spring (15). First observed during the early 1970s, when its interval was very regular at 50 minutes, it actually proved to be an irregular performer. However, whatever the interval, the eruptions always lasted 5 minutes, spraying water to about 2 feet. With declining frequency through the 1970s, Fifty entered dormancy by 1980 and its site is now difficult to find.

17. UNNG-SHO-3 was active for a short while during the late 1970s. The eruptions came from a symmetrical vent at the apex of a triangle formed with White Hot Spring (15) and Fifty Geyser (16). Few details about the eruptions of SHO-3 are known. The play reached 4 feet high.

18. UNNG-SHO-4 might be one recipient of the energy lost by other members of the Orion Group. Prior to the first known activity during 1978, the site was a depression sometimes containing a bit of tepid water. Now there is a large crater lined with spiny geyserite. It is clear that the crater had been buried by erosion during a very long dormancy and that it has simply been reopened by the current activity. The geyser plays muddy water. It is always regular in its performances, with intervals that range between 15 and 30 minutes. The play lasts around 2 minutes, sending bursts as much as 12 feet high.

Table 31. Geysers of the Orion Group

Name and Number	Interval	Duration	Height (ft)
Taurus Spring (12)	rare	seconds	4
Union Geyser (13)	hrs–yrs	40–60 min	100–125
UNNG-SHO-1 ("Sea Green") (14)	rare	seconds	10
UNNG-SHO-2 ("Fifty") (16)	irregular	5 min	1–2
UNNG-SHO-3 (17)	unrecorded	unrecorded	4
UNNG-SHO-4 (18)	15–30 min	2 min	12
White Hot Spring (15)	irregular	minutes	2

North and South Groups

The springs and geysers on the west side of Shoshone Creek were separated into these two groups by the earliest researchers. There is actually only a slight natural divide between them, so they will be considered here as a single unit.

The greatest number of hot springs at Shoshone are in this area. Aside from the several geysers, there are many beautiful pools and brilliant algal and mineral colorations. Among the pools are Three Crater Spring and Coral Spring (at "Z" on Map BB). This area is accessible via an old trail, with a still usable footbridge, that splits from the main trail near Minute Man Geyser. Immediately south of this trail is an exceptionally deep pool. Shown at "Y" on Map BB, this was identified as Funnel Spring in the first edition of this book. It turns out that the real Funnel Springs (there are two) are to the south and very small by comparison. The large pool has no name. It evidently formed as a result of a steam explosion sometime during the 1920s.

The following descriptions will note several name changes. From the time of first explorations during the 1870s until 1980 virtually no research was done at Shoshone. Through the intervening years a number of names were shifted from one place to another. This edition sets the names right.

19. UNNG-SHO-5 was called Grotto Spring in the first edition of this book. The error, of many years standing, was understandable since the geyserite formation here strongly resembles that of Grotto Geyser in the Upper Geyser Basin. In fact, the real Grotto Spring is a rather small pool about 100 feet to the east of SHO-5. Located in a depression, SHO-5 itself does not discharge any water during an eruption, but a nearby pool does overflow at those times. The activity is erratic. At times the geyser is extremely regular, but it is more often unpredictable in its action. Intervals are known to range from less than 1 to several hours. The play lasts from 5 to 30 minutes. Bursts from the main vent can reach up to 10 feet high.

20. UNNG-SHO-6 was called "TB" in the first edition of this book, but that name has been dropped and no new name suggested. "Teardrop" might be a good name, based on the shape of the crater. The vent, at the narrow end of the pool, extends vertically downward to a considerable depth. The geyser is probably cyclic in its activity. Active cycles are brief, but then eruptions can recur as often as every 5 minutes. Lasting up to 4 minutes, this play reaches as much as 30 feet high. More commonly the geyser is in a relatively dormant phase when intermittent overflow may be punctuated by occasional bursts to 1 foot.

21. PEARL SPRING is little more than an intermittent spring, but its periods of overflow may include bursting to 2 feet high. These periods may last as long as 2 hours. Following the play the water level of the pool drops very slowly, requiring about 2 hours to drop 12 inches. Refilling takes another 2 hours, and a rather long overflow period is necessary before another bit of splashing occurs.

22. GLEN SPRING is situated in a deep alcove in the hill, largely out of sight of the rest of the Shoshone Basin. It is a geyser but is only seen to play on rare occasions. The wide, shallow pool is colored a strange yellow-green everywhere away from the vent. Along the front of the pool is a series of logs, appearing to have been placed there long ago. The infrequent eruptions are a series of individual bursts of water, separated from one another by as much as 30 seconds, sometimes reaching as much as 5 feet high. The duration is probably several hours.

23. BROWN SPONGE was so named because of a brown mineral stain on the inside of the crater, which is composed of a porous geyserite. Brown Sponge probably plays rather frequently, but because of the small size of the play only scant attention has been paid to it. The height is generally less than 1 foot.

24. YELLOW SPONGE plays from a water level well below the surrounding ground surface. The geyserite is tinted a pale, pure yellow by a trace of iron oxide minerals. One of the more vigorous geysers in the area, Yellow Sponge plays every 10 seconds. Each eruption lasts 2 to 4 seconds and jets spray to between 4 and 8 feet.

25. SMALL GEYSER has evidently changed its behavior considerably since the 1870s. Back then it erupted frequently as high as 20 feet. Nothing of that sort now exists in the area. A number of craters, all of them spouting water on occasion, lie in the area. Small is recognizable because there are nearly always steam bubbles entering the bottom of the crater, causing a flickering appearance. These steam bubbles produce the nearly constant eruptive activity. There is some periodicity to the splashes, but the flickering never stops. The splashes are mostly less than 3 feet high; an exceptional one may reach 8 feet.

26. KNOBBY GEYSER was identified as Frill Spring in the first edition of this book. Frill is now known to be a shallow pool lined with orange algae a short distance to the north. Knobby has also been confused with Bead Geyser (27). The crater of Knobby is squarish in outline and entirely decorated with exceptionally ornate geyserite. The vent is at the uphill corner of the crater. Knobby is known to be affected by Velvet Spring (28). Its best performances occur when Velvet Spring is dormant, as has been the case since 1982. Then Knobby is clearly cyclic in its activity. Dormant periods generally are 1 to 2 hours in length. Active

periods last from 1½ to 3 hours, during which there are both minor and major intervals. If an eruption lasts less than 1½ minutes, then the following interval will be less than 3 minutes; if the duration is longer than 3 minutes, then the interval will exceed 7 minutes. There are essentially no intermediate values. Eruption type also controls the height of the play. Minor eruptions seldom exceed 10 feet, while the majors may reach 25 feet or more.

This cyclic behavior of Knobby has only been clear since the 1982 dormancy of Velvet Spring. Before then Knobby was comparatively inactive. Eruptions were erratic, and some dormant intervals between cycles were more than 24 hours long.

27. BEAD GEYSER is the name that was given to an impressive geyser that was active during the 1870s. What happened to Bead during the years between then and now is uncertain. For many years it was confused with what is now positively known to be Velvet Spring (28). At other times it was thought to be what is now called Knobby Geyser (26). There is a chance that Bead has entirely disappeared. If it does still exist, then it is most likely a small pool a few feet northwest of Knobby. This spring has a crater lined with an intricately designed geyserite that makes it appear to be layered (though it really isn't). This spring is a geyser, but it plays very infrequently and no details about its modern activity are known.

28. VELVET SPRING was believed to be Bead Geyser (27) until a comparison of an 1870s drawing with the modern crater revealed the error. Clearly, this was not a geyser during the early exploration of Yellowstone, but it was actively erupting from some early date until 1982. The eruptions by Velvet were remarkably regular, only a few seconds variation making it one of the most regular geysers in Yellowstone. The play recurred every 12 to 14 minutes and lasted 2½ minutes. Velvet has two vents. The main crater contains a deep, blue pool. Its bursting eruption would spray water up to 20 feet high. The smaller vent to the west would play with more of a jetting action, at an uphill angle, to a height of as much as 25 feet. Since the current dormancy began in 1982, Velvet has performed as an intermittent spring. The times of overflow correspond to a few seconds of increased, superheated boiling. The decline in activity is apparently due to an exchange of function with Knobby Geyser (26).

29. LION GEYSER is one of the most regular geysers in the Shoshone Basin, except that it is subject to frequent, long dormant spells. When active, which might be as little as one year out of every three, the intervals range from 50 to 70 minutes; as is often the case, however, at any given time there is seldom more than a few minutes variation from the current average. The eruptions last 4 minutes. Most of the bursts are only 2 to 4 feet high, but because Lion's vent is slit-like and penetrates the ground at an angle, some bursts squirt water at a sharp angle to the south. These may reach as much as 12 feet high and 25 feet out. At the end of the eruption the crater drains, forming a sucking whirlpool over the vent. Very little refilling of the crater takes place until immediately before the next eruption.

30. BRONZE GEYSER rarely erupts now but evidently did so rather frequently during early days of the Park. It is located a few feet south of Lion Geyser (29), and the most notable thing about it is the color of the geyserite rim. The sinter has incorporated iron oxide in such a way as to give it an almost perfect bronze-like luster. When Bronze does erupt the play lasts no more than a few seconds and reaches 3 feet high.

31. IRON CONCH SPRING forms the third point of a triangle, along with Lion (29) and Bronze (30) Geysers. The crater is even more heavily stained with iron oxide than is Bronze's; the result is a brilliant red-orange vent surrounded by bumpy, bronzy mounds of geyserite. Iron Conch is a regular geyser. Intervals range from 9 to 30 minutes but usually average near the lower figure. The play lasts 1 minute and reaches 2 to 3 feet high.

32. UNNG-SHO-7 was listed by the Hayden Survey as South Group Spring #2. It is now a geyser and appears to have been so for a long time. Eruptions are very frequent. From the vent at the uphill end of a rift in the surrounding geyserite shield, the play reaches up to 4 feet high.

33. UNNG-SHO-8 ("OUTBREAK" GEYSER) was created by a steam explosion during 1974. At first the eruptions were extremely erratic, but Outbreak has settled down to a very reliable behavior. The eruptions are extremely regular, at times being accurate to within 2% of the 33-minute average interval. The play lasts almost exactly 2 minutes and jets water as high as 15 feet.

Fall Creek Group

Through the woods and around the hill to the southwest of the South Group is the Fall Creek Group. It is an area of many large and very active hot springs. Aside from the one geyser and one large perpetual spouter described here, it includes numerous small spouters, pretty pools, and mud pots.

34. UNNG-SHO-9 is an interesting geyser in that most of the time, although active, its water temperature is considerably below boiling. This kind of spring is still a true geyser, involving boiling at depth within the plumbing system, but the eruptions are triggered by the evolution of gases other than steam. At such times this geyser plays frequently but to only 2 feet high. During 1985 it was found to have increased its temperature to the boiling point, and its activity was more regular and stronger. The play recurred every 4 minutes. Lasting about 1½ minutes, some of the bursts reached 6 feet high.

35. BOILING CAULDRON is the hot spring of the Fall Creek Group that produces most of the runoff of the area, forming a very large stream of scalding water. It is a perpetual spouter, jetting from several vents. One vent plays to about 6 feet; another jets mostly steam, producing a roaring that can be heard for several hundred feet.

One of the most delicately colored springs in Yellowstone is just a few feet southwest of Boiling Cauldron. The pool of Cream Spring is of the palest blue-green, filling a crater of pure white sinter.

Table 32. Geysers of the North, South, and Fall Creek Groups

Name and Number	Interval	Duration	Height (ft)
Bead Geyser (27)	infrequent	unrecorded	unknown
Boiling Cauldron (35)	steady	steady	6
Bronze Geyser (30)	rare	seconds	3
Brown Sponge (23)	unrecorded	minutes	1
Glen Spring (22)	irregular	hours	5
Iron Conch Spring (31)	9–30 min	1 min	1–2
Knobby Geyser (26)	1–20 min	sec–8 min	3–25
Lion Geyser (29)	50–70 min	4 min	2–12
Pearl Spring (21)	hours	2 hrs	1–2
Small Geyser (25)	seconds	seconds	2–8
UNNG-SHO-5 (19)	30 min–5 hrs	5–30 min	10
UNNG-SHO-6 (20)	irregular	1–4 min	1–30
UNNG-SHO-7 (Hayden #2) (32)	seconds	seconds	4
UNNG-SHO-8 ("Outbreak") (33)	33 min	2 min	10–15
UNNG-SHO-9 (34)	4 min	1½ min	6
Velvet Spring (28)	12–14 min	2½ min	15–25
Yellow Sponge (24)	10 sec	3 sec	4–8

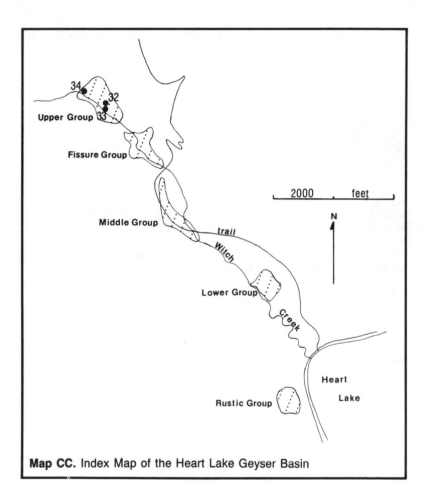

Map CC. Index Map of the Heart Lake Geyser Basin

Chapter 12

Heart Lake Geyser Basin

The Heart Lake Geyser Basin (Map CC) lies in a setting rather different from those of the other geyser basins. Instead of hot springs being found in a contiguous group, they are a series of widely spaced clusters. Hiking into the area, after having walked through about 5½ miles of dense lodgepole pine forest, the hiker suddenly emerges from the trees to find himself at the edge of a deep valley. There, standing with muddy hot springs right at his feet, the view is down Witch Creek toward Heart Lake, still 2½ miles away. Spotting the length of the green valley are small white spots, the sinter deposits of the several hot springs groups. Beyond is the lake and, farther still, the snowy peaks of the Absaroka Range. The view is one of the prettiest in Yellowstone.

The Heart Lake Basin is divided into five naturally separated groups. Geysers are found in the Rustic, Lower, Fissure, and Upper groups; the Middle Group contains several pretty pools but no geysers. Most of the geysers here are of small size, and only two geysers of significant size are known. Rustic Geyser is not quite the largest in the area, but it has been the most reliable performer in the basin; Glade Geyser plays higher than does Rustic, but it is erratic and generally infrequent. Overall, in spite of the small size of the eruptions, the activity at Heart Lake is intense.

Since its geysers do tend to small sizes, the Heart Lake Geyser Basin has not attracted much attention. The only detailed map ever published was printed in 1883, and the most recent descriptive work prior to this book was published in 1935. Right up to the present time, Heart Lake has been Yellowstone's most ignored geyser basin.

The descriptions that follow are based on observations made between 1970 and 1977, with revisions dating from 1985. All of the data presented have been checked against figures obtained by the U.S. Geological Survey (USGS) in 1973. The fact that the two sets of figures are often different proves only that the activity here is constantly changing. There can be little question but that much about these geysers is unknown.

As with any other geyser basin described in this book, the names used here are those commonly recognized or are based on numerical designations taken from the USGS studies. For those, the technique used elsewhere in this book for unnamed geysers is a bit different – the final number is accompanied by a letter, indicating that the spring was first described as either a geyser ("G") or a spring ("S").

Heart Lake is one of the least impacted areas of Yellowstone despite the heavy foot traffic into the lake. The trail leaves the South Entrance highway at a point about 6 miles south of the Grant Village junction and just north of Lewis Lake. From the trailhead it is 5½ miles to the overlook at the head of the valley and another 2½ miles from there to Heart Lake itself. The Heart Lake Ranger Station is often manned during the summer months and, if so, can provide assistance and outside communication in case of emergency. But that cannot be counted on. In this backcountry area, as in all others, your safety is your own responsibility.

Rustic Group

The Rustic Group (Map DD, Table 33), named for Rustic Geyser, is the closest hot spring group to Heart Lake. Set against the base of Mt. Sheridan, it is about ½ mile south of the Heart Lake Ranger Station and about 1,000 feet from the lakeshore. The best approach is to take the shortest route from the lake as possible. The meadow outside the treeline is normally extremely soggy, and it is usually impossible to find a totally dry route.

Rustic Geyser is the most important geyser in the Heart Lake Basin. Aside from it there are at least five other geysers in the group. Columbia Pool ("X" on Map DD) is among the prettier pools in Yellowstone. It is 25 feet deep and a rich azure-blue color, but it cannot be approached closely because of an extensive overhanging geyserite rim.

1. **RUSTIC GEYSER** is both important and spectacular. For most of its known history it has been the only large and frequently active geyser in the Heart Lake Geyser Basin. Always regular, its intervals have been known to range from 10 to 90 minutes. There is evidence that the length of the interval is dependent on the level and temperature of the subsurface water table. As the summer season progresses the level drops and the temperature rises, causing shorter intervals. For example, during June of 1974 the average was about 25 minutes; by August it had decreased to just 14 minutes, and it lowered further in September to just 10 minutes, the shortest average ever recorded. In the long run, an average of 26 minutes seems to be typical.

Eruptions begin with little warning. Water slowly rises in the crater. When it is still about 6 inches below the rim the water suddenly surges, filling the crater to overflowing within a few seconds. Bursts come in a rapid succession with perhaps 100

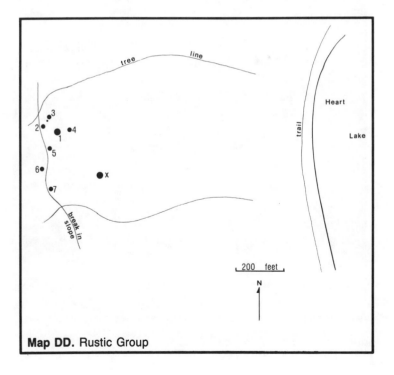

Map DD. Rustic Group

Rustic Geyser, reaching 50 feet high, is the only frequently erupting geyser of considerable size in the Heart Lake Basin.

of them during the usual 40- to 60-second eruption. The water is thrown into the air as steam bubbles explode within the shallow pool, and the pop can be heard with each one. The explosions vary in their forcefulness; most are only 10 to 20 feet high, but every eruption also includes a few reaching 35 to 50 feet. The play ends as abruptly as it began.

Rustic Geyser was active without any known interruption from the discovery of Yellowstone until sometime during the winter of 1984–85. With this dormancy the water has remained at a low level while its temperature has dropped so low as to allow orange algae to grow. The cause of this dormancy is clear: an exchange of function has shifted the energy flow to UNNG-HLR-S2 (3) which has simultaneously changed from a rather infrequent and weak geyser into one of powerful and regular eruptions. How long Rustic's dormancy might last is, of course, unknown, but the general lack of well-defined runoff leading away from S2 implies that such vigorous activity is exceptional.

At some time in the distant past Rustic was altered by man. Logs were placed around the crater, giving it a squarish outline. Now completely covered by pale brown sinter, they appear virtually unchanged since the early days of the Park. It is probable that the logs were placed by Indians as long as 200 or 300 years ago. Why they would do such a thing is not known, but it does indicate that they were not afraid of the geysers.

2. UNNG-HLR-G2 lies at the base of a grassy slope a few feet from Rustic Geyser (1); a fallen tree partially covers the crater. About 10 feet long, the crater is coated by a brown geyserite identical to that at Rustic and, indeed, there is evidence of a connection between the two. This geyser is usually very regular in its activity. Most of the time the average interval is near 25 minutes, but some as short as 5 minutes have been seen. This is a vigorous little geyser, madly throwing its water in all directions. Most bursts are only 5 feet high, but some of 15 feet occur with every play. Even during the eruptions the water level stays far down in the crater, and there is never any overflow. The eruptions last from 1½ to 5 minutes. With the 1985 activation of HLR-S2 (3), HLR-G2 showed clear relationships in its activity to that of the new geyser. G2 would not erupt when S2 was playing, and an eruption of either would lower the water level in the other.

3. UNNG-HLR-S2 is a few feet from both HLR-G2 (2) and Rustic Geyser (1), forming the third apex of a triangle. This shallow pool is clearly related to both of the other geysers. Always an infrequent performer before 1985, HLR-S2 has undergone powerful eruptions with the consequent dormancy of Rustic. There was evidence of some powerful eruptions by HLR-S2 during 1974, when a large runoff channel was produced in the loose gravel surrounding the crater. It can be surmised that that activity also caused Rustic to be dormant. The modern eruptions recur regularly, with intervals ranging from 1½ to 3 hours. The play is a massive bursting and jetting as much as 20 feet high, which persists throughout the 5-minute duration. A small hole in the geyserite a few feet toward HLR-G2 also plays during the eruptions, sending a steady jet to about 12 feet.

4. UNNG-HLR-G3 erupts from a small, boiling pool in a deep hole. About 50 feet from Rustic Geyser (1), it is very infrequently active and apparently did not benefit from the 1985 exchange of function. Eruptions are always infrequent, and active periods are probably exceptional. Observed intervals have been as short as 1½ hours but usually much longer, while the play lasts only a few seconds. Some bursts reach 10 feet above the ground level.

5. UNNG-HLR-S4 was always a quiet spring with steady slight discharge prior to 1985. Sometime during the exchange of function episode that affected virtually all of the Rustic Group, it underwent an explosion. The crater was considerably enlarged and runoff channels indicated powerful activity. No eruptions have been observed, however.

6. PROMETHEUS SPRING has behaved as a flowing, non-erupting spring, as a perpetual spouter, and as a geyser during its known history. Just how dominant each of these kinds of action has been is unknown. When a perpetual spouter, the play is about 6 feet high. When acting as a true, periodic geyser, then Prometheus is more spectacular. Intervals range from 8 to 15 minutes. The jetting eruption lasts less than 1 minute, sending spray at an angle away from the hillside to as much as 15 feet high.

The crater of Prometheus Spring is brilliantly colored by a mixture of reds, browns, yellows, and black because of iron and manganese oxide minerals. At least, it was. A report made during late 1985 indicated that Prometheus, like nearby geyser S4 (5), had undergone a steam explosion. Instead of the colorful vent on a grassy hillside there was a yawning crater. If this is indeed Prometheus, then it has certainly changed its activity as well as its appearance.

7. UNNG-HLR-G4 is almost a perpetual spouter. The eruption is only about 1 foot high. Just in front of the crater is an old geyserite cone within which the water level slowly rises and falls. It may erupt at times. Just in front of the cone is spring #8, whose rate of overflow varies in sympathy with the eruption of HLR-G4.

Table 33. Geysers of the Rustic Group

Name and Number	Interval	Duration	Height (ft)
Prometheus Spring (6)	8–15 min	1 min	6–15
Rustic Geyser (1)	10–90 min	40–60 sec	35–50
UNNG-HLR-G2 (2)	5–25 min	1½–5 min	5–15
UNNG-HLR-G3 (4)	rare	seconds	10
UNNG-HLR-G4 (7)	steady	steady	1
UNNG-HLR-S2 (3)	1½–3 hrs	5 min	20
UNNG-HLR-S4 (5)	unknown	unknown	10?

Lower Group

Until the early 1970s the Heart Lake trail passed through the center of the Lower Group. Now it runs across the hillside through the forest above the springs, about 300 feet from the nearest spring. The Lower Group (Map EE, Table 34) is a very compact cluster containing a total of about thirty hot springs. Eight of them are geysers, none of which have been named.

8. UNNG-HLL-G1 splashes out of a 2-foot-high cone. The activity of the geyser is cyclic. Most of the time the eruption is confined to within the cone. Some spray rises above the rim but it all falls back inside. During such periods there are infrequent surges when the splash reaches 3 feet above the top. Rarely, HLL-G1 undergoes a more powerful eruption. For a few seconds water is thrown to over 10 feet with enough discharge to create a considerable but short runoff stream.

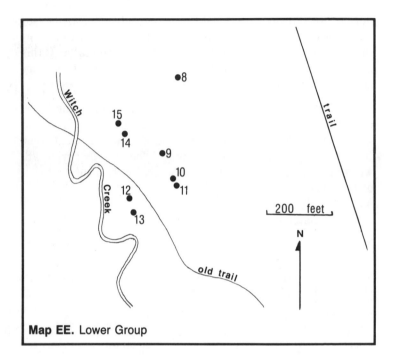

Map EE. Lower Group

9. UNNG-HLL-G3 is the smallest known geyser in the Heart Lake Basin and one of the smallest anywhere. Centered in an unobtrusive splash zone covered with beaded sinter, the 1-inch-wide vent spatters a fine spray of water a few inches high; some droplets may occasionally reach 1 foot. The eruptive activity is cyclic. Recurring every 60 seconds, preliminary eruptions last about 5 seconds. The main activity is identical to these except that the duration is 20 seconds. Following the "major" eruption the geyser is quiet for about 5 minutes. Geyser HLL-G3 is subject to dormant periods, and then the shallow crater all but disappears.

10. UNNG-HLL-S8 is a very pretty little pool. The rim of the crater is beautifully beaded and scalloped with pearly gray sinter. HLL-S8 is a perpetual spouter with eruptions 1 foot high. As is common to most springs in the Lower Group, there is no discharge from this spring.

11. **UNNG-HLL-G2** is another small pool with no discharge. It periodically splashes to 1 foot for durations of 5 seconds to 1 minute.

12. **UNNG-HLL-G4** is the largest regularly spouting spring in the Lower Group. The light blue pool sits within a 2-foot by 5-foot crater. The steady boiling frequently increases in vigor and water is thrown 2 to 6 feet high. Some eruptions last as long as 2 minutes although most are much shorter. The crater and runoff channel of HLL-G4 are both highly colored by hot water algae; the very dark color within the vent is probably due to manganese oxide minerals.

13. **UNNG-HLL-S21**, about 60 feet south of HLL-G4 (12), is another small perpetual spouter. About 1 foot high, the splashing eruption creates one of the heaviest discharge streams in the group – between 5 and 10 gallons per minute. As with HLL-G4, the vent is nearly black in color.

14. **UNNG-HLL-S15** spouts constantly from a small crater. Located near the top of a low sinter knoll, this might once have been the site of an older, more important hot spring or geyser. The steady eruption of HLL-S15 is only 1 foot high, but a wide splash zone and considerable runoff channels suggest that it undergoes infrequent eruptions several feet high. None has ever been recorded.

15. **UNNG-HLL-S16** is yet another perpetual spouter, 1 foot high. From all appearances it is identical to HLL-S15; however, this spring shows no signs of any periodic, more powerful activity.

Table 34. Geysers of the Lower Group

Name and Number	Interval	Duration	Height (ft)
UNNG-HLL-G1 (8)	infrequent	seconds	3–10
UNNG-HLL-G2 (11)	frequent	5 sec–1 min	1
UNNG-HLL-G3 (9)	1–5 min	5–20 sec	inches
UNNG-HLL-G4 (12)	frequent	sec–2 min	2–6
UNNG-HLL-S8 (10)	steady	steady	1
UNNG-HLL-S15 (14)	steady	steady	1
UNNG-HLL-S16 (15)	steady	steady	1
UNNG-HLL-S21 (13)	steady	steady	1

Fissure Group

The Fissure Group (Map FF, Table 35) is the most important hot spring group in the Heart Lake Basin. The continuous splashing, bubbling, roaring, and steaming creates a scene like that of an old steam works. Thus, the mountain behind the springs is known as Factory Hill. Geyser activity is most intense on the sinter-covered rise near the upper end of the group. Here is a long crack in the geyserite from which arise several geysers and numerous other hot springs. A southward continuation of this fissure lines up with a sharp change in the slope of the hillside, and both may be evidence of recent fault activity. Witch Creek flows through the center of the Fissure Group and much of its volume actually runs below ground in the fissure area. With a temperature of 85°F (30°C), Witch Creek is almost entirely hot spring runoff.

16. UNNG-HLF-S1a sits well apart from the main portion of the Fissure Group. It was not observed in the course of the USGS studies in the early 1970s and might, therefore, have developed since then. Less than 200 feet from the Heart Lake trail, it is all but hidden by trees and the tall grass of a small meadow. The constant play splashes 1 to 2 feet high.

17. UNNG-HLF-S1 plays steadily from a 2-foot-wide crater on top of a sinter platform directly above Witch Creek. The central part of the vent is colored black by mixed iron and manganese oxides, while the rim is Indian red because of iron oxide alone. The eruption is usually about 3 feet high.

18. UNNG-HLF-G9 is the modern successor to a large pool or geyser. The crater is over 12 feet wide and 8 feet deep. Inactive for a long time, its sinter walls are deeply weathered. HLF-G9 erupts through a long, narrow crack near the bottom of the western crater wall. Were it to erupt vertically it would be a considerable geyser, spouting a steady stream several feet high. As it is, the play is almost horizontal, reaching completely across the bottom of the old crater. The intervals are highly irregular; they can be as short as 15 minutes, but most are several hours long. The action lasts less than 1 minute.

Heart Lake Geyser Basin / *245*

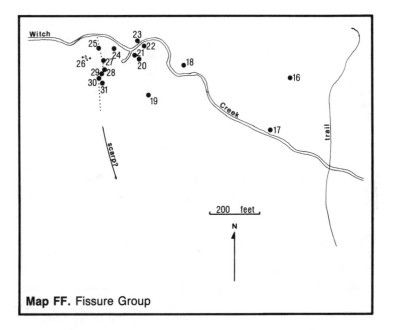

Map FF. Fissure Group

19. GLADE GEYSER is the tallest in the Heart Lake Geyser Basin. It erupts from a small cone near the top of which is a circular vent about 1 foot across. The steady water stream shoots at a slight angle so that the water lands in the alcove below the cone.

Glade's activity is, unfortunately, highly variable and always uncertain. In addition, it is apparently cyclic. The first recorded eruptions were seen in 1964. At that time the play recurred regularly every 35 minutes. Those eruptions were 30 feet high and lasted about 1 minute. By 1973 Glade was erupting infrequently although still somewhat regularly in a cyclic pattern. The intervals ranged from 40 to 60 hours long, and eruptions always came in a series of two. Separated by as little as 10 minutes or as long as several hours, these plays would be 40 to 50 feet high for most of the 2-minute duration. By 1984 Glade had changed further, to the point that it was quite frequent and reliable. A full cycle of activity required about 18 hours to complete. Following one cycle, the next would begin with 6 to 8 hours of quiet.

Then a series of minor eruptions began. Such play recurred every 2 to 3 hours, each eruption lasting 10 minutes and reaching 30 feet high. Finally, the cycle would end with a major eruption. It would initially look the same as a minor, but the play extended to as much as 20 minutes. As Glade began to run out of water the height could reach between 45 and 60 feet high. On no other occasion has Glade been known to perform for such great durations and heights. The entire show was very much like that of Atomizer Geyser (#131 in the Upper Basin). Unfortunately, Glade has continued to show its erratic side. After all the great activity of 1984, by 1985 it had slowed considerably. Although certainly active, it was not seen by any reporting observer.

20. UNNG-HLF-G3 is located in a sandy basin about 10 feet upslope from Triple Bulger Geyser (21). The eruption is only 1 to 2 feet high, but it is regularly periodic. Intervals of about 2 hours lead up to eruptions that last 13 to 25 minutes. Like nearby Triple Bulger, G3 sometimes goes dormant. The two geysers evidently are active or dormant at the same time, but there is no other evidence of control by one spring on the other. When dormant, HLF-G3 all but disappears from sight as the crater is filled with rubble from the slope above.

21. TRIPLE BULGER GEYSER is one of the most impressive springs in the Fissure Group. The oval pool is colored aquamarine over each of the three vents. During an eruption the water is bulged up to 3 feet high over each crater. On occasion the bulges burst sending spray to 6 feet, and even more rarely all three bulges will burst at once, sending droplets to over 10 feet. When active, Triple Bulger is in eruption nearly 40% of the time: the intervals average 42 minutes, the durations 24. Dormant periods of unknown length sometimes afflict Triple Bulger, but even then its water discharge of 25 gallons per minute is the highest of any single spring in the Fissure Group.

22. UNNG-HLF-S20 was probably once a more powerful geyser than it is now. The cone is large and massive with the rim rising fully 2½ feet above its surroundings. The present activity is far smaller than that required to form such a cone. There is a constant boiling of the water within the crater. Some splashes throw out a little water and an exceptional surge may reach 2 feet above the rim.

23. UNNG-HLF-S12 plays from a beautiful small crater right next to Witch Creek. The delicately scalloped sinter rim is lightly stained by iron oxides, giving it a pinkish and orangish cast. HLF-S12 is a perpetual spouter. The maximum height is 2 feet.

24. SHELL SPRING is a geyser but because of its position the activity is almost impossible to see clearly. The deep crater is carved into a nearly vertical sinter cliff, 10 feet above Witch Creek. The back side of the crater is fluted like a clam shell. The play of the geyser splashes against this wall. Constantly boiling, the small pool periodically surges upward, throwing its water with a violent spraying action. Most of the water falls back into the pool, but some does escape to reach 5 feet into the air. If Shell were more exposed, some of the water would reach well over 10 feet and it would be a very noticeable geyser.

25. HOODED SPRING is a perpetual spouter. It lies at the north end of the rift that gave the Fissure Group its name. Hooded Spring was so named because of a sinter projection that extends partially out over the crater, deflecting the eruption. This "hood" appears to be the remains of an old geyserite cone. The eruption, hood notwithstanding, is 3 to 4 feet high. Just behind Hooded Spring, hidden back within the fissure, is another perpetual spouter; it plays 1 foot high.

26. UNNG-HLF-S26 and S27 are nearly identical. Between the two is Shelf Spring, a lovely robin's-egg-blue pool. The small cones of HLF-S26 and HLF-S27 are intricately beaded and each contains a vent about 6 inches in diameter. Boiling up from superheated water, the highest spray reaches about 2 feet. From all appearances, these two springs look capable of much stronger eruptions, but none have ever been recorded.

27. UNNG-HLF-G7 is a small double pool. It was created by a steam explosion that opened the craters within the fissure. The play is constant from both vents, but the greatest height is only 1 foot.

The final four members of the Fissure Group are situated along the south-central portion of the rift within about 30 feet of each other. These springs are related to one another and just a brief period of observation reveals their competitive activity.

28. UNNG-HLF-G4 is the most active of the four geysers. It is nearly, but not quite, a perpetual spouter. With pauses only a few seconds long, HLF-G4 spouts to 5 feet from a vent nearly 8 feet long. The fan-shaped spray will be continuous for as long as 2 minutes, although its normal duration is only a few seconds. The activity of HLF-G4 seems largely independent of that of the other geysers in the complex, except that it is nearly always quiet when HLF-G6 undergoes its stronger form of eruption.

29. UNNG-HLF-G6 spouts from the next opening along the fissure, south of HLF-G4 (28). Its eruptions recur about every minute and last 5 to 10 seconds. Most of the play does not reach the ground level, but when HLF-G4 falls quiet some surges may reach 4 feet high. A small cone at the south side of HLF-G6 occasionally splashes during these stronger eruptions.

30. UNNG-HLF-G8 lies in a very narrow opening in the rift. The vent is never more than 2 inches wide but more than 6 feet long. The activity of HLF-G8 is closely tied to that of HLF-G5 (31). When HLF-G5 is dormant, which is the usual case, HLF-G8 erupts frequently. The most powerful bursts then come in concert with eruptions by HLF-G6 (29). Some of the surges will reach about 3 feet above the ground. When HLF-G5 is active, however, the play of HLF-G8 is very brief and weak.

31. UNNG-HLF-G5 is the largest geyser of the fissure complex. During its active periods eruptions recur every 11 to 15 minutes. The geyser discharges slightly during the quiet interval. As the play begins, the overflow suddenly becomes very heavy, totalling at least 20 gallons during the 15-second eruption. Water is jetted as a steady stream, sometimes reaching 8 feet high. During dormant periods the nearby geyser HLF-G8 (30) is more active and HLF-G5 discharges a steady flow of about 5 gallons per minute. The crater of HLF-G5 shows no signs of extended activity and runoff channels leading from it are almost non-existent. It is likely that eruptive activity from this hole is unusual.

Table 35. Geysers of the Fissure Group

Name and Number	Interval	Duration	Height (ft)
Glade Geyser (19)	hrs–days	1–20 min	30–60
Hooded Spring (25)	steady	steady	3–4
Shell Spring (24)	frequent	seconds	5
Triple Bulger Geyser (21)	42 min	24 min	3–10
UNNG-HLF-G3 (20)	2 hrs	13–25 min	1–2
UNNG-HLF-G4 (28)	seconds	sec–2 min	5
UNNG-HLF-G5 (31)	11–15 min	15 sec	8
UNNG-HLF-G6 (29)	1 min	5–10 sec	4
UNNG-HLF-G7 (27)	steady	steady	1
UNNG-HLF-G8 (30)	irregular	seconds	3
UNNG-HLF-G9 (18)	15 min–hrs	1 min	3–4
UNNG-HLF-S1 (17)	steady	steady	3
UNNG-HLF-S1a (16)	steady	steady	1–2
UNNG-HLF-S12 (23)	steady	steady	2
UNNG-HLF-S20 (22)	steady	steady	2
UNNG-HLF-S26–27 (26)	frequent	seconds	2

Upper Group

The Upper Group (Map CC, Table 36) covers a large area but most of its activity is in the form of relatively cool, muddy acidic springs. Alkaline springs with clear water are few and mostly confined to a limited area immediately next to Witch Creek, but three of them are geysers. They are distinctive and easily found. To reach the Upper Group simply follow Witch Creek upstream from the Fissure Group.

32. DELUGE GEYSER is about ¼ mile upstream from the Fissure Group. Named in the 1870s, it and Columbia Pool in the Rustic Group are the only deep blue pools in the Heart Lake Geyser Basin. Deluge is surrounded by a broad, thick sinter deposit. It appears to have once been a much larger geyser than it is now. The modern activity consists of frequent boiling periods. The level of the quiet pool rises to a heavy overflow. Super-heated water reaches the surface, resulting in a sizzling, spluttering eruption. The maximum height is generally about 1 foot, but some reports of 4-footers are occasionally heard.

33. UNNG-HLU-G1 plays from a crater next to Witch Creek directly below Deluge Geyser (32). Its activity was first observed during 1985. Eruptions were frequent, each lasting about 1 minute and reaching 2 to 4 feet high.

34. SPIKE GEYSER lies about 600 feet upstream from Deluge Geyser (32). In several ways Spike is one of the most intriguing geysers in Yellowstone. The cone, although only 2 feet tall, most closely resembles the dead and dying cones of the Monument Geyser Basin. It stands near one end of a geyserite bridge that spans Witch Creek. Spike was reported in eruption by some of the early expeditions to Yellowstone but never again until 1974. It seems to have been in continuous eruption since then. The play is as curious as the cone. Very little water issues from the tiny vent at the top of the cone; what does is squirted about 6 inches high. The tallest spout comes from a pencil-sized vent near the base of the cone. It briefly squirts, every second or so, a steady stream about 2 feet high. A small pool at the backside of the cone surges steadily and boils, throwing some water to about 1 foot. It has certainly taken Spike a long time to form its cone, yet the surrounding area is badly weathered. It looks as though the geyser has seen better days, with long active periods separated by very much longer dormancies.

Table 36. Geysers of the Upper Group

Name and Number	Interval	Duration	Height (ft)
Deluge Geyser (32)	2–10 min	1–3 min	boil–3
Spike Geyser (34)	steady	steady	2
UNNG-HLU-G1 (33)	frequent	1 min	2–4

Chapter 13

Other Yellowstone Geysers

Geysers are known to occur in several other areas of Yellowstone National Park. Although most of these localities are relatively inaccessible, this book would not be complete without some mention of them. These geysers occur as members of hot spring groups that cover such small areas that they cannot be considered to be actual geyser basins. These areas are shown on Map GG.

1. Seven Mile Hole

Seven Mile Hole is a portion of the Grand Canyon of the Yellowstone that is accessible by trail. About 7 miles downstream from the Lower Falls of the Yellowstone, it is famed for its fishing. The trail to the area follows the canyon rim then abruptly drops into the canyon; the elevation difference is about 1,200 feet in 1½ miles.

Hot springs occur in several small, scattered groups within Seven Mile Hole. Within one group about half-way to the bottom of the canyon are two geysers. One, surprisingly, has an official name. Safety-valve Geyser erupts every 10 to 20 minutes, has a duration of 2 to 3 minutes, and splashes about 3 feet high. Nearby is a second geyser, but its height is not more than 2 feet. The Seven Mile Hole area includes several perpetual spouters among its other hot springs.

2. The Grand Canyon of the Yellowstone

The Grand Canyon is brilliantly colored from the Lower Falls downstream about 2 miles. The coloration is the result of hydrothermal rock alteration that has formed a mixture of numerous oxide minerals. The thermal area at the Grand Canyon has been

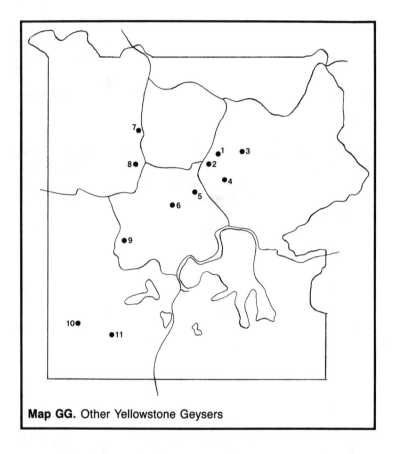

Map GG. Other Yellowstone Geysers

active for a very long time. Some old geyserite deposits above the rim near Artist's Point are estimated to be between 300,000 and 600,000 years old. Today's hot springs are largely confined to the bottom of the canyon. They can be seen from the various viewpoints but none are accessible by trail. Several geysers are included.

On the east side of the river just downstream from the Lower Falls (so close as to sometimes be within the spray) is a tiny hot spring group. The Uncle Tom's Trail, which drops into the canyon, used to extend to these springs, so the springs received names in spite of their small sizes. Included are Tom Thumb, Fairy, and Watermelon Geysers.

A short distance downstream and across the river is the site of another geyser. Directly below Red Rock Point, this Red Rock Geyser erupted 15 feet high, but the only recorded year of activity was 1947.

Most visible from Artist's Point, both upstream and downstream from there, are several other hot springs and geysers. None are named. The most important of these is a geyser that plays from a vent at the river's edge. It usually shows itself only with a bit of steam at a narrowing of the canyon a short distance upstream from the viewpoint. Eruptions are infrequent but will jet water completely across the river. Downstream from the point are one additional geyser and at least six perpetual spouters.

3. Joseph's Coat Hot Springs

Joseph's Coat is one of the extremely inaccessible hot spring areas east of the Grand Canyon. No trail leads to the area, and the springs have rarely been visited. The topographic maps of Yellowstone show a "Whistler Geyser" at Joseph's Coat, but that spring was probably never a geyser at all. There is a geyser there, however. Informally known as "Broadside Geyser," its eruption is a nearly steady fine spray, which jets almost horizontally from the vent.

4. Bog Creek Hot Springs

Along Bog Creek, southeast of Canyon Village and east of Hayden Valley, and again not accessible via trail, are some small unnamed thermal areas. In one of these there is a single geyser. Observed on only three known occasions, it has been active each time but with considerable change in its performance. Overall, however, the intervals tend to several minutes in length. Eruptions last only a few seconds but spray water to between 6 and 15 feet high.

5. Crater Hills

The Crater Hills area is within Hayden Valley, about 1 mile west of the highway. Getting to the area is very dangerous. In 1983 a Park ranger was mauled by a grizzly bear while walking in the area; there's a lot of room for grizzlies to hide among the tall sagebrush of Hayden Valley. In any case, there are numerous hot springs in the Crater Hills, only one of which is depositing geyserite. This Crater Hills Geyser is eruptive for a greater percentage of time than it is quiet. The play reaches about 8 feet.

6. Highland Springs Area

Along Alum Creek in the far northwestern portion of Hayden Valley are several hot spring areas. One of these is known as Highland Springs; it contains some small perpetual spouters but, apparently, no true geysers. Nearby, within a small canyon and not indicated on any map, is another group. Here are several more perpetual spouters and some small geysers. None of the eruptions reach more than 2 or 3 feet high.

7. Clearwater Springs

The Clearwater Springs are just north of the Roaring Mountain area, on the road between Mammoth and Norris. The only geyser activity known here occurred during 1922. Since that year was Yellowstone's 50th Anniversary, the geyser was named Semi-Centennial Geyser. The eruptions reached 75 feet high.

8. Unnamed Area Near Norris

About 2 miles west of the Norris Museum is a thermal area that has been visited perhaps only a half-dozen times over the years. Access is difficult, involving trekking through wet meadows, fording high streams, and bushwacking dense forest. The area turns out to contain a variety of springs, everything from mud pots to geysers. Little is known about the activity, but it seems as though the geysers are active for very long periods and/or have extremely short intervals, as they have been in eruption during most visits to the area. The larger of the two geysers erupts from a crack in the ground, sending a fan-shaped spray to as much as 30 feet. The other geyser plays from a pool, the highest splashes reaching only a few feet.

9. Rabbit Creek

The Rabbit Creek area is really a part of the Midway Geyser Basin. It is discussed separately because there is no trail into the area and it seems to have been visited as seldom as some very remote backcountry areas. The geyser activity is confined to the canyon of South Rabbit Creek. One perpetual spouter is known to vary its play considerably in a regular, pulsing pattern. The height ranges between 1 and 10 feet. Several other springs also show signs of periodic behavior.

10. Boundary Creek

In the southwestern portion of Yellowstone are the hot springs of Boundary Creek. Because this is the closest thermal group in Yellowstone to the Island Park area outside the Park (where geothermal well drilling is possible), these hot springs have been monitored closely in the last few years. The hope is to understand their activity well enough to be able to detect any slight change in water flow because of distant drilling. The surprise was that these springs include two geysers. They are both small but eruptions are frequent.

11. Ferris Fork of the Bechler River

Within a deep canyon along the Ferris Fork, perhaps two miles upstream from Three River Junction, is a small thermal area. Among the hot springs is a spouter. Whether it is actually a geyser or a perpetual spouter is uncertain. If perpetual, then it may have ceased activity, as no eruption has been seen recently. If it is a geyser, then its interval, though long, must be much shorter than the durations. The height of play is about 10 feet.

As of now, geysers are not known to occur in any other thermal area of Yellowstone. However, the geysers of areas 4, 8, 10, and 11 described here were only discovered during the 1970s. Also, geysers and geyser-like action have been seen at both the Mud Volcano Area and the Mary Mountain Hot Springs. It is definitely possible that more geysers are out there.

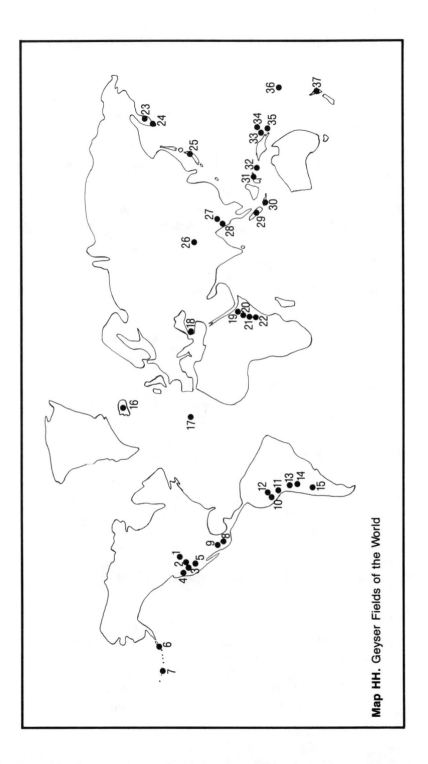

Map HH. Geyser Fields of the World

Appendix

Geyser Fields of the World

This appendix, as it appeared in the first edition of *The Geysers of Yellowstone,* was the first public presentation of information about all known geyser fields of the world. Since then much more has been learned. Geysers have been found in new areas, while other places have been proven to not involve geysers. As with the rest of this book, this section is revised to a great extent.

The sources of information presented here are diverse. Geysers have been noted in the course of numerous geologic studies – they are rare enough to make their existence an important part of any geologic situation – but few of these studies have been published for wide distribution. Nearly as often as not, these reports are written in some language other than English. Some are as much as 140 years old. Because of a misunderstanding among many early researchers, some artesian springs have been listed as geysers although they most definitely are not. It has turned out, then, that the most valuable source of information about geysers in the modern world has been personal communications, mostly letters from geologists all around the world.

All of these studies have made one thing especially clear: Yellowstone National Park is far and away the greatest geyser field anywhere. Any one of its larger geyser basins, taken alone, would be the largest geyser field in the world. The small area of the Upper Geyser Basin alone contains at least 25% of all the geysers on Earth, and the total for the Park – the 436 plus geysers described here – may make up as much as 75% of the world total.

Just why geysers are so common in Yellowstone is not known with certainty. Their existence is a complex matter, involving details such as water temperature, water supply, degree of self-sealing within the geothermal system, and, perhaps of the utmost importance, the extent to which the water has been both over-pressured beyond normal hydrostatic pressure and over-heated (or superheated) above the normal boiling point for a given depth and pressure. In any case, geysers make up a greater percentage of the total number of hot springs in Yellowstone than they do elsewhere. For example, Iceland contains more hot springs than Yellowstone does, yet the geysers there number only about

30. Even that small number is big enough to make Iceland one of the most important geyser fields on Earth.

The fact that no place in the world can compare with Yellowstone must not be taken as any belittlement of other geysers. Icelanders and New Zealanders are very proud of their geysers and the Russians have established a national park around theirs. One is hard put to convince these people that Yellowstone really is better. These nations and others can claim several large, justifiably famous spouters. Yet the combination of *all* the other geyser fields of the world, listed here as 36 in number, includes little more than 200 geysers. This figure includes known active and inactive geysers as well as a number of areas for which the only available information simply states "several geysers." All of the world's known geyser fields are shown on Map HH.

Each of the following descriptions is followed by a numerical listing of references. The descriptive section is then followed by an annotated bibliography of these references. It is hoped that the entire work is accurate, but there are bound to be some errors. However, this section is definitely not designed as a guidebook, but only as a source of information. In that capacity it gives an accurate idea as to the nature and distribution of geyser fields.

Finally, it must be noted that many of these geyser fields are not what they once were. Man's ever widening search for energy has destroyed many of these geothermal systems, and a number of those remaining will soon have a similar fate. Even Yellowstone has been threatened by geothermal drilling in the Island Park Caldera, just outside the western boundary of the Park. Geysers are disappearing from our world. Yellowstone is the one geyser field that *must* be saved. Someday it might well be the last geyser field.

1. YELLOWSTONE NATIONAL PARK, WYOMING. In terms of the number of geysers, the power of the activity, or any other category one would like to consider, Yellowstone is far and away the world's largest and best geyser field. Its more than 400 geysers are scattered among nine individual geyser basins, which range in size from the Upper Basin with over 180 geysers to smaller areas with as few as 9 geysers. With nearly three out of every four of the world's geysers, Yellowstone simply cannot be compared with any place else.

2. BEOWAWE, NEVADA. Beowawe is a small community, little more than a whistle-stop on the railroad, halfway between Battle Mountain and Elko in northern Nevada. The geysers are found about 4 miles southwest of the town, near the head of Whirlwind Valley. The gold rush pioneers of the 1850s saw the steam clouds and took them to be permanent dust devils; the area was not reported to contain geysers until

The last geyser of any significance in the field at Beowawe, Nevada, jets a few feet high beneath the spectacular but destructive presence of drilled steam wells on the Main Terrace.

1869. A graded public road leads to the springs. The geysers themselves, however, are on private land, which has been leased for geothermal development, so whether they are accessible now is uncertain.

The Beowawe Geysers did not receive detailed study until 1934. At that time the small field contained more than a dozen spouters, enough to have made Beowawe the fifth or sixth largest geyser field in the world. Indeed, out of only 50 hot springs, about 30 have been known to erupt, probably the highest proportion of spouting vents in any geyser area.

The hot springs were distributed about two groups: a sinter terrace on the hillside and a lower, sinter-covered shield on the valley floor near the base of the terrace. Most of the activity was on the Main

The geothermal field at Beowawe, Nevada, once boasted as many as thirty geysers. Now only three remain. The largest plays a few feet high from a shallow pool.

Terrace. Among the several geysers was one (the original "Beowawe Geyser") that erupted to about 30 feet high, and others that played frequently to as much as 15 feet high. The sinter shield in the valley below included just three geysers.

One of the earliest United States geothermal exploration programs was begun at Beowawe in the 1950s. Three deep steam wells were drilled on the Main Terrace. Testing of the wells for steam pressure and temperature robbed most of the natural springs of water and heat. All of the geysers were destroyed and most pools dried up, leaving only a few muddy springs and steam vents in their places. Then in the early 1970s somebody used dynamite on two of the well caps. Both became steady spouters, erupting comingled steam and water to as high as 70 feet. Although these two wells have been recapped, the Main Terrace only vaguely resembles what was there before.

The sinter shield in the valley was less affected by the drilling, and the clear alkaline springs remain. Three of them are still geysers. One, a deep, blue pool, erupts rather infrequently. Its activity ranges from a spray 10 feet high to a mildly turbulent overflow. Another geyser here erupts even more rarely from a narrow crack in the geyserite. The third geyser, when active, is the best performer of the three. Sometimes called "Beowawe Geyser" (but not to be confused with the original Beowawe Geyser on the Main Terrace), its 2-foot-wide vent is centered in a shallow, 10-foot-wide basin. This geyser erupts erratically, with intervals ranging from 2 to 24 hours. The play lasts 10 minutes, sending some bursts up to 10 feet high and ending with a weak steam phase. The total water discharge amounts to several hundred gallons per eruption. Elsewhere on the valley floor are a few small perpetual spouters.

A recent transaction has transferred geothermal rights from one company to another, and a large-scale commercial geothermal power facility is in the works. That will certainly doom the remaining geysers. It's too bad. Beowawe was known as a geyser area before Yellowstone was proven. It was one of the most concentrated such areas anywhere, and among the largest, too. And now it's all but gone.

References: 3, 4, 5, and 32.

3. STEAMBOAT SPRINGS, NEVADA. Steamboat Springs is almost too accessible. The area is astride U.S. Highway 395 just 9 miles south of downtown Reno, Nevada. Consequently, it has suffered severe damage because of a lack of management, while most of the local population is unaware of just how rare such an area is. The situation is beginning to change and a park may soon be established.

The geyser activity at Steamboat Springs is continuously changing. Seldom does any given spouter persist for more than a few months before an exchange of function causes its death or dormancy. On the other hand, there has always been at least some degree of eruptive activity in the area.

Most of the action is on the Main Terrace west of the highway. Many different geysers have been active there. During the 1870s one of them was very regular and played as high as 75 feet. It became so well known that the residents of Virginia City made frequent trips to the area to watch it, and Dan DeQuille mentions the geyser in his famous book, *The Big Bonanza*. Other geyser activity on the Main Terrace has generally been small. At least eighteen have been seen.

The Lower Terrace, near the resort east of the highway, contains fewer springs, among which have been eight observed geysers. None of these have matched the scale of activity on the Main Terrace, but one has proven to be the most persistent geyser at Steamboat Springs. Though not always vigorous, it has apparently been active to some extent for over 50 years.

A part of the Main Terrace is under the ownership of the federal Bureau of Land Management. The private holder of the rest of the terrace is negotiating with the government to exchange her land for an equal acreage elsewhere. Should that take place then the Main Terrace will become a Washoe County Park, with nature trails and interpretive displays about the geysers. Meanwhile, a private organization known as the Geyser Observation and Study Association is conducting periodic observations of the activity at Steamboat. Perhaps the area is finally getting the recognition it deserves. For those interested, reference #6 contains accurate maps of the terraces.

References: 1, 2, 3, 6, and 32.

4. MORGAN SPRINGS, CALIFORNIA. Located just outside the south entrance of Lassen Volcanic National Park, Morgan Springs is a small collection of very hot, flowing springs and pools. During the mid-1950s at least three of them were active as geysers. No such action has been seen before or since, but the one known episode is enough to include the area among the world's geyser fields.

Nearby, within the national park, is Terminal Geyser. It is probably not a true geyser but rather a perpetual spouter or maybe even only a hot artesian spring. However, it certainly does play with a fluctuating geyser-like action reaching as much as 30 feet high during some years.

References: 3 and 32.

5. LONG VALLEY CALDERA, CALIFORNIA. The Long Valley Caldera is a huge volcanic explosion crater very much like that of Yellowstone and formed at about the same time. It is, therefore, logical that it should contain similar hot springs. It does, but geysers have been unusual. Reports about geysers are scattered through the literature, but the reliability of the reports is sometimes questionable. The current situation is not.

Starting in May 1980 and continuing through the years since, the Long Valley area has been subject to several earthquake swarms. Some of the Richter magnitudes have been greater than 6. This has been shown to be the result of an intrusion of molten magma at a shallow depth, possibly presaging a new episode of volcanic eruptions in the area. The intrusion has altered the heat flow of the area, increasing the temperatures in several hot spring groups and producing a few geysers.

At the Casa Diablo Hot Springs, near the junction of U.S. Highway 395 and State Highway 203, where geysers have been reported in the past, is now one geyser. Its activity is directly related to the status of a nearby steam well. If the well is turned on and spouting, then the geyser is all but dormant; when the well is off, the geyser plays frequently. Its height is as much as 30 feet.

At the swimming area at Hot Creek, which is operated by the U.S. Forest Service, reports are that at least one geyser was created by the 1980 earthquakes, spouting for a while to 40 feet. A number of other springs there were also reported to have erupted following the shocks, but all geyser action at Hot Creek has now died out.

Last is the Hot Bubbling Pool, near the sheriff's station. It may not be a true geyser, but it is at least an intermittent spring, varying its water level and degree of boiling with a total period of 4 to 5 hours.

References: 3, 7, and 32.

6. **UMNAK ISLAND, ALASKA.** Umnak Island is one of the first in the Aleutian Chain, quite close to the mainland of Alaska. In the narrow midsection of the island are several hot spring groups. Two of these, in Geyser Valley along Geyser Creek, which drains into Geyser Bight, contain geysers. Though small, their activity is vigorous. All have recorded intervals ranging between 3 and 10 minutes, durations of around 3 minutes, and heights of 3 feet. These data, virtually the same for all six geysers present, were obtained in 1948. Umnak was visited again during the late 1970s. At that time the geysers were still active, but much less frequently. That report indicates that the hot springs are more notable for their great depths and beautiful coloration, matching some of the larger pools of Yellowstone.

References: 2, 8, and 32.

7. KANAGA ISLAND, ALASKA. Kanaga Island is another of the Aleutian Chain, but much farther from the mainland near Adak Island. During a general geothermal survey of resources in Alaska it was discovered that Kanaga's hot springs include a number of small geysers. Nothing further is known about them.

Reference: 32.

8. COMANJILLA, GUANAJUATO, MEXICO. Comanjilla is a fancy hot spring spa and hotel between the cities of Leon and Guanajuato, northeast of Guadalajara. All of the bathing pools are fed by the runoff from the hot springs. The first description of these geysers was written in 1910. The activity of the area is stable enough that all of the geysers described then can still be identified. The largest is Geyser Humboldt, nearly always dormant but playing up to 10 feet high when active. Another plays regularly about every 2 hours, the eruption lasting several minutes and reaching around 4 feet high. At least four other, smaller geysers are also found at Comanjilla.

References: 3, 9, and 32.

9. IXTLAN DE LOS HERVORES, MICHOACAN, MEXICO. The name roughly translates as "boiling pools," and Ixtlan certainly has its share of them. Located about midway between Guadalajara and Morelia, it is a large geothermal area. Because of its great number of mud pots, pools, and geysers, it has sometimes been promoted as "Mexico's Little Yellowstone." Unfortunately, it has also been the site of geothermal drilling, and that has severely altered the natural springs.

The hot springs occur in several groups scattered along a 2-mile stretch of the valley. Geysers used to occur in all of the clusters. With descriptive names translating to such as Black, Coyote, White Rock, and Kitchen, at least fourteen geysers were active in 1906. As recently as the 1950s at least most were still active, including Tritubulario (Three Vent) and Pozo Verde (Green Spring), each playing 10 to 15 feet high.

The geothermal drilling has all but destroyed the natural springs at most of Ixtlan de los Hervores. One of the wells is spouting continuously, reaching perhaps 50 feet high. That area is fenced and operated as something of a park. The guard charges a few pesos for admission.

A part of the easternmost area, behind the village of Salitre, has been relatively unchanged although drilling also occurred there. At least two large geysers are still active, one playing on unknown intervals for as long as 10 minutes; it reaches about 3 feet high. However, the old large geysers Tritubulario and Pozo Verde have both been dormant

for a long enough time to have allowed large cacti to grow in their runoff channels.
References: 3, 10, 11, 32.

10. CARUMAS, MOQUEGUA, PERU. The vicinity of Carumas, at about 12,000 feet elevation in the Andes of southern Peru, is filled with hot springs. All are of significantly high temperatures, and geysers are known to occur in three of the groups.

The best area is Sicoloque, where there are four geysers, one reaching over 12 feet high, one about 10 feet, and two around 4 feet.

At Putina there are three geysers. One is again around 12 feet high while both others play to less than 3 feet.

Sayasayani is the site of a single geyser 3 feet high.

The waters of all these areas and more are used for bathing, and evidence of Inca usage is found in several areas.
References: 2, 3, and 32.

11. CALIENTES, CANDARAVE, TACNA, PERU. As in the Carumas area (see #10, above), the hot water from the springs at Calientes has been used for medicinal bathing for hundreds of years. Incan ruins are abundant in the area. The elevation of the area is nearly 14,500 feet above sea level. There are many boiling springs here, but only one certain geyser. In 1979 it erupted with extremely regular 55-minute intervals; the duration was 2 minutes and the height over 20 feet.
References: 2 and 32.

12. PUENTEBELLO, PUNO, PERU. The geysers of Puentebello occur within and immediately in front of a single limestone cavern. Generally, limestone is considered an improper material for the existence of geysers as it does not have the inherent strength of siliceous sinter. Nevertheless, geysers do seem to occur at Puentebello. Within the cave (and inaccessible because of the hot water and inhospitable atmosphere) are "many" geysers, all playing 3 to 6 feet high; these may be perpetual spouters. Just outside the cave is a truly periodic geyser with heavy discharge. It plays every 10 seconds, lasts 2 seconds, and reaches 4 to 5 feet high.
Reference: 32.

13. SURIRI, TARAPACA, CHILE. Many of the geyser fields of the world are in very remote areas, but Suriri is certainly one of the remotest. It is nearly 15,000 feet up in the Andes of far northern Chile, and no roads come anywhere near approaching the area. Essentially the only access would be via helicopter, and even then it would be a very long

trip. It makes sense, obviously, that very little observation has been done at Suriri. As part of a geothermal study of the country, it was surveyed during the 1960s and a report was published in 1972. No geyser was active at that time, but one was observed back in 1944. It was very small – but it was a geyser. At least 230 hot springs occur in the area, and a few intermittently boiling springs were seen in 1972.
References: 12 and 32.

14. PUCHULDIZA, TARAPACA, CHILE. Also located in northern Chile and high in the Andes Mountains, Puchuldiza is at least slightly more accessible than Suriri. Overland travel of about four days is needed to reach the area. At an elevation of just about 14,000 feet, it contains a few small geysers. No details about their activity have been published, but at least four geysers were present during the mid-1970s.

About 3 miles down the river draining the Puchuldiza field is a smaller thermal area known as Tuja. It also contains at least four small geysers.
References: 13 and 32.

15. EL TATIO, ANTOFAGASTA, CHILE. El Tatio is one of the world's premier geyser fields, even now in spite of considerable geothermal drilling in the area. The basin lies high in the Andes, at an elevation of 13,800 feet above sea level; it is, however, served by a rough but passable road. The valley is almost completely ringed by active volcanoes, making El Tatio one of the most directly volcanic of geyser fields, too. The geothermal exploration of the area was intended as the start of actual power developments. That is temporarily on hold, so the geysers remain.

El Tatio has contained as many as 67 geysers. Not all have ever been active at the same time, and the record for a single observation is 37 geysers. El Tatio is somewhat notable among geyser fields in not containing any significantly large geysers. The tallest eruptions observed have been on the order of 20 feet high. However, the existence of 67 geysers through the years makes El Tatio the third largest geyser field in the world, after Yellowstone and New Zealand.
References: 2, 3, 14, and 32.

15. ICELAND. Most discussions of the geysers of Iceland always seem to generalize, giving the impression that there is a single geyser basin. Reality is that while the large geysers of fame are confined to one small area, hot spring groups with geysers are scattered widely about the island. They total a large enough number to make Iceland probably the fourth largest geyser field in the world.

The names of the geyser areas are fascinating. Icelandic is a Viking tongue, largely unrelated to any other modern language, and many of these names are all but unpronounceable by English-speaking people. The geyser basins bear names such as Torfastathir, Hruni, Reykir in Ölfus, and Borgarfjartharsysla. The geysers themselves also have some stupendous names such as Sturlureykir, Svathi, Eyvindarhver, and Opherrishola. Each name has some specific meaning, often very descriptive, as those of Yellowstone.

Most famous of all is Geysir. It is the namesake of all the geysers in the world. Translated, the name means "gusher" or "spouter." The Icelandic people are proud of Geysir; the name is actually copyrighted so that it can never be applied to any other geyser.

Geysir is at Haukadalur. It rarely erupts now. Why this is so is uncertain; perhaps it is simply dormant because of an exchange of function with other springs in the area, or perhaps it was damaged after suffering too many artificially induced eruptions during the 1950s. When active, the eruption may reach 200 feet high. It truly is one of the world's major spouters and probably deserves its rank as the most famous geyser on Earth. After all, it was first described way back in the year 1294.

Another important geyser at Haukadalur is Strokkur, whose name means "churn." Before 1900 it played in concert with Geysir, some of its spouts also reaching 200 feet high. After a long dormancy, Strokkur reactivated around 1970. Now it gushes forth every 15 to 20 minutes, the single burst of most eruptions reaching 75 feet high. Strokkur is presently the largest geyser in Iceland. Three or four other, much smaller geysers occur at Haukadalur, which is maintained with a park-like atmosphere.

Another great concentration of geysers was at Reykir in Ölfus. Most of these can no longer be identified because of drilling for geothermal energy, most of which is used for heating greenhouses. Gone are the famous Gryla, which played every 2 to 3 hours as high as 40 feet, and Littli, which could reach 80 feet. Gone, too, are the once famous man-made geysers known as Bogi I, Bogi II, and Gosi II, all of which played when the owner desired to about 35 feet.

Probably the most active basin in Iceland now is at Hveravellir, almost dead center on the island. It contains about 15 active geysers; most are small but one erupts to about 15 feet. Other geysers have been known in at least fifteen other areas in Iceland. Many of these places included only a single geyser.

Iceland is, to be sure, one of the foremost geyser fields in the world. Of course, the nation has virtually no other energy reserves of its own, and geothermal energy is vital to the future existence of the country. Therefore, there has been virtually no attempt to preserve the geysers. Only the small area at Haukadalur has any real measure of protection, and any nearby drilling in the future would take them as well.

References: 1, 2, 3, 15, 16, and 32.

17. VOLCAN FURNAS, ISLA SAN MIGUEL, AZORES ISLANDS, SPAIN. The name "Furnas" translates just as it sounds – "furnace." It is a volcano, probably only dormant rather than dead, within which are numerous hot springs. At the turn of this century there were several geysers, one erupting frequently as high as "several feet." By 1955, none were active. The hot springs still include a number of boiling springs, some of them intermittent in their action. If there are no geysers now, there certainly may be again.

References: 2 and 3.

18. AYVACIK, TURKEY. Boiling hot springs would not be expected near the northwest coast of Turkey, but several occur near the town of Ayvacik. This is, in turn, near the site of ancient Troy. Gayzer Suyu is the single geyser in the area. In 1952 it was reported to erupt frequently to 6 feet. The only other known reference may not refer to Gayzer Suyu, but it's nice to think that it does, for it would then be the oldest reference to any known geyser. This is *The Iliad,* written by Homer around 800 B.C.

Reference: 2.

19. ALLALLOBEDA, DANAKIL AREA, ETHIOPIA. The Danakil Depression is a forbiddingly stark desert in east-central Ethiopia. It is a volcanic area within the northern part of the East African Rift System. Not far from Allallobeda is Hadar, where the remains of Lucy, First Family, and other early hominids were found during the 1970s. At Allallobeda the hot springs are aligned along a fault zone. The Allallobeda Spouter plays constantly as much as 20 feet high. Another spring is a true geyser, but its eruption is less than 1 foot high. Other intermittent springs also exist in the area.

References: 17 and 32.

20. THE LAKES DISTRICT, ETHIOPIA. The highlands of southern Ethiopia, while still dry, are markedly different from the Danakil. A series of large lakes occupies low areas in the Rift Valley. Hot springs are numerous and geysers are known in at least two places. A very early report about these geysers referred to them under the name "Ta'hou." The name is obsolete now, for no modern reference to such a place can be found. Just which geysers were Ta'hou – these in Ethiopia or perhaps even some in Kenya – is uncertain.

Along the northwest shore of Lake Abaya is an extensive hot spring area. The geyserite platform is dotted with small cones and beaded deposits, both of which indicate geysers. In the mid-1960s no eruptions could be seen, but one spring was active in late 1979. Its action was erratic but reached 6 feet high.

In Lake Langano's North Bay is Geyser Island. Following an earthquake in 1906 one spring erupted powerfully, some of the play reaching over 60 feet. The play was extremely brief, perhaps a single burst, but recurred every 30 seconds. Through the years the activity declined and by 1966 it had regressed to intermittent overflow.

References: 2, 3, 17, and 32.

21. LOGKIPPI, KENYA. Logkippi (Logipi, Lokipi, etc.) is a small lake a few miles south of the southern end of Lake Turkana, in northern Kenya. It would be a part of Lake Turkana except for some recent lava flows, which act as a dam. The Logkippi area includes several hot springs. Logkippi Geyser itself plays almost constantly, reaching 8 to 10 feet above a raised sinter platform. A few of the other springs may also be geysers.

References: 2, 3, and 20.

22. LAKE BOGORIA, KENYA. Lake Bogoria in central Kenya is famed as one of the better flamingo nesting areas anywhere. Relatively little attention has been paid to the hot springs near the south end of the lake. Among these is a single geyser. Loburu Geyser erupts every 5 minutes, sending its water to a height of 5 feet or more. The East African Power & Light Company has done exploratory drilling in the Lake Bogoria area. While this has resulted in a thorough documentation of the hot spring activity, it may also soon spell the end of Loburu.

References: 2 and 32.

23. GEYSERNAYA RIVER, UZON CALDERA, KAMCHATKA PENINSULA, U.S.S.R. The Kamchatka Peninsula is that long, fat extension of Siberia that points south into the north Pacific Ocean. Geysers are known to exist in two places on the peninsula; by far the better is near the Uzon Caldera, a large and recent rhyolitic volcano.

The valley of the Geysernaya River is so remote that it wasn't explored until 1941. T. I. Ustinova was so excited by her find that the Russian government, even during World War II, sponsored an additional expedition to the area. That was followed by several others through the 1950s. Now the area has become the Kronotski National Park, and a recent report claims that such tourist facilities as a visitor center, campground, trails, and so on are being constructed to be ready

Zhemchuzhnyi Geyser ("The Pearl") is one of the larger geysers in Kam-chatka's Kronotski National Park, playing 40 feet high every 4 to 5 hours. (Photo by Steinberg.)

for use by 1987. So far, no non-Russian has been invited to see the area; perhaps that is about to change.

Twenty-two geysers are known to exist along a 2-mile stretch of the river. Their activity is certainly on par with that of Yellowstone. The Three is a geyser that plays from three different vents, each one spouting at a different angle and height. Active several times per day, it reaches 75 feet high. Across the stream from the Three is the Neighbor. As the time for an eruption of the Three approaches, Neighbor's own eruptions become more frequent and more powerful. Finally, the geysers complete a cycle with concerted eruptions, after which both fall silent for some time. Fountain is another important spouter. It plays every 16 minutes, jetting water over 60 feet high. Largest of them all is Velikan ("Giant"). One of the world's largest geysers, it erupts every 4 to 6 hours to heights ranging over 130 feet.

As remote as it is, there is little likelihood that any geothermal development will take place along the Geysernaya River any time in the near future. Its geyser field is therefore one of the very few being preserved for the future. The Russian efforts to do so should be applauded. References: 2, 3, 18, and 32.

24. PAUZHETSKIE, KAMCHATKA PENINSULA, U.S.S.R. Not far south of Petropavlovsk, the largest city in Kamchatka, is the geothermal field of Pauzhetskie. In years past the area contained several small geysers. Some authors considered them to be artesian springs, the spouting caused by gravity rather than boiling, but the action is periodic, which gravity certainly is not. Being close to a large city, Pauzhetskie was a natural choice for geothermal development. It has been intensive and, as is always the case, most natural springs have been destroyed as a result. In 1984 the area contained two geysers, both erratic in their activity and no more than 1 or 2 feet high. References: 2, 3, and 32.

25. JAPAN. Considering the number of rhyolite fields and active volcanoes in Japan, geysers are very few in number. Although there are eruptions to be seen in several areas around the country, only one basin contains any natural geysers. These are the Onokobe Springs, Miyagi Prefecture, in northern Japan. Among several hundred hot springs, the two geysers each play to about 5 feet high. Elsewhere in the group are numerous sparkling clear pools, some of which show signs of geyser activity in the past.

Artificial geysers, both hot springs whose water levels have been altered and drilled wells, are found in several other areas in Japan. These include the "geysers" of Tsuchiya, Shikabe, Yunotani, and Tamatsukuri. These spouters are generally small.

Malyi Geyser ("Small Geyser") is one of the largest of the Kamchatka geysers, in spite of its name. (Photo by Steinberg.)

The hot spring area at Atami, a resort city about 100 miles south of Tokyo, used to contain a very famous and frequently active geyser. Eruptions would occur as often as once per day, maintaining a 30-foot height for several hours. The Atami Geyser ceased activity in the late 1920s when a nearby landslide caused a change in its water level, and nothing similar has been observed in the vicinity since then.
References: 2, 3, and 32.

26. XIZANG (TIBET), PEOPLE'S REPUBLIC OF CHINA. "We marched for three successive days without coming to tents. Then we saw in the distance a great column of smoke rising into the sky. We wondered if it came from a chimney or a burning house, but when we got near we saw it was the steam rising from hot springs. We were soon gazing at a scene of great natural beauty. A number of springs bubbled out of the ground, and in the middle of the cloud of steam shot up a splendid little geyser fifteen feet high. After poetry, prose! We all naturally thought of a bath . . ."

So wrote Heinrich Harrer in describing his *Seven Years In Tibet.* Unfortunately, there is no way of identifying his nice geyser. Xizang is known to have geysers in several individual localities. Indeed, none of those recently studied seems to be either Harrer's or those described during the 1870s.

The La Chu River is a tremendously remote place, its headwaters rising at an elevation of over 17,000 feet. Roughly halfway between Lhasa and Lake Tengri Nor, the region was first described in 1875, when the geyser areas were identified, and then again in 1912, when details were provided. The better of the two geyser basins was Peting Chuja. In 1912 it contained at least twelve geysers, the *smallest* of which was reported to play 20 feet high, among several dozen other hot springs. A few miles farther downstream from Peting Chuja is Naisum Chuja. It reportedly included only two geysers, but both were said to spout 50 to 60 feet high. It must be recognized that the observer might actually have been measuring steam clouds rather than water jets. Even so, the existence of this many geysers along the La Chu River makes the region one of the larger geyser fields in the world. Unfortunately, no modern confirmation of these geysers is available.

Modern studies have been conducted at several other places in Xizang. Geysers are known in three of these geothermal fields and a large perpetual spouter in another.

The most extensive area is Tagajia, at an elevation of about 14,000 feet near the headwaters of the Lagetzanbo River. There are four geysers. The two largest both play to heights of more than 60 feet. The interval of one is 3 hours. The other has intervals of 36 hours and a duration of only 10 minutes, but it is a pretty geyser as it plays at a 45-degree angle.

A second geyser basin is Chapu. Geysers such as Quzun and Semi are reported to have increased the frequency of their eruptions by up to five times following an earthquake in 1959.

Geysers are also reported for an area called Guhu, but no data are available.

The perpetual spouter is at Namling. Named Bibiling, its steady play reaches over 30 feet.

With this many individual geyser occurrences, there is surely no question about Xizang being a major geyser field. Of course, the unfortunate point is that the Chinese research that has revealed these geysers is aimed at geothermal developments.

References: 2, 19, 20, 21, 22, and 32.

27. THAILAND. Thailand is certainly a well-explored place, yet the fact that its hot springs include geysers is a discovery of the 1970s. Geysers are now known to occur in three localities, each at least 50 miles from the nearest other.

There is some question as to whether or not true geysers, rather than simple spouting springs, were being described in all of the three areas, but one for which there is no doubt is Pa Pai. There are only seven hot springs there, but four are geysers. All have intervals of around 30 seconds, durations of 12 to 15 seconds, and heights of 6 feet.

At Fang, just across the border from Laos, are several small geysers among about thirty springs. They typically play every 15 to 45 seconds and reach 2 feet high.

More questionable is the geyser reported at Pong Hom. It may be a perpetual spouter, but it is certainly impressive at up to 20 feet high.

Reference: 23.

28. PAI, BURMA. The listing of a geyser at Pai, in the Tavoy District of the Burmese panhandle, seemed unlikely until the discovery of geysers in nearby Thailand. The only written reference to the geyser was penned in 1864. It described the geyser as being 6 feet high.

References: 3 and 24.

29. SUMATRA, INDONESIA. Sumatra, the largest and northwesternmost of the Indonesian islands, is intensely volcanic, and geysers are known to occur in at least four areas. They are separated from one another by great enough distances for them to be considered as individual geyser fields. From northwest to southeast, the localities are:

TAPANULI. Within a restricted zone, geysers occur in four hot spring groups. Near the village of Sibanggor Jae is a single geyser, erupting 8 feet high. Tarutung has a single geyser, which reaches about 10 feet.

The most extensive of these hot spring groups is at Silangkitang, where one geyser plays from a large pool, the play being frequent and 8 feet high. Finally, a muddy perpetual spouter at Sipirok jets a steady stream of strongly acid water to about 60 feet.

PASAMAN. Within a small hot spring area about 1½ miles from the town of Panti is a single geyser, 5 feet high.

KERINCI. The Geyser Gao Gadang is probably the largest geyser in Indonesia. Near the village of Dusan Baru, it is most active when the air temperature is exceptionally high or the barometric pressure is very low. Then it may erupt frequently and has been seen to play more than 70 feet high. At other times it rarely erupts and then reaches only 3 feet high.

LAMPUNG-SEMANGKO. A caldera within this district used to contain geysers in a number of places, including one geyser basin that reportedly contained a dozen or more geysers. A few decades ago the area was disrupted by a series of powerful phreatic (steam) eruptions, and most geysers were destroyed. Geysers are now found in just two hot spring groups. Near Waimuli there are two geysers, both playing only 1 foot high. At Waipanas is a single geyser, showing intervals of 10 seconds, durations of 5 seconds, and a height of 12 feet during late 1971.

References: 25 and 32.

30. CISOLOK, JAVA, INDONESIA. Cisolok is on the southwest coast of Java. Most of the hot springs arise from the bed of the Cipanas River, and it is only those whose deposits have grown above the river level that erupt. The deposits are unusual for a geyser area in that they are calcium carbonate (calcareous sinter) rather than siliceous sinter. Two geysers have been described. One reaches 12 to 17 feet high, while the other plays to just 1 foot. According to one author these are not geysers at all but only hot artesian springs; but they are listed as geysers by volcanologists with the Geological Survey of Indonesia.

References: 3 and 32.

31. MINAHASA, SULAWESI, INDONESIA. Sulawesi (or Celebes) is a large, very irregularly shaped island between the main Indonesian islands and the Philippines. The northeastern arm of the island contains the volcanic area of Minahasa. Although hot springs are extremely common throughout the district, geysers occur in only one group. Near the village of Toraget, a deep, clear pool erupts every 3 to 5 minutes. The play lasts only a few seconds and reaches 1½ to 2 feet high. Other geysers have been recorded in this area, but most of their activity has been restricted to short periods of time following earthquakes.

Also in the Minahasa District is Nolok Volcano which, during the

1950s, contained a boiling lake that periodically erupted as high as 150 feet.

References: 2, 3, and 32.

32. BACAN ISLAND, MOLLUCAN CHAIN, INDONESIA. Bacan Island (also spelled Bactian, Batjan, and Bacjan) is the largest of the Mollucas, historically important under their old name of "Spice Islands." Bacan lies just off the west coast of the large island of Halmahera. The hot springs of the island are almost all of boiling temperatures, and several were reported as geysers during the 1800s. The largest was named Atoe Ri. No modern geothermal survey has been conducted in the area, so the present status of these geysers is unknown.

References: 3 and 32.

33. NEW BRITAIN ISLAND AND VICINITY, PAPUA-NEW GUINEA. The Bismark Archipelago contains a great many islands, mostly quite small. New Britain and New Ireland are, however, among the largest islands in the South Pacific. Geysers, actually comprising several distinct fields, are found on New Britain and one of the islets.

At Garua Harbor on the north-central coast of New Britain are found two major hot spring groups. At the settlement of Talasea there are no geysers at the present time, but extensive geyserite deposits, small cones, and boiling temperatures make their former and possible future existence likely. Across the bay, near the village of Pangalu, is a smaller hot spring cluster, which does contain two geysers. Both seem to come and go through time, sometimes being inactive, sometimes acting as perpetual spouters, and at other times behaving as true periodic geysers. The larger of these can play as high as 25 feet; the other more typically reaches 6 feet.

About 50 miles southeast of Talasea and 10 miles inland from the coastline at Cape Hoskins is the Kasiloli thermal area. Although the active area is very small, measuring less than 1,000 feet in any direction, it contains at least fourteen geysers, making it among the largest geyser fields anywhere. Tabe Geyser erupts with intervals ranging from 15 minutes to several hours in length, probably because of cyclic action; the duration is 3 minutes and the height in excess of 30 feet. The other geysers, none of which have been named, all play to between 1 and 4 feet.

North of New Britain is the Witu Group of small islands. Among these is Narage Island, a speck of dormant volcanism less than 1 mile across. Hot springs are numerous, especially near the beaches, and among them is one geyser. When observed during the 1800s it played as much as 30 feet high. Now it is much weaker. In 1970 it exhibited intervals of 2 to 3 minutes, durations of 20 to 30 seconds, and a height of around 3 feet.

Geysers have also been reported in the literature to occur on "Hannam Island north of New Britain." Such a place does not exist. Hannam was the original name for what is now recognized as part of the New Britain mainland, the Willaumez Peninsula, and the reference to geysers there is apparently to those of the Talasea-Pangalu areas.

References: 1, 2, 3, 26, and 32.

34. LIHIR AND AMBITLE ISLANDS, NEAR NEW IRELAND ISLAND, PAPUA-NEW GUINEA. These islands lie off the east coast of New Ireland, forming the easternmost lands of the sprawling nation of Papua-New Guinea.

Lihir (or Lir) Island is small, measuring about 5 by 3½ miles. There are several hot spring groups, and two of them *may* contain geysers. Near the coastline is a deep vent known as Roaring Spring. Its water level periodically rises and falls, accompanied by much noisy evolution of steam. A second area contains the Hot Air Blow Hole. This sounds like a steam vent, but its activity is described as periodic. Both of these springs are possible geysers.

Ambitle (or Anir, or Feni) Island is larger and contains more hot springs than does Lihir, and here geysers positively exist. At a low elevation, near a plantation, are numerous hot springs. Several show intermittent activity, and one is clearly a geyser, erupting irregularly but frequently to about 1½ feet high. Inland about 2 miles is another thermal area. It contains several very hot, geyserite-lined pools. At least one of these is thought to be a large but infrequent geyser, playing as much as 30 feet high. Elsewhere in this group may be as many as five other geysers plus one 10-foot perpetual spouter.

References: 1, 2, 3, 26, and 32.

35. FERGUSSON ISLAND, D'ENTRECASTEAUX ARCHIPELAGO, PAPUA-NEW GUINEA. Fergusson is the largest of the d'Entrecasteaux Islands, located off the southeastern tip of New Guinea itself. Among the dozens of thermal areas are Deidei and Iamelele.

At Deidei there are several geysers. Unfortunately, no written report has specified the number, but one researcher seemed to recall, twenty-five years after his visit, about a dozen. Most of the eruptions are quite small, but one geyser is reported to reach 15 feet while another plays between 5 and 10 feet high. This is all that's known about one of the world's larger geyser fields.

A few miles away is Iamelele. Though there are many more hot springs than at Deidei, geyser activity is much less intense. The several clusters of hot springs all contain at least some sinter deposits, but only two areas contain any large formations of geyserite. These are broad sinter terraces dotted with small cones. The cones alone are indications of geyser activity, but small eruptions are only rarely seen. The extent of erosion in the area as well as geochemical information imply that Iamelele is on the wane.

References: 1, 3, 26, and 32.

36. NASAVUSAVU, VANUA LEVU, FIJI. Vanua Levu is the largest of the Fiji Islands, but not the one of greatest population. Until recently it was rarely visited by outsiders, but tourist facilities have recently been built almost right at the Nasavusavu Hot Springs. Here are several small hot spring groups, each including a few boiling springs. At one, located about ½ mile from the hotel, are three related springs within 30 feet of each other. Known as Nakama Springs, they are geysers. Eruptions consist of vigorous boiling and occasional splashes to the grand height of several inches. Eruptions last for several hours. Some of the other springs in this compact group are periodic in their overflow, making them intermittent springs.

References: 3, 27, and 32.

37. NEW ZEALAND. The thermal areas of New Zealand's North Island comprise the second largest geyser field in the world – or, at least, they did. As many as 200 active geysers have been known during the recorded history of the Rotorua-Taupo Volcanic Zone. Because of recent geothermal and hydroelectric developments, perhaps no more than 40 geysers remain.

The most important of the remaining geyser basins is at Whakarewarewa, just outside the city of Rotorua. The area is a Maori Preserve, operated as a park where admission is charged, and protected from any direct geothermal developments. It is threatened by geothermal drilling outside the area, however, and has already suffered some losses. Several of the geysers are large and worthy of special note. Wairoa used to be one of the largest and most regular geysers in the world. Its eruptions resembled Old Faithful's. The maximum height was between 120 and 150 feet, but eruptions have been rare since the 1920s. The Pohutu ("Big Splash") Geyser Complex behaves in much the same way as does Yellowstone's Grand Geyser Complex. As the time for an eruption approaches, Te Horo becomes agitated with much splashing about in the crater. Its height is usually only a few feet, but it has been known to reach as much as 50 feet high. Just a few minutes before Pohutu erupts, the Prince of Wales Feathers Geyser plays from a narrow rift on the shoulder of Pohutu's crater. Shot out at an angle, its height is between 30 and 50 feet. Finally, Pohutu suddenly begins to play. Ranging up to more than 100 feet high, its eruptions last 20

Pohutu Geyser, joined by the arching play of Prince of Wales Feathers Geyser, is now the largest of New Zealand's geysers, with some play reaching over 100 feet high.

minutes. The Feathers continues throughout Pohutu's activity. The entire display may be repeated as often as every 2 hours. Besides these, Whakarewarewa contains at least eight other geysers.

The country around Lake Rotomahana was once the site of two of the largest siliceous sinter terraces in the world. The Pink and White Terraces were over 50 feet high and several hundred feet broad. Playing in the crater atop the White Terrace was Te Terata, a geyser that sometimes put on spectacular displays. Not a trace of the terraces remains today; they were completely blown away by the explosive Mt. Tarawera-Rotomahana volcanic eruptions of 1886. But in the aftermath of those destructive blasts new and equally fascinating thermal features were formed. Star of them all—star of all the world's known geysers—

was the great Waimangu. Beginning in 1900 and lasting four years, Waimangu Geyser (whose name means "Black Water") played like no other geyser has ever done. A typical eruption would last several hours. Each included some bursts of 600 to 1,000 (yes, 1,000) feet high. Larger bursts were common, and Waimangu sometimes even exceeded 1,500 feet! It might seem impossible that any geyser could contain that much pressure and energy, but Waimangu continued to play as often as every 1½ days for all of its four years of existence. When it died it wasn't because of changes in its plumbing system, but because of landslides causing water level changes in the surrounding area. The dominant feature in the area is now Frying Pan Lake, and two or three small geysers have been recently active around its shore. The largest is Taha Roto, up to 15 feet high.

Until 1961 Orakeikorako was a geyser basin to match the Upper Basin of Yellowstone. Over 100 geysers and intermittent springs were active, 20 of which were of major proportions. Orakeikorako Geyser would sometimes erupt to 180 feet. Whenever it was dormant, nearby Minguini Geyser would play, infrequently reaching a measured 295 feet high! Meanwhile, Rameka played to 30 feet, Terata to 50, Porangi to 80, Diamond to 25, and Te Mimi-a-homai-te-rangi to 75, just to name a few. Most of the geysers are gone now. In 1961 they were covered by the waters of Lake Ohakuri, backed up by the relatively small Waikato River Dam just a few miles downstream. The Orakeikorako area is still maintained as a tourist attraction, and several geysers remain. The largest is Aorangi, which played up to 100 feet high shortly after the lake had filled.

Wairakei was another important geyser basin. Its Geyser Valley contained upwards of 40 geysers, some of them large and spectacular. A geothermal power plant spelled their end. Now only empty craters mark the site. Even the geysers at The Spa, near Lake Taupo several miles away, have been affected to the point that they almost never erupt.

Geysers are known to exist or to have existed in a few other thermal groups within this zone. These include Waiotapu, Tokaanu, and Te Kopia. The activity of these areas is either so uncommon or so small that they are better known for their pools and mud pots.

The distance from Rotorua to Lake Taupo is about 50 miles. A recent count found only 18 active geysers within this stretch of countryside. None have a guaranteed future. As with Iceland, New Zealand is a nation of limited energy sources. The geothermal energy is used for space heating and electrical generation. The government has shown a tendency toward continued developments, to the eventual destruction of all the geysers remaining. Some geologists and citizens in New

Zealand think there must be a better way and have filed suit against future drilling, especially at Whakarewarewa and Waimangu. We hope for their success.
References: 1, 2, 3, 28, 29, 30, 31, and 32.

The 37 regions just described are those positively known to contain geysers at this time or in the recent past. In addition to them, a number of other localities around the world have been reported to contain geysers. Whether they actually do is going to have to wait for future explorations, but for the record, they are:

BOILING SPRINGS, GERLACH, NEVADA. First reported on by John C. Fremont in 1845, when irregular periodic boiling was described, the Boiling Springs at least include geyser-like activity. Eruptions were reported as much as 5 feet high during the winter of 1984–85. The area also contains large mud pots that have been known to throw their mud as much as 100 feet high.

AMEDEE HOT SPRINGS, CALIFORNIA. Current evidence is that the Amedee area would never have contained geysers. However, the town of Amedee (now long gone) once had a newspaper named *The Amedee Geyser,* and another reference contains the following report, which stands on its own: "The greatest novelty of the area were the hot springs and geysers which erupted from the soil. . . . Even the geyser was harnessed for a novel purpose – Amos Lane invented a clock which moved foreward exactly 38 seconds with each spurt of the water, thereby keeping perfect time" (D. F. Myrick, *The Railroads of Nevada and Eastern California* [Berkeley: Howell-North Books, 1962], 353–54).

ARARO, MICHOACAN, MEXICO. In 1952 this scenic area near the eastern shore of Laguna Cuitzeo north of Morelia was reported to contain several clear intermittent springs and perhaps one geyser or perpetual spouter among its sinter-lined pools and mud pots.

QUETZALTENANGO DISTRICT, GUATEMALA. North of the bathing resorts of Aguas Georginas and Aguas Amargas are said to be "fumaroles and geysers for the traveller to see." Also, southeast of the town of Zunil another thermal area is reported to contain "geysers and fumaroles." This may be the same locality seen by a member of the U.S. Geological Survey to include a large perpetual spouter.

VOLCAN PURACE NATIONAL PARK, COLOMBIA. The hot springs at Termales de San Juan are near this national park's visitor center and traversed by an interpretive trail. The hot springs are described as being geysers with eruptions a few feet high. Unfortunately, the description also states that one can tell the temperature of the water by the color of its algae. Since hot water algae will not survive above 167°F (71°C), this implies that these pools cannot be geysers.

VOLCAN ALCEDO, ISLA ISABELA, GALAPAGOS ISLANDS, ECUADOR. Several references state that geysers occur within this caldera. It is more likely that the "geysers" are fumaroles, as the geology of the area is basaltic volcanism, with the wrong chemistry for geysers.

QUIGUATA, ANTOFAGASTA?, CHILE. Quiguata is listed by a 1967 reference as containing geysers, but it does not seem to be mentioned by any other report. The location is about 100 miles north of El Tatio.

"EL TATIO," BOLIVIA. The El Tatio geothermal system extends over the mountains and across the international border into Bolivia. Because of political tensions, visitors to the Chilean side are not welcome to visit the other side. Anyone doing so would, however, unquestionably encounter geysers. This is, of course, not a separate geyser field but it is listed separately here because of the national difference.

HELLS GATE, KENYA. Hells Gate is a long canyon traversed only by a trail south of Lake Naivasha. It certainly contains hot springs, which are listed as a major attraction of the area by at least two published tourist guides and by the Kenya Ministry of Tourism and Wildlife. These sources talk of water jets several feet high. Geologists, on the other hand, report that they believe (they apparently do not know for certain) these to be fumaroles.

KERGUELEN ISLAND, SOUTH INDIAN OCEAN. Kerguelen, a large but virtually unknown island, lies in the sub-Antarctic. Hot springs are known to occur in the southern part of the island, where seals warm themselves in the steam. A television documentary showed these springs to be hot, clear, deep pools, while the narrator mentioned splashing.

FLORES ISLAND, INDONESIA. Geysers are rumored to exist at Magekabo, Ende District, in western Flores. Numbers cited are "several" and heights "considerable." The area has not yet been included in the Indonesian geothermal surveys.

ALA RIVER, NEW BRITAIN ISLAND, PAPUA-NEW GUINEA. Deep in the heart of New Britain, along the Ala River, is a thermal area that definitely does include some spouting springs. They seem to be perpetual spouters rather than true geysers. They also may have temperatures below boiling so that their eruptions are partly due to gases other than steam.

Finally, the following localities have been reported as containing geysers, but definitely do not:

BRADY'S HOT SPRINGS, NEVADA. One spouter was possible during the late 1840s, and maybe again during the 1920s, but all natural springs have been destroyed by geothermal development.

COSO HOT SPRINGS, CALIFORNIA. High temperature springs and siliceous sinter deposits exist, but no geysers have ever been observed.

AHUACHAPAN, EL SALVADOR. An acid area of mud pots and fumaroles, the "Hell's Half Acre" never included geysers in spite of travel guides to the contrary.

LARDARELLO, ITALY. Site of the world's first operating geothermal power plant, there certainly were some very hot springs, but true geysers were never observed.

ZAMBIA AND ZIMBABWE, AFRICA. Several spots in each of these countries have been reported to contain geysers. One or two do involve spouting artesian springs of warm to hot temperatures, but they are powered by gravity rather than boiling. The other localities contain only a few lukewarm springs, and at the reported site of the Chilambwa Geyser there is no form of thermal activity whatsoever.

THE GEYSERS, CALIFORNIA. In spite of the name, The Geysers never included geysers – it was named because of the steam clouds, which were mistaken for geysers during California's earliest history.

ARTIFICIAL "GEYSERS" IN THE WESTERN UNITED STATES. Highway maps often indicate geysers here and there around the west. These are all drilled wells, spectacular but artificial. They include the "geysers" at Calistoga, California; Lakeview and Adel, Oregon; and Soda Springs, Idaho. The Crystal and Woodside "geysers" near Green River, Utah, are even more different, being drilled wells that act as "soda pop geysers." They play cold water, with the eruptions powered by the evolution of carbon dioxide gas. Both of these spouters are abandoned, unsuccessful wildcat oil wells.

Annotated Bibliography
Geyser Fields of the World

1. Allen, E. T., and A. L. Day. 1935. *Hot springs of Yellowstone National Park.* Carnegie Institute of Washington Publication Number 466.

An early but intensive study containing descriptions of nearly all of Yellowstone's geyser areas and mention of some of the world's other geyser fields.

2. Van Padang, M. N., ed. 1951–65. *Catalogue of the active volcanoes of the world, including solfatara fields.* 21 vols. Naples, Italy: International Volcanological Association. A good source of all kinds of volcanic data, this is the only reference to several of the smaller geyser fields; information about geysers is often sketchy, though. Only 1,000 copies printed in English.

3. Waring, G. A. 1965. *Thermal springs of the United States and other countries of the world.* U.S. Geological Survey Professional Paper 492. Not all-inclusive, and not entirely reliable because of differences in the definition of a geyser and because of age, but still excellent as a comprehensive, general reference. Outstanding bibliography of 3,733 references.

4. Nolan, T. B., and G. H. Anderson. 1934. Geyser area near Beowawe, Eureka County, Nevada. *American Journal of Science* 27:215–29. The only detailed reference to Beowawe as it was before geothermal drilling, with maps and photos.

5. Zoback, M. C. 1979. *A geologic and geophysical investigation of the Beowawe geothermal area, North-central Nevada.* Stanford University Publications, Geological Sciences, vol. 16. A work that concentrates on the overall geology of the Beowawe system, but does include information about current activity and a detailed map.

6. White, D. E. 1968. *Hydrology, activity, and heat flow of the Steamboat Springs thermal system, Washoe County, Nevada.* U.S. Geological Survey Professional Paper 458-C. Includes a map showing and tables listing all the important springs at Steamboat, including the geyser activity observed from 1946 to 1952.

7. Bezore, S. P., and R. W. Sherberne. 1985. *Monitoring geothermal wells and spring conditions in selected areas of California for earthquake precursors.* California Division of Mines and Geology Open File Report OFR 85-12 SAC. Mentions various activity changes among the Long Valley Caldera hot springs since the earthquakes of May 1980.

8. Byers, F. M., and W. W. Brannock. 1949. Volcanic activity on Umnak and Great Sitkin Islands, 1946–1948. *Transactions of the American Geophysical Union* 30:719–34. The only written reference to the geysers of Umnak to provide details of the activity and maps.

9. Wittich, E. 1910. Geysers y mantiales termales de Comanjilla (Guanajuato). *Soc. Geologica Mexicana Bulletin* 6:183–88. A short descrip-

tive work on the nature of geyser activity in 1906 with a map accurate enough to allow the individual springs to be identified today. (In Spanish)

10. Singletary, C. E. 1952. The hot springs, geysers, and solfatara of the northern part of Michoacan, Mexico. *Texas Journal of Science* 4:413–20. Includes very brief descriptions of the thermal areas at Ixtlan de los Hervores and Araro, but no substantive details about the geyser activity. Photos.

11. Waitz, P. 1906. Los geysers d'Ixtlan. Paper delivered at the 10th International Geological Congress, Mexico City. A field-guide sort of report, this provides a lot of details about the individual geysers and other hot springs. Map and photos. (In French)

12. Trujillo, P. 1972. *Estudio de las manifestaciones termales de Suriri.* 15 pp. An in-house report to the Geological Survey of Chile. Provides considerable detail about the current activity at Suriri and a mention of the geyser of 1944. Detailed map. (In Spanish)

13. Lahsen, A. 1976. *La actividad geotermal y sus relaciones con la tectonica y el volcanismo en el norte de Chile.* Primer Congreso Geologico Chileno, Santiago, 2–7 August 1976, pp. B105–27. Provides general information about numerous geothermal areas in Chile, especially noting Suriri, Puchuldiza, and El Tatio. (In Spanish)

14. Trujillo, P. 1969. *Estudio para el desarrollo geotermico en el norte de Chile—Manifestaciones termales de El Tatio.* 11 pp. An in-house report to the Geological Survey of Chile. Provides great detail about the geysers of El Tatio and a very detailed map. (In Spanish)

15. Barth, T. F. W., Jr. 1950. *Volcanic geology, geysers, and hot springs of Iceland.* Carnegie Institute of Washington Publication Number 587. A very complete coverage of all of Iceland's geyser basins (and other hot spring groups). The data is, however, considerably out-of-date, as most was gathered during the 1930s. Good maps and many photos.

16. Einarsson, T. 1967. *The Great Geysir and the hot spring area at Haukadalur Iceland.* Geysir Committee, Reykjavik, Iceland. A small tourist guide to the area at Haukadalur, with photos and a map.

17. United Nations Development Program. 1973. *Geology, geochemistry, and hydrology of hot springs of the East African Rift System within Ethiopia.* Technical Publication DP/SF/UN/116. Provides great detail about the many dozens of geothermal areas within Ethiopia, many detailed maps, and photos of springs at Allallobeda.

18. Raik, A. 1963. *Nature investigations in the Far East.* Academy of Sciences of the Estonian S.S.R., Tartu State University. Entirely

about the geyser field along the Geysernaya River, one chapter is about the geyser activity specifically. (In Russian, with English chapter summaries)

19. Montgomerie, T. G. 1875. Narrative of an exploration of the Namcho, or Tengri Nur Lake, in great Tibet, made by a native explorer in 1871-2. *Royal Geographical Society* (of London) *Journal* 45: 315-30. Includes mention of the localities and activity of geysers at Peting Chuja and Naisum Chuja on the La Chu River.

20. Sapper. 1914. A narrative of a journey through Thibet. *Danckelmann's Mitteil.*, Ergänz III, 44. A very short article in which the geysers of the La Chu River are mentioned as to numbers and heights. (In German)

21. Liao, Z. 1979. *Setting of the geothermal fields of Tibet and a discussion of associated heat source problems.* Geothermal Institute, University of Auckland, New Zealand. Report Number 79.17. Describes, mostly in passing, the geysers of Tagajia, Chapu, Guhu, and Namling.

22. Liao, Z., et al. 1979. Heat beneath Tibet. *Geographical Magazine* (London), May 1979, 560-66. A popularized and somewhat disorganized account in which the geysers of Tibet are described. Includes an excellent photograph of a geyser at Tagajia.

23. Ramingwong, T., et al. 1979. *Geothermal resources of northern Thailand: A compilation.* Department of Geological Sciences, Chiang Mai University. A short report in which a tabulation of hot spring areas includes mention of the geysers in the area. Mostly general and no specific details provided.

24. Stevenson, J. F. 1864. Account of a visit to the hot springs of Pai in the Tavoy District. *Asiatic Society Bengal Journal* 34:383-86. Makes special note of the single geyser at Pai and also discusses general hot spring conditions and deposits.

25. Healy, J. 1972. *Geothermal reconnaissance, Lampung District, South Sumatra.* Report to Volcanological Section, Geological Survey of Indonesia, 37-41. Locates and provides eruptive data for the existing geysers of the Semangko geyser field.

26. Reynolds, M. A. 1950s. Several reports on the geothermal activity within the former territories of Papua and New Guinea. Australian Bureau of Mineral Resources, unpublished reports 1954/63, 1956/9, and 1956/25. These reports are brief descriptions of the thermal areas and their activity, covering Deidei, Iamelele, Kasiloli, and Lihir and Ambitle Islands. They enlarge and update earlier reports. Sketch maps included.

27. Healy, J. 1960. *The hot springs and geothermal resources of Fiji.* New Zealand Department of Scientific and Industrial Research Publication Number 136. Includes a description of the Nasavusavu Hot Spring area and detailed notes about the periodic activity of the Nakama Springs.
28. Grange, L. I. 1937. *Geology of the Rotorua-Taupo subdivision.* Geological Survey of New Zealand Bulletin 37. The Rotorua-Taupo area contains all of New Zealand's geyser basins. The descriptions here are usually complete, though sometimes sketchy, and therefore give good information about the geysers as they were before development of the area destroyed most. Many maps and photos.
29. Keam, R. F. 1955. *Volcanic wonderland.* Auckland, New Zealand: G. B. Scott. Contains brief descriptions of all of New Zealand's more important thermal areas, with frequent mention and emphasis on geyser activity. Many photos.
30. Lloyd, E. F. 1972. *The geology and hot springs of Orakeikorako.* New Zealand Geological Survey Bulletin 85. An absolutely outstanding book, this contains detailed descriptions of the geyser activity both historically and just before the inundation by Lake Ohakuri. Numerous photos, detailed maps, a table listing every hot spring in the area, and reams of other data.
31. Lloyd, E. F. 1975. *Geology of Whakarewarewa Hot Springs.* New Zealand Department of Scientific and Industrial Research, Information Series Publication Number 111. Designed for visitors to the Whakarewarewa preserve, this colorful booklet includes detailed descriptions of the geyser activity of the area plus some information about the nearby Arikikapakapa mud pot area. Includes detailed, large-scale map.
32. Personal experiences of the author: personal visits, movies, television documentaries, slide shows, numerous small foreign language publications, conversations, and so on, but especially written communications with geologists world-wide. It is these people above all who have provided much valuable data to this research. They cannot be thanked enough for their time and efforts in providing information and publications about the geysers (or non-geysers) in their own and other countries:
Dr. Donald E. White, U.S. Geological Survey
Dr. Robert Christianson, U.S. Geological Survey
Dr. Thomas P. Miller, U.S. Geological Survey
Mr. Alberto Parodi I., Arequipa, Peru
Dr. Alfredo Lahsen A., University of Chile

Dr. Stefan Arnorsson, University of Iceland
Mr. Sebastian Bwire-Ojiambo, East African Power and Light Co., Nairobi, Kenya
Mr. Colin D. Kerr, Geological Survey of Zambia
Dr. L. A. Lister, University of Rhodesia (Zimbabwe)
Dr. Genrich Steinberg, Academy of Sciences of the U.S.S.R., Yuzhno, Sakhalin
Mr. Wishnu S. Kartokusumo, Volcanological Survey of Indonesia
Mr. R. J. S. Cooke, Senior Government Volcanologist, Papua-New Guinea
Dr. R. W. Johnson, Australian Bureau of Mineral Resources
Mr. Bradley J. Scott, New Zealand Geological Survey
Dr. E. F. Lloyd, New Zealand Geological Survey
Dr. James Healy, New Zealand Geological Survey
Dr. R. F. Keam, University of Auckland, New Zealand

Glossary

ALGAE: colonial, single-celled plants; in Yellowstone, brightly colored forms of blue-green algae (now called cyanobacteria) live in thermal waters cooler than 167°F (71°C).

BURST: applicable to fountain-type geysers, a burst may be a single throw of water or, in the case of those geysers having a series of short, closely-spaced eruptions, a burst may be one of the periods of spouting.

COMPLEX: a cluster of springs or geysers that are so intimately associated that the activity of any one member will affect that of the others.

CONCERTED: simultaneous eruptions by two or more geysers of a complex, usually the eruption of one triggering the eruption of the other.

CRATER: may be synonymous with *vent;* more often, the crater is a broad shallow depression within which is centered a comparatively small vent. A crater is also a wide, deep hole containing a pool.

CYCLE: the time span from the start of one active phase of a geyser, through the following dormancy, to the start of the next active phase. Sometimes incorrectly used as a synonym for *period.*

DORMANCY: a span of time during which a geyser temporarily ceases to erupt. Many geysers will be active for long periods of time and then go dormant. Note that dormant does not mean dead.

DURATION: the period of time from the start of an eruption to the end of the same eruption.

ERUPTION: the spouting action of a geyser.

EXCHANGE OF FUNCTION: the shift of energy and/or water from one geyser or hot spring group to another, resulting in a decline of activity in the first and an increase in the latter.

FREQUENT: the term for eruptions that are irregularly spaced in time yet occur often, usually separated by only a few minutes.

FUMAROLE: a steam vent; a fumarole is a hot spring in which the water supply is so limited that all water is completely and constantly converted to steam.

GEYSER: a hot spring in which eruptive activity is induced by the boiling of water at depth within a plumbing system, which forcibly ejects water out of the vent in an intermittent fashion.

Cone-type: a geyser whose eruption is a steady column of water, usually issuing from a cone or mound with a small vent.

Fountain-type: a geyser whose eruption is a series of separate explosions or bursts of water, issuing from a pool with a large vent or crater.

GEYSER BASIN: an area of hot springs within which geysers are found.

GEYSER FIELD: an expanse of land, large or small, that encompasses all of the geyser basins of a geographical region.

GEYSERITE: the form of silica deposited by geysers and perpetual spouters, usually with a beaded surface; also, a general synonym for "siliceous sinter."

GROUP: a set of hot springs that are considered as a unit on the basis of some geographical separation from other nearby sets.

HEIGHT: the distance from the ground to the top of a geyser's erupted water jet. The height listed in the tables and descriptions is invariably the maximum height and not necessarily characteristic of the entire eruption.

INFREQUENT: the term for eruptions that are very irregular, usually with intervals days to weeks long.

INTERVAL: the period of time from the end of one eruption to the beginning of the next; with most geysers the interval is so much longer than the duration that "interval" is used as a synonym for "period."

IRREGULAR: the term for eruptions that show no evident pattern of distribution, intervals ranging from minutes to days in length.

MUD POT: a hot spring with a limited water supply; not enough is present to carry away clay muds that are brought to the surface, so they accumulate forming a thick, bubbly material within the crater.

PERIOD: the interval plus the duration; that is, the span of time from the start of one eruption to the start of the next.

PERPETUAL SPOUTER: a spouting spring resembling a geyser but whose eruptive activity does not stop; though included as such throughout this book, important mechanical differences mean that a perpetual spouter is not a true geyser.

PLAY: the eruptive activity of a geyser; a synonym for "eruption."

PLUMBING SYSTEM: the subsurface network of tubes, cavities, and channels that make up the water supply system of a hot spring; it is especially important for geysers in that it must contain a near-surface constriction, be pressure tight, and have a large volume.

PREPLAY: any activity by a geyser, such as heavy overflow or splashing, preceding an eruption; useful in that preplay is an indication that the time of eruption is near.

RARE: the term for eruptions that almost never occur, many months to years sometimes passing between them.

SELDOM: the term for eruptions that are very widely spaced, several months often passing between them.

SPUT: the term for a small geyser or perpetual spouter whose activity is relatively insignificant compared to surrounding features but whose action can have deleterious effect on nearby geyser activity; also, a general term for the members of a large group of small features.

SILICEOUS SINTER: the deposit of opaline silica that is formed by hot springs and geysers.

UNCOMMON: a synonym for "infrequent."

VENT: the surface opening of the plumbing system; in geysers it is the point from which the eruption issues.

Suggested Reading

Allen, E. T., and A. L. Day. 1935. *Hot springs of Yellowstone National Park*. Carnegie Institute of Washington Publication Number 466.

Bonney, O. H., and L. Bonney. 1970. *Battle drums and geysers—the life and journals of Lt. Gustavus Cheney Doane, soldier and explorer of the Yellowstone and Snake River regions*. Chicago: The Swallow Press.

Brock, T. D., and M. L. Brock. 1971. *Life in the geyser basins*. Yellowstone National Park: Yellowstone Library and Museum Association.

Bryan, T. S. 1990. *Geysers: What they are and how the work*. Niwot, Colorado: Roberts Rinehart, Inc.

Haines, A. L. 1955. *Osborne Russell's journal of a trapper*. Lincoln: University of Nebraska Press.

———. 1977. *The Yellowstone story: a history of our first national park*. 2 vols. Yellowstone Library and Museum Associated University Press.

Keefer, W. R. 1972. *The geologic story of Yellowstone National Park*. U.S. Geological Survey Bulletin 1347.

Kirk, R. 1972. *Exploring Yellowstone*. Seattle: University of Washington Press.

Langford, N. P. 1972. *The discovery of Yellowstone Park*. Lincoln: University of Nebraska Press.

Lystrup, H. T. 1969. *Hamilton's guide—Yellowstone National Park*. West Yellowstone, Montana: Hamilton's Stores Inc.

Marler, G. D. 1951. Exchange of function as a cause of geyser irregularity. *American Journal of Science* 249:329–42.

———. 1964. *Effects of the Hebgen Lake earthquake of August 17, 1959 on the hot springs of the Firehole Geyser Basins, Yellowstone National Park*. U.S. Geological Survey Professional Paper 435, 185–97.

———. *Studies of geysers and hot springs along the Firehole River, Yellowstone National Park, Wyoming*. Yellowstone National Park: Yellowstone Library and Museum Association.

Macdonald, G. A. 1972. *Volcanoes.* Englewood Cliffs, New Jersey: Prentice-Hall.

White, D. E., et al. 1975. *Physical results of research drilling in thermal areas of Yellowstone National Park, Wyoming.* U.S. Geological Survey Professional Paper 892.

White, D. E., R. A. Hutchinson, and T.E.C. Keith, 1988. *The geology and remarkable thermal activity of Norris Geyser Basin, Yellowstone National Park, Wyoming.* U.S. Geological Survey Professional Paper 1456.

Whittlesey, L. H. 1988. *Yellowstone place names.* Helena: Montana Historical Society Press.

———. 1989. *Wonderland Nomenclature.* Sacramento: The Geyser Observation and Study Association in cooperation with Montana Historical Society Press; typescript manuscript, 2,242 pages.

———. 1973. *Inventory of thermal features of the Firehole River Geyser Basins and other selected areas of Yellowstone National Park.* National Technical Information Service Publication Number PB–221289.

Marler, G. D., and D. E. White. 1975. Seismic Geyser and its bearing on the origin and evolution of geysers and hot springs of Yellowstone National Park. *Geological Society of America Bulletin* 86:749–59.

Index of Geyser Names

Addenda

The following items cover some of the more important changes to Yellowstone's geyser activity since this edition of *The Geysers of Yellowstone* was released in 1986. Additional alterations have been incorporated directly into the text. Anything listed here is current as of June 1990.

Upper Geyser Basin

Page 25. Because some perceived the century-old name to be derogatory, Chinaman Spring is now officially **Chinese Spring.**

The round pool located a few yards southeast of Little Squirt Geyser is **Bronze Spring.** It began erupting during 1987 and, with somewhat decreased frequency, has persisited into 1990. Eruptions are generally infrequent (1 or 2 per day), but the splashes of 4 to 6 feet can persist for several minutes. **Silver Spring,** the sinter-rimmed pool west of Bronze, has had a few boiling eruptions, also since 1987.

Cascade Geyser had a few eruptions during January of 1988, the stronger of which reached 12 feet high.

Page 42. Several small geysers exist around the northern base of the cone of Castle Geyser. The largest of these, informally known as **"Gizmo Geyser"** (also as "Castle's Vent"), began strong eruptions during 1986. Its action is cyclic and, interestingly, is *not* related to that of Castle. Intervals range from a few minutes to several hours, while the duration is from 1 to 8 minutes. Eruptions begin with small water bursts, then develop into a very noisy steam eruption that jets watery spray as high as 15 feet at a sharp angle.

Page 43. Terra Cotta is now known to include at least four geysers among its vents, Terra Cotta "C" and "D" being added to the list since 1986. Terra Cotta "C" is generally infrequent but has occasional episodes of frequent eruptions as much as 6 feet high. Terra Cotta "D" must be termed rare. The two or three eruptions seen during 1989 reached up to 20 feet high, whereas those of 1990 hit only 1 to 2 feet.

Between the boardwalk and **Chimney Cone** is a small oval spring that erupted at least once during April 1990 to about 4 feet.

Page 47. A couple of the text statements about **Crystal Spring** are incorrect. It is a geyser. A few eruptions sprayed muddy water as high as 20 feet during both 1974 and 1983. Much smaller but more frequent eruptions of 2 feet were observed during 1987.

Page 54. Just east of the boardwalk between Grand and Economic Geysers is a small double spring where the smaller vent flows a constant trickle of water into the larger. It is not a pretty feature, but "**Key Spring**" had a series of eruptions in August 1988. The play was at an angle, 10 feet high and 25 feet outward across the boardwalk.

Page 59. South Purple Pool underwent a series of very significant, 30-foot eruptions during the fall of 1987, and these definitely seem to have been precursors to Giant Geyser's better record of performance since then.

Page 62. Giant Geyser is considered to be in an active phase. It has continued having occasional eruptions, although not with anything approaching either frequency or regularity since the eruption and onset of hot periods in September 1987. Some publications state that Giant has not played since 1955; here is the complete record of the 12 known eruptions that have taken place since then: 9/18/1964; 9/09/1978; 9/27/1982; 10/12/1984; 8/20/1986; 9/12/1987; 6/28/1988; 9/12/1988; 12/18/1988; 4/17/1989; 1/6–7/1990; and 1/26–27/1990.

Page 63. Although the perfectly round spring next to the trail has been called the name, the real **Round Spring** lies near Pear Geyser, more than 100 feet west of the trail. In May 1990 it underwent the most powerful series of eruptions ever witnessed in the Round Spring Group. Many of the bursts were over 30 feet tall, and one eruption unquestionably reached above 50 feet.

Although none were actually seen, powerful eruptions by **Pear Geyser** carved a deep and wide channel during the 1989–90 winter season.

Page 71. The correct number of eruptions by **Splendid Geyser** during 1985 was 44. It had another 99 eruptions during 1986, 26 in 1987, only 3 in 1988, none during 1989, and 2 as of June 1990.

Page 78. The feature that had been buried during the road construction, and which apparently led to the development of the present Culvert Geyser, began to reappear during 1988. Under the name "**Persistent Spring,**" it has broken out of a ceramic pipe and through the edge of the trail south of Culvert. It acts as a perpetual spouter.

Page 90. The southernmost feature of the "Westside Group" is a pretty, greenish pool shown on USGS maps as having been a geyser shortly after the 1959 earthquake. Possibly stimulated by another quake in July 1989, this **"South Pool"** had numerous eruptions over the next several months. Some of the play was up to 15 feet high, and the water discharge was huge. These eruptions apparently ended during April 1990.

Page 91. As pointed out in the text, UNNG-WSG-4 became a major geyser in April 1986. **Fantail Geyser** persisted throughout that summer, with highly regular and spectacular eruptions. During most of the season, the intervals were around 6 hours. The play came from both of the two craters in the form of massive bursts and jets as much as 75 feet high. These did not significantly decrease their strength until near the end of the 45 minute duration, when a powerful steam phase began. Fantail abruptly became irregular and weaker in mid-August, 1986, and the duration simultaneously decreased to only 10 minutes with no steam phase. Eruptions ceased completely before the end of October.

At the edge of the river nearby, another spring activated as a geyser along with Fantail. **Ouzel Geyser's** eruptions reached up to 50 feet high, but its irregular and brief performances never matched those of Fantail.

Both Fantail and Ouzel have continued infrequent activity since 1986. Fantail has played perhaps a dozen times, most of the eruptions resembling those of late 1986. Ouzel can still burst as high as 20 feet but only when the Firehole River is at a low level.

Pages 96 and 99. The geyser shown and described as #162 is really **Coral Geyser,** which continues to have frequent subterranean eruptions. **Black Pearl Geyser,** which is virtually inactive, lies within the crater across the boardwalk southwest of Coral.

Pages 100–103. Several name revelations and activity changes have occurred at Black Sand Basin. **Whistle Geyser** had its first eruption since 1968 on July 1, 1990. It is now known that the noisy, spouting vent between Spouter Geyser and the road is properly called **The Grumbler.** And sorry, but #166 is not available to be named after all; it was given the long-forgotten name **Ragged Spring** during the 1880s. The small geyser left (east) of Green Spring has reappeared. **Handkerchief Geyser** erupts 12 to 15 feet high from near Handkerchief Pool, and a strong 4-foot spouter has developed where the boardwalk once lay near the Emerald Pool junction. Along Iron Spring Creek to the north, **"Pentagonal Geyser"** is in frequent eruption, sometimes as much as 10 feet high.

Page 106. An "energy surge" of unknown origin affected most of the Myriad Group during the winter of 1987–88, and some of the resulting activity continues. A vent within North Sister (known as **Mugwump Geyser** during the 1880s) erupted as high as 20 feet. **Trail and West Trail Geysers** had their first eruptions since 1959; West Trail was the stronger of the two this time, with some bursts of 15 feet. It continues to act as a small perpetual spouter. Nearby (and not previously discussed in this book) are **Bell, Pit, and Strata Geysers** along with numerous smaller eruptive features. Although most of the eruptions have been small, they are considered significant in that they were not earthquake induced. **Round, Spectacle, and** (briefly) **Abuse Geysers** were also active for a short time.

Midway Geyser Basin

Page 115. Silent Pool is a small but deep blue spring containing numerous logs next to the trail across the river from River Spouter. It erupted as high as 4 feet during early 1990, the first activity ever known from it. The frequency is unknown.

Lower Geyser Basin

Page 138–139. There has been confusion as to which feature should have which name within the Firehole Lake Group (which itself can also be called the Black Warrior Group). What is *probably* correct is this: #26, **Young Hopeful Geyser** is only some of those eleven vents. Those nearer the break in slope immediately below the boardwalk separately comprise **Gray Bulger.** And spring #27, identified in the text as Gray Bulger, in reality is **Artesia Spring,** which is how it was identified in the first edition of this book way back in 1979.

Within the same group, UNNG-FLG-1 is probably the one named **Primrose Spring** in 1878. It continues to have small, infrequent eruptions.

Page 148. The area of UNNG-FTN-3 is now known to be the site of at least three independent geysers, each of which can reach over 20 feet and one, rarely, sometimes over 50 feet high. It is impossible to tell from the boardwalk which vent is which, unless more than one happens to erupt at the same time.

Pages 150. The tall angled jet of spray near Deep Blue Geyser is now informally known as "**The Firehose.**" Although nearly a perpetual spouter, it has been observed to briefly quit playing (for as long as 30 minutes every few days), and so it is actually a geyser. The play at times is over 50 feet high.

Page 159. Many observers have had difficulty locating UNNG-RVG-1. This is because it is located south of Mound Geyser, not north, and at a distance of more like 1,000 rather than 700 feet!

Norris Geyser Basin

Page 170. Valentine Geyser (which first erupted in 1907, not 1902) rejuvenated during the summer of 1989. Although few eruptions were actually witnessed, and they were mostly only 20–30 feet high, it was playing often enough to keep its runoff channel fresh. A series of small earthquakes on June 16, 1990 apparently stimulated Valentine to erupt to over 50 feet high. Further indicating a possible shift of energy back to this portion of Porcelain Basin, the eruptions of Valentine are preceeded, just as before, by brief eruptions from **Guardian Geyser**.

Page 177. The general Porcelain Terrace area is alive with geysers and spouters that change so rapidly that it can be difficult to keep track of them. Nevertheless, one that appeared during February 1990 was given a name ("**Inclined Geyser**"). It erupted at an angle against the hillside and eventually got so powerful as to resemble **Daisy Geyser,** except that it was bigger at as much as 110 feet high. As expected because of the unstable location, this strong action quickly decreased, but **Inclined** was still active into August.

Page 183. Steamboat Geyser might have recovered from the dormancy begun in 1984. It erupted on 1/15/1989; 5/05/1989; 10/09/1989; and 6/04/1990.

Page 189. During a disturbance on September 5, 1989, **Porkchop Geyser** literally exploded. Its beautiful crater was replaced by a ragged jumble of broken boulders. Debris was found more than 220 feet away from the site. The new Porkchop is a pool, roughly 6-by-12 feet, filled with beautifully opalescent water (see Blue Mud Spring for a description). Occasional boiling eruptions, up to 6 feet high, are seen, but with seemingly decreasing frequency.

West Thumb Geyser Basin

Page 195. A brief rejuvenation of the **West Thumb Geyser Basin** resulted in several springs becoming active geysers again during 1986–87. Included were **Collapsing Spring, Surging Spring, Ledge Spring, Thumb Geyser, and Roadside Steamer.** The culmination was an eruption by **Abyss Pool** (its first and only known), which gouged deep runoff channels over a wide area. Unfortunately, all this action was short-lived and the main section at West Thumb was again devoid of geysers by 1988.

Gibbon Geyser Basin

Page 207. One aftermath of the forest fires of 1988 was severe mud slides during heavy rains in August 1989. One of them thoroughly buried **Gibbon Hill Geyser** and seems to have ended its career. Given the amount of water and energy that had been released by Gibbon Hill, that it has not managed to rejuvenate and clear itself of the debris is surprising. However, ten months after the slide, only the barest wisps of steam were visible at the site.

Shoshone Geyser Basin

Page 217 ff. Further names work, and many activity changes have taken place in the Shoshone Geyser Basin. Some of the "new" names date way back to 1872! UNNG-SHO-5 bears the name **Mangled Crater Spring.** UNNG-SHO-6 is the real **Frill Spring.** UNNG-SHO-9 can be called **Pecten Geyser,** and the Fall Creek Group where it is located is more properly called the **Western Group.**

A vague 1988 report had **Little Giant Geyser** playing over 20 feet high, which would be its most powerful eruptions in decades. **Minute Man's Pool** has had frequent small (to 10 feet high) eruptions on a continuing basis. **Velvet Spring** recovered from its dormancy in late 1987, and the eruptions by **Knobby Geyser** underwent the expected decline in force and frequency. There has been no change in the water levels or activities within the **Orion Group.**

The footbridge across Shoshone Creek was removed during 1986, so the only way to reach the western half of Shoshone Basin is to either wade across the creek or cross via some downed logs at the extreme southern end of the basin.

Heart Lake Geyser Basin

Page 235. Two small geysers have been discovered within the **Middle Group** of the Heart Lake Geyser Basin. They are located some distance upstream from the Witch Creek trail crossing.

Page 239. You might say that **Rustic Geyser** has again been altered by people. Sometime during the 1989–90 winter season, somebody thoroughly jammed and wedged a log into Rustic's vent. An attempt to remove it was completely unsuccessful; we hope the wood will decay rather than silicify. Log or no log, Rustic remains dormant.

Page 240. The text statements about **UNNG-HLR-S4** and **Prometheus Spring** are incorrect. Change definitely occurred, but HLR-S4 exists as it did before. However, UNNG-HLR-S6, not described before because it was a small and unimportant feature, did begin erupting. It now has a large crater that gives rise to bursts up to 10 feet high. And Prometheus certainly did not explode. Instead it has simply become so dormant that wildflowers are growing within its vent.

About the Author

T. Scott Bryan has been a seasonal employee in Yellowstone National Park since 1970, working in the maintenance division at Canyon Village for four years and as a ranger-naturalist at Norris and Old Faithful since then. He has held other National Park Service positions in Glacier National Park, Death Valley National Monument, Glen Canyon National Recreation Area, and the Los Angeles Field Office. After serving in the Navy (when he was able to visit the geysers of Japan and New Zealand), he received his Bachelor of Science degree in geology at San Diego State University; his education continued at the University of Montana, where he received the Master of Science degree in 1974. He is now the instructor of geology and physical sciences at Victor Valley College in Victorville, California. *The Geysers of Yellowstone* is his first book; he has also published several articles on the history and geology of the American West.